FTCE Middle Grades General Science 5-9

Teacher Certification Exam

By: Sharon A. Wynne, M.S.

XAMonline, Inc.
Boston

Library of Congress Cataloging-in-Publication Data
Wynne, Sharon A.

FTCE Middle Grades General Science 5-9: Teacher Certification / Sharon A. Wynne.
ISBN 978-1-64239-011-7

1. Middle Grades General Science 5-9   2. Study Guides.   3. FTCE
4. Teachers' Certification & Licensure.   5. Careers

Disclaimer:
The opinions expressed in this publication are the sole works of XAMonline and were created independently from the National Education Association, Educational Testing Service, or any State Department of Education, National Evaluation Systems or other testing affiliates.

Between the time of publication and printing, state specific standards as well as testing formats and website information may change that is not included in part or in whole within this product. XAMonline developed the sample test questions and the questions reflect similar content as on real tests; however, they are not former tests. XAMonline assembles content that aligns with state standards but makes no claims nor guarantees teacher candidates a passing score. Numerical scores are determined by testing companies such as NES or ETS and then are compared with individual state standards. A passing score varies from state to state.

Printed in the United States of America
FTCE: Middle Grades General Science 5-9
ISBN: 978-1-64239-011-7

Table of Contents

Great Study and Testing Tips!

What to study in order to prepare for the subject assessments is the focus of this study guide but equally important is *how* you study.

You can increase your chances of truly mastering the information by taking some simple, but effective steps.

Study Tips:

1. Some foods aid the learning process. Foods such as milk, nuts, seeds, rice, and oats help your study efforts by releasing natural memory enhancers called CCKs (*cholecystokinin*) composed of *tryptopha*n, *choline*, and *phenylalanine*. All of these chemicals enhance the neurotransmitters associated with memory. Before studying, try a light, protein-rich meal of eggs, turkey, and fish. All of these foods release the memory enhancing chemicals. The better the connections, the more you comprehend.

Likewise, before you take a test, stick to a light snack of energy boosting and relaxing foods. A glass of milk, a piece of fruit, or some peanuts all release various memory-boosting chemicals and help you to relax and focus on the subject at hand.

2. Learn to take great notes. A by-product of our modern culture is that we have grown accustomed to getting our information in short doses (i.e. TV news sound bites or USA Today style newspaper articles.)

Consequently, we've subconsciously trained ourselves to assimilate information better in neat little packages. If your notes are scrawled all over the paper, it fragments the flow of the information. Strive for clarity. Newspapers use a standard format to achieve clarity. Your notes can be much clearer through use of proper formatting. A very effective format is called the *"Cornell Method."*

Take a sheet of loose-leaf lined notebook paper and draw a line all the way down the paper about 1-2" from the left-hand edge.

Draw another line across the width of the paper about 1-2" up from the bottom. Repeat this process on the reverse side of the page.

Look at the highly effective result. You have ample room for notes, a left hand margin for special emphasis items or inserting supplementary data from the textbook, a large area at the bottom for a brief summary, and a little rectangular space for just about anything you want.

3. Get the concept then the details. Too often we focus on the details and don't gather an understanding of the concept. However, if you simply memorize only dates, places, or names, you may well miss the whole point of the subject.

A key way to understand things is to put them in your own words. If you are working from a textbook, automatically summarize each paragraph in your mind. If you are outlining text, don't simply copy the author's words.

Rephrase them in your own words. You remember your own thoughts and words much better than someone else's, and subconsciously tend to associate the important details to the core concepts.

4. Ask Why? Pull apart written material paragraph by paragraph and don't forget the captions under the illustrations.

Example: If the heading is "Stream Erosion", flip it around to read "Why do streams erode?" Then answer the questions.

If you train your mind to think in a series of questions and answers, not only will you learn more, but it also helps to lessen the test anxiety because you are used to answering questions.

5. Read for reinforcement and future needs. Even if you only have 10 minutes, put your notes or a book in your hand. Your mind is similar to a computer; you have to input data in order to have it processed. *By reading, you are creating the neural connections for future retrieval.* The more times you read something, the more you reinforce the learning of ideas.

Even if you don't fully understand something on the first pass, *your mind stores much of the material for later recall.*

6. Relax to learn so go into exile. Our bodies respond to an inner clock called biorhythms. Burning the midnight oil works well for some people, but not everyone.

If possible, set aside a particular place to study that is free of distractions. Shut off the television, cell phone, pager and exile your friends and family during your study period.

If you really are bothered by silence, try background music. Light classical music at a low volume has been shown to aid in concentration over other types. Music that evokes pleasant emotions without lyrics are highly suggested. Try just about anything by Mozart. It relaxes you.

7. Use arrows not highlighters. At best, it's difficult to read a page full of yellow, pink, blue, and green streaks. Try staring at a neon sign for a while and you'll soon see that the horde of colors obscure the message.

A quick note, a brief dash of color, an underline, and an arrow pointing to a particular passage is much clearer than a horde of highlighted words.

8. Budget your study time. Although you shouldn't ignore any of the material, *allocate your available study time in the same ratio that topics may appear on the test.*

Testing Tips:

1. Get smart, play dumb. Don't read anything into the question. Don't make an assumption that the test writer is looking for something else than what is asked. Stick to the question as written and don't read extra things into it.

2. Read the question and all the choices twice before answering the question. You may miss something by not carefully reading, and then re-reading both the question and the answers.

If you really don't have a clue as to the right answer, leave it blank on the first time through. Go on to the other questions, as they may provide a clue as to how to answer the skipped questions.

If later on, you still can't answer the skipped ones . . . **Guess.** The only penalty for guessing is that you might get it wrong. Only one thing is certain; if you don't put anything down, you will get it wrong!

3. Turn the question into a statement. Look at the way the questions are worded. The syntax of the question usually provides a clue. Does it seem more familiar as a statement rather than as a question? Does it sound strange?

By turning a question into a statement, you may be able to spot if an answer sounds right, and it may also trigger memories of material you have read.

4. Look for hidden clues. It's actually very difficult to compose multiple-foil (choice) questions without giving away part of the answer in the options presented.

In most multiple-choice questions you can often readily eliminate one or two of the potential answers. This leaves you with only two real possibilities and automatically your odds go to Fifty-Fifty for very little work.

5. Trust your instincts. For every fact that you have read, you subconsciously retain something of that knowledge. On questions that you aren't really certain about, go with your basic instincts. **Your first impression on how to answer a question is usually correct.**

6. Mark your answers directly on the test booklet. Don't bother trying to fill in the optical scan sheet on the first pass through the test.

Just be very careful not to miss-mark your answers when you eventually transcribe them to the scan sheet.

7. Watch the clock! You have a set amount of time to answer the questions. Don't get bogged down trying to answer a single question at the expense of 10 questions you can more readily answer.

COMPETENCY 1.0   CONCEPTUAL AND QUANTITATIVE KNOWLEDGE
                    OF THE STRUCTURE AND BEHAVIOR OF
                    MATTER

SKILL 1.1   Analyze the physical and chemical properties of matter (e.g.
               mass, volume, density, chemical reactivity).

Everything in our world is made up of **matter**, whether it is a rock, a building, or an animal. A rock or a piece of wood is not a single substance since is a combination of different materials. A substance is a material with uniform properties throughout. Salt, steel, gold, and water are substances. Milk is not a substance, though it appears to be uniform, because it contains tiny drops of fat.

Mass is a measure of the amount of matter in an object. Two objects of equal mass will balance each other on a simple balance scale no matter where the scale is located. The unit of mass in SI units is the kilogram, which is the mass of a particular piece of metal maintained by the International Bureau of Weights and Measures in Sèvres, France. In English units mass is measured in pounds, a unit of force, but mass should not be confused with weight, which is the force of gravity.

A **physical property** of a substance is its density, which is the mass of an object made of the substance divided by its volume ($D = m/V$). The density of water is 1 $gm/(cm)^3$ and the density of lead is 11.3 $gm/(cm)^3$. Other physical properties of a substance are its color, hardness, resistivity, viscosity, solubility, and ductility. A physical property can be observed without changing the identity of a substance. Dissolving salt in water is considered a physical change because the salt and water can be easily separated. Also, even though the freezing and melting of water changes the physical properties of the water and ice, the change is considered a physical change.

Chemical properties describe the ability of a substance to be changed into new substances. When exposed to air, iron rusts. The properties of the rust are different from the properties of iron, so this is a chemical change. Baking powder goes through a chemical change as it changes into carbon dioxide gas when mixed with water.

SKILL 1.2   Distinguish between the states of matter

The **phase of matter** refers to its three possible states: solid, liquid, and gas. A **solid** has a definite shape and volume. A **liquid** has a definite volume and assumes the shape of its container. A **gas** has will spread out to occupy the entire space of whatever container it is in.

The three states can be understood in terms of kinetic theory of matter, which states that all matter consists of atoms or molecules in a state of constant motion. In a solid, the molecules or atoms have strong forces holding them together and the molecules vibrate with small amplitudes. In a gas, the forces between the molecules are very small and the molecules are free to move anywhere in the container. In a liquid, the forces holding the molecules together are greater than in a gas, but less than in a liquid.

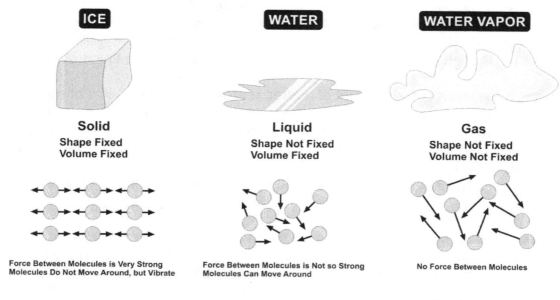

Udaix/Shutterstock.com

A **plasma** is a partially ionized gas in which some of the electrons are not bound to any atoms or molecules. Plasmas are electrically conductive and can be generated inside vacuum tubes with a beam of electrons. Plasmas are the most common form of matter in the universe because stars are composed of plasmas.

SKILL 1.3   Apply knowledge of the gas laws

The physical properties of a gas are it temperature (T), volume (V), mass (n), and pressure (P). Temperature is measured with a thermometer in Fahrenheit or Celsius degrees. The lowest possible temperature is -273.15 C° and corresponds to the absence of molecular motion. The SI unit for temperature is the kelvin (K). The lowest temperature is 0 K in SI units. The average kinetic energy of the atoms or molecules of the gas determines its temperature.

Mass is measured in moles (n), which is the number of molecules in the gas expressed in terms of Avogadro's number, which is 6.02×10^{23}.

The pressure of a gas is the force the gas exerts on a wall of the container divided by the area of the wall (P = F/A). It is a property of the gas itself because the pressure can be measured at any point in the container. The SI unit of force is the newton (N) and the SI unit of pressure is the pascal (Pa). Other units of pressure are the atmosphere (atm), millimeters of mercury (mm Hg), and pounds per square inch (lb/in^2, psi). The pressure of our atmosphere at sea level is 14.7 psi = 1 atm = 101,325 pa = 760 mm Hg.

The ideal gas law is based on the assumption that there are no forces acting between the molecules of the gas. The law is based on measurements of pressure, volume, temperature, and mass:

$$PV = nRT$$

R is the universal gas constant and has the same value for all gases. That PV is constant if T is constant can be understood from the mechanics of a single gas molecule bouncing back and forth inside a container. The smaller the container and the greater the speed of the molecule, the more collisions on the wall there will be. Also, the greater the speed of the molecules, the greater the force exerted by the molecules on the wall.

Adding or removing heat will change the pressure, volume, and temperature of a gas. Also, compressing the gas or letting the gas expand will change these parameters. The ideal gas law can be re-written as the combined gas law:

$$\frac{P_1V_1}{T_1} = \frac{P_2V_2}{T_2}$$

It is a combination of Boyle's law, Charles' law, and Gay-Lussac's law. In Boyle's law, the temperature is constant and pressure and volume are inversely related. In Charles' law, pressure is constant and volume and temperature are directly related. In Gay-Lussac's law, the volume is constant.

SKILL 1.4   Identify the major discoveries in the development of the atomic theory.

The atomic theory of matter was first suggested by a Greek named Democritus. In the 1780's, a scientist named John Dalton expanded on Democritus' idea. Dalton, a school teacher, made some observations about air: Air is a mixture of different kinds of gases; these gases do not separate on their own; it is possible to compress gases into a smaller volume. He also thought that particles of different substances must be different from each other and must maintain their own mass when combined with other substances. Dalton's atomic model is

1. Matter is made up of atoms.

2. Atoms of an element are similar to each other.
3. Atoms of different elements are different from each other.
4. Atoms combine with each other to form new kinds of compounds.

During the 1870s, William Crookes created "cathode rays" in a vacuum tube by connecting a high voltage battery to an anode and cathode. In 1896, British physicist J. J. Thomson showed that the mysterious rays were composed of negatively charged particles with a mass almost two thousand times smaller than the mass of the hydrogen atom. Thus, Thomson discovered the electron.

Thompson developed the plum pudding model of the atom. In this model, the atom consists of electrons equally mixed in a sphere of positive material. The electrons were the plums and the positively charged matter was the pudding.

In 1896, radioactivity was discovered. In addition to electrons (beta rays) and gamma rays, radioactive atoms emit alpha particles, which turned out to be the nuclei of the helium atom. The British scientist Ernest Rutherford used the alpha particles to test Thomson's model. Rutherford aimed a beam of alpha particles at a piece of gold foil. Most of the alpha particle penetrated the foil with only a few degrees of scattering. But a significant percent scattered 180°, that is, they bounced back. Rutherford said it was as if you shot a cannon ball at tissue paper and it bounced back. The result of his experiment gave way to Rutherford's atomic Model:

1. Most of an atom consists of empty space.
2. At the center of the atom is a nucleus that contains most of the mass and all of the positive charge of the atom.
3. The region of the space outside the nucleus is occupied by electrons.
4. The atom is neutral because the positive charge on the nucleus equals sum of the negative charges on the electrons.

The Danish scientist Niels Bohr created a new model of the atom in 1913. It was based on the recent discoveries in quantum mechanics and the discrete spectrum of light emitted by hydrogen atoms. According to this model:

1. Electrons orbit the nucleus, but only in discrete orbits or energy levels.
2. Electrons don't emit radiation when orbiting the nucleus.
3. When an electron moves from an outer orbit or higher energy level to an inner orbit or lower energy level, it emits a photon with an energy equal to the energy difference.

In later years, developments in quantum mechanics enabled physicists to derive the energy levels in hydrogen from fundamental principles.

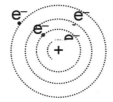

SKILL 1.5   Identify the characteristics of elements, compounds, and mixtures.

Passing an electric current through water will cause it to change into two flammable gases: oxygen and hydrogen. When hydrogen and oxygen are combined there is a tremendous release of energy in the form of light and water forms. Water is a **compound**, but oxygen and hydrogen are elements. An **element** is a substance that cannot be broken down into other substances. The most common isotope of hydrogen consists of one proton and one electron and is the first element on the periodic table. The second element is helium with 2 protons, 2 neutrons, and 4 electrons. Currently there are 118 elements on the periodic table built up by increasing the number of protons and neutrons in the nucleus.

A **compound** is made of two or more elements that have been chemically combined. A **molecule** is the smallest particle of substance that can exist independently and has all of the properties of that substance. A water molecule is made up of two hydrogen atoms and one oxygen atoms and has the **chemical formula** H_2O. The subscript 1 is not used when there is only one atom in the molecule.

A **mixture** is any combination of two or more substances in which the substances keep their own properties. A fruit salad is a mixture of different kinds of fruit. The amount of each type of fruit in the salad can vary from salad to salad or within the salad. In a compound, there is always ratio of elements. The other difference is that the substances in a mixture can be separated by physical means. For example, you can dissolve 1 gram of salt (NaCl) in 1 liter of water or 7 grams of water. The salt can be separated from the water by evaporation. In the case of salt itself, there is always one sodium atom and one chlorine atom. The sodium and chlorine can be separated only by melting the salt and running an electric current through it. The sodium is bonded to the chlorine with strong chemical forces.

Common compounds are **acids, bases, salts**, and **oxides** and are classified according to their characteristics.

An **acid** contains hydrogen ions (H^+). Although it is never wise to taste a substance to identify it, acids have a sour taste. Vinegar and lemon juice are both acids, and acids occur in many foods in a weak state. Strong acids can burn skin and destroy materials. Common acids include:

Name	Formula	Use
sulfuric acid	H_2SO_4	fertilizers, explosives, cleaning materials
Nitric acid	HNO_3	medicines, alcohol, dyes, car batteries
Carbonic acid	H_2CO_3	soft drinks
Acetic acid	$HC_2H_3O_2$	plastics, rubber, photographic film, solvent

Bases have a bitter taste and the stronger ones feel slippery. Like acids, strong bases can be dangerous and should be handled carefully. All bases contain hydroxyl ions (OH^-). Many household cleaning products contain bases. Common bases include:

Name	Formula	Use
sodium hydroxide	NaOH	soap, paper, vegetable oils, refining petroleum
ammonium hydroxide	NH_4OH	deodorants, bleaching compounds, cleaning compounds
potassium hydroxide	KOH	soaps, drugs, dyes, alkaline batteries, purifying industrial gases
calcium hydroxide	$Ca(OH)_2$	cement, plaster

An **indicator** is a substance that changes color when it comes in contact with an acid or a base. Litmus paper is an indicator. Blue litmus paper turns red in an acid. Red litmus paper turns blue in a base. A substance that is neither acid nor base is **neutral**. Neutral substances do not change the color of litmus paper.

PH SCALE

Salt is formed when an acid and a base combine chemically. Water is also formed. The process is called **neutralization**. Table salt (NaCl) is an example of this process. Salts are also used in toothpaste, Epsom salts, and cream of tartar. Calcium chloride ($CaCl_2$) is used on frozen streets and walkways to melt the ice. **Oxides** are compounds that are formed when oxygen combines with another element. Rust is an oxide formed when oxygen combines with iron.

SKILL 1.6   Apply knowledge of symbols, formulas, and equations for common elements and compounds (e.g., acids, bases, salts, carbon compounds) and their reactions.

One or more substances are formed during a **chemical reaction**. Energy is released in exothermic chemical reactions and is required for endothermic chemical reactions. Sometimes the energy release is slow and sometimes it is rapid. In a fireworks display, energy is released very rapidly. However, the chemical reaction that produces tarnish on a silver spoon happens very slowly.

Chemical equilibrium occurs when the quantities of reactants and products are no longer changing, but the reaction may still proceed forward and backward. The rate of forward reaction must equal the rate of backward reaction and the reaction is said to be in a steady state.

We can represent the reactants and products of a reaction in a chemical equation. Carbon and oxygen gas react to form carbon dioxide. The chemical equation can be written:

$$C + O_2 \rightarrow CO_2$$

The mass of the reactants is equal to the mass of the products. This means the chemical equation must be balanced and there must be the same number of atoms on both sides of the equation. Remember that the subscripts indicate the number of atoms in the elements. If there is no subscript, assume there is only one atom.

SKILL 1.7   Identify characteristics and functions of the components of an atom.

The **nucleus** is the center of the **atom**. The positive particles inside the nucleus are called **protons**. The mass of a proton is about 2,000 times that of the mass of an electron, but the magnitude of the charge is the same. The number of protons in the nucleus of an atom is called the **atomic number**. All atoms of the same element have the same atomic number. Atoms have no charge because the number of electrons moving around the nucleus equals the number of protons.

Neutrons are the second type of particle in the nucleus. Neutrons are slightly more massive than protons and have no charge. The number of neutrons in a nucleus can vary. **Isotopes** of an element have the same number of protons in the nucleus, but have a different number of neutrons.

The mass of an element on the periodic table is expressed in **atomic mass units** (amus). An amu is equal to 1/12 of the mass of carbon-12, the most common isotope of carbon. Carbon-12 has 6 protons, 6 neutrons, and 6 electrons. The mass of carbon as shown on the periodic table is slightly more than 12 amus because there are small amounts of carbon-13 and carbon-14 in the carbon found on Earth. The **mass number** of an atom is the sum of its protons and neutrons.

Electrons orbiting the nucleus occupy quantized or discrete energy levels. Planets orbiting the sun can be any distance from the sun, but electrons have wavelike or quantum properties that require them to be fixed distances from the nucleus. The electrons closest to the nucleus have the least amount of energy. According to the Pauli Exclusion Principle, electrons in an atom all have to be different, that is, have different *quantum numbers*, as they are called. There are two electrons in the lowest energy level, and not one, because electrons spin on their own axis. A spin can be either up or down. At the higher energy levels, electrons can have more angular momentum and hence more quantum numbers. The elements in the periodic table are built up by adding protons, neutrons, and electrons to the hydrogen nucleus. Electrons fill the lowest energy levels first. When the levels or shells are filled up, the next shell starts to fill up.

Energy level	Name	Number of electrons
first	K shell	2
second	L shell	8
third	M shell	18
fourth	N shell	32

Atoms react with each other when their outer levels are unfilled. The inert gases, helium, neon, and argon do not form compounds because their outer shells are filled.

When an electron gains energy by absorbing a photon or by a collision, it moves from one energy level to a higher energy level. The electron cannot leave one level until it has enough energy to reach the next level. **Excited electrons** are electrons that have absorbed energy and have moved farther away from the nucleus. Electrons can also lose energy. When they do, they fall to a lower level. However, they can only fall to the lowest level that has room for them.

SKILL 1.8   Identify chemical or physical properties of elements based on their placement on the periodic table.

The **periodic table of elements** is an arrangement of the elements in rows and columns so that it is easy to locate elements with similar properties. The elements of the modern periodic table are arranged in numerical order by atomic number.

The **periods** are the horizontal rows of the table and are named Period 1, Period 2, and so on, up to Period 7. The vertical columns of the periodic table are called **groups**, or **families.** Elements in a family have similar properties. The following is a key to each element on the periodic table:

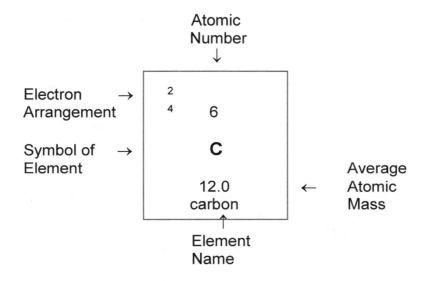

There are two systems for naming groups and many periodic tables show both naming systems. The International Union of Pure and Applied Chemistry (IUPAC) recommends the names Group 1, Group 2, and so on, up to Group 18.
There are three types of elements: metals, nonmetals, and metalloids.

Periodic Table of the Elements

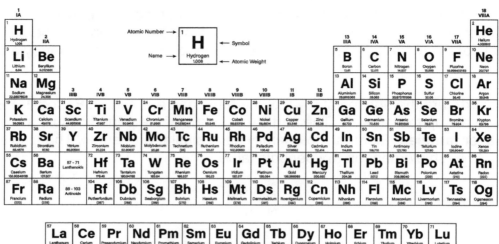

Humdan/Shutterstock.com

Metals

With the exception of hydrogen, all elements in Group 1 are alkali metals. These metals are shiny, softer and less dense than other metals, and are the most chemically active. Group 2 metals are the alkaline earth metals. They are harder, denser, have higher melting points, and are chemically active. The transition elements can be found in Period 4 to Period 7 under Group 4 to Group 12. They are hard and have high melting points. Compounds of these elements are colorful, such as silver, gold, and mercury.

Nonmetals

Nonmetals are not as easy to recognize as metals because they do not always share physical properties. However, in general the properties of nonmetals are the opposite of metals. They are dull, brittle, and are not good conductors of heat and electricity. Nonmetals include solids, gases, and one liquid (bromine).

Nonmetals have four to eight electrons in their outermost energy levels and tend to attract electrons. As a result, the outer levels are usually filled with eight electrons. This difference in the number of electrons is what caused the differences between metals and nonmetals. The outstanding chemical property of nonmetals is that they react with metals.

The **halogens** can be found in Group 17. Halogens combine readily with metals to form salts. Table salt, fluoride toothpaste, and bleach all have an element from the halogen family. The **noble gases** got their name from the fact that they did not react chemically with other elements, much like the nobility did not mix with the masses. These gases (found in Group 18) will only combine with other elements under very specific conditions. They are **inert** (inactive). In recent years, however, scientists have found this to be only generally true, since chemists have been able to prepare compounds of krypton and xenon.

Metalloids

Metalloids have properties in between metals and nonmetals. They can be found in Group 13 to Group 16, but do not occupy the entire group. They are arranged in stair steps across the groups. As to physical properties, all are

1. solids having the appearance of metals.
2. white or gray, but not shiny.
3. conduct electricity, but not as well as a metal.

As to chemical properties,

1. all have some characteristics of metals and nonmetals.
2. their properties do not follow patterns like metals and nonmetals. Each must be studied individually.

Silicon is the second element in Group 14. It is a **semiconductor** because it has a conductivity between that of an insulator and a conductor. Sand is made of a silicon compound, silicon dioxide. Silicon is also used in the manufacture of glass and cement.

SKILL 1.9   Identify characteristics of types of chemical bonding (e.g., covalent, ionic, metallic, hydrogen).

The outermost electrons in atoms are called **valence electrons.** Because they are the only electrons involved in the bonding process, they determine the properties of the element.

A **chemical bond** is a force of attraction that holds atoms together. When atoms are bonded chemically, they cease to have their individual properties. When hydrogen and oxygen combine to form water, their properties change entirely.

A **covalent bond** is formed when two atoms share electrons in order to get completely filled shells. Covalent bonding happens between nonmetals. An example is hydrogen gas (H_2). The atoms of the hydrogen gas molecule are held together because the two shared electrons give each hydrogen nucleus a filled outer shell. **Covalent compounds** are compounds whose atoms are joined by covalent bonds. Table sugar, methane, and ammonia are examples of covalent compounds.

An **ionic bond** is a bond formed by the transfer of electrons from one atom to the other. It happens when metals and nonmetals bond. Before chlorine and sodium combine, the sodium has one valence electron and chlorine has seven. Neither valence shell is filled, but the chlorine's valence shell is almost full. During the reaction, the sodium gives one valence electron to the chlorine atom. Both atoms then have filled shells and are stable. Something else has happened during the bonding. Before the bonding, both atoms were neutral. When one electron was transferred, it upset the balance of protons and electrons in each atom. The chlorine atom took on one extra electron and the sodium atom released one atom. The atoms have now become ions. **Ions** are atoms with an unequal number of protons and electrons. To determine whether the ion is positive or negative, compare the number of protons (+ charge) to the electrons (– charge). If there are more electrons the ion will be negative. If there are more protons, the ion will be positive.

Compounds that result from the transfer of metal atoms to nonmetal atoms are called **ionic compounds.** Sodium chloride (table salt), sodium hydroxide (drain cleaner), and potassium chloride (salt substitute) are examples of ionic compounds.

Metallic bonding exists only in metals, such as aluminum, gold, copper, and iron. In metals, the electrons are not fixed to any particular nuclei and are free to move. There is an interaction between the electrons and the metallic nuclei that bonds the atoms together. This special situation is responsible for the unique properties of metals, such as their malleability and electrical conductivity.

Hydrogen bonding is an example a force that acts between two molecules of a liquid or a solid and holds the molecules together. An example of this is the water molecule. While the total charge of H_2O is zero, the oxygen end of the molecule is negative and the hydrogen end is positive. We say the oxygen-hydrogen bond is *polar*. This can be understood as the result of the large positive charge of the oxygen nucleus as compared to the small positive charge on the hydrogen nucleus. This creates an attractive force between water molecules that keeps the molecules connected.

The boiling point of water, for example, is much greater than would be the case if such bonding did not exist. This fact alone should make the human race (and the rest of life) grateful for hydrogen bonding since water would otherwise be a gas at room temperature.

Hydrogen bonds can occur within and between other molecules. For instance, the two strands of a DNA molecule are held together by hydrogen bonds. Hydrogen bonding between water molecules and the amino acids of proteins are involved in maintaining the protein's proper shape.

SKILL 1.10   Identify types of chemical reactions and their characteristics.

In a **composition reaction**, two or more substances combine to form a compound.

$$A + B \rightarrow AB$$
$$C + O_2 \rightarrow CO_2$$

Another example is that silver and sulfur combine to yield silver dioxide.

In a **decomposition reaction**, a compound breaks down into two or more simpler substances.

$$AB \rightarrow A + B$$
$$2H_2O \rightarrow 2H_2 + O_2$$

An electric current is needed to split water molecules into hydrogen and oxygen gas.

In a **single replacement reaction**, a free element replaces an element that is part of a compound.

$$A + BX \rightarrow AX + B$$
$$CuSO_4 + Fe \rightarrow FeSO_4 + Cu$$

Iron plus copper sulfate yields iron sulfate plus copper.

In a **double replacement reaction**, parts of two compounds replace each other. In this case, the compounds seem to switch partners.

$$AX + BY \rightarrow AY + BX$$
$$HCl + NaOH \rightarrow NaCl + H_2O$$

Sodium chloride plus mercury nitrate yields sodium nitrate plus mercury chloride.

COMPETENCY 2.0   CONCEPTUAL AND QUANTITATIVE KNOWLEDGE OF FORCES AND MOTION AND THEIR RELATIONSHIP

SKILL 2.1   Differentiate between the types and characteristics of contact forces and forces acting at a distance, and their interactions.

Dynamics is the study of the relationship between motion and the forces affecting motion. **Forces** cause objects to move and can be understood as a push or a pull.

The force of **gravity** is the force that causes objects to fall to Earth. We can feel the force of gravity when we lift something up. The force of gravity also keeps the moon rotating around Earth and Earth rotating around the sun. The universal law of gravity states that there is a gravitational attraction between all objects on Earth determined by the equation:

$$F_{\text{gravity}} = G\frac{m_1 m_2}{d^2}$$

where G is the universal gravitational constant and d is the distance between the two masses. Mass and weight are not the same quantities. Weight refers to the force of gravity between an object and Earth.

Electrostatic forces between objects are attractive when the charges are different and repulsive when charges are the same. Charges are measured in the units coulombs and Coulomb's law states:

$$F_{\text{electric}} = k_e \frac{q_1 q_2}{d^2}$$

where k_e is Coulomb's constant. Coulomb's law is what keeps electrons rotating around the nucleus in atoms. Coulomb's law also explains ionic bonding.

Electrostatic forces can be easily observed by rubbing a glass rod with silk. Electrons on the silk transfer to the glass rod, giving the glass rod a negative charge.

Magnetic forces are observed when examining lodestones, which are pieces of an iron ore found in nature. Lodestones are magnetized, which means they have a north pole and south pole. In addition, magnets have the property of attracting iron (Fe) and a number of other ferromagnetic materials, as they are called. As with electrostatic forces, like poles repel each other and unlike poles attract each other. But unlike charges, magnetic poles always come in pairs.

Gravitational forces can be understood as objects acting at a distance. To understand electric and magnetic forces, the concept of electric and magnetic fields must be introduced. When a charge is stationary it produces an electric field in the space around it. When a charge is moving, it also produces circular magnetic fields that are perpendicular to the direction of motion. By the latter half of the nineteenth century, physicists developed a full understanding of the relationship between electric and magnetic fields and showed that light consisted of electric and magnetic fields, broken off from charges, and traveling through space.

The existence of nuclear forces is apparent from the fact that the repulsive electrostatic force between protons does not drive the protons apart. It is apparent that the neutrons in the nucleus serve as a kind of glue, because the larger the nucleus the more neutrons there are. Aluminum, for example, has one more neutron than protons, but lead has over 40 more neutrons than protons. When protons are very close to each other, there is an attractive force called the strong force. The strong force is the same when a neutron is in contact with another neutron or a proton. The lack of stability in large nuclei can be understood from the fact that all the protons in a nucleus are repelling each other, and nuclear forces only affect the adjacent proton or neutron.

Statics is the study of physical systems at rest or moving with a constant speed. This occurs when the net force acting on an object is zero. When a book is resting on a table, for example, the force of gravity is in equilibrium with the force of the table acting upward on the book. The force of the table on the book is called the normal force.

Static friction describes the force of friction of two surfaces that are in contact but do not have any motion relative to each other, such as a block sitting on an inclined plane. **Kinetic friction** describes the force of friction of two surfaces in contact with each other when there is relative motion between the surfaces. Both static and kinetic friction these rules:

1. The materials that make up the surfaces determines the magnitude of the frictional force.
2. The frictional force is independent of the area of contact between the two surfaces.
3. The direction of the frictional force is opposite to the direction of motion for kinetic friction.
4. The frictional force is proportional to the normal force between the two surfaces in contact.

SKILL 2.2 Identify applications of Newton's laws of motion.

Newton's first law of motion states that an object at rest will remain at rest and an object in motion will remain in motion at a constant velocity unless acted upon by an external force. This is also called the law of inertia and can be derived from the following law.

Newton's second law of motion states that if a net force acts on an object, it will cause the object to accelerate:

$$\vec{F} = m\vec{a}$$

The arrows indicate that force and acceleration have direction and are vector quantities. Mass is a scalar quantity because no direction is associated with it.

Newton's third law states forces on objects come from other objects and hence always exist in pairs: The force of object 1 on object 2 is equal and opposite to the force of object 2 on object 1.

Newton's third law leads mathematically to the law of conservation of momentum, which governs a collision or any interaction between two objects. Momentum is the mass of an object times its velocity: $\vec{p} = m\vec{v}$. When there is a collision between two objects, the momentum before the collision is equal to the momentum after the collision.

Newton's second law leads to the concept of work, which is force acting through a distance. Energy is the ability to do work and kinetic energy is the energy of motion. Potential energy can be defined when the force depends on the relative locations of the objects, as is the case of electric and gravitational forces. The force exerted by a spring depends on how much the spring is stretched or compressed and is a conservative force. Friction is not a conservative force. One can see this by comparing the motion of a pendulum with the motion of an object stopped by the force of friction. The law of conservation of mechanical energy can be written:

$$\frac{1}{2}mv^2_{\text{initial}} + PE_{\text{initial}} = \frac{1}{2}mv^2_{\text{final}} + PE_{\text{final}}$$

One of the great historical achievements of Newton's laws was to derive Kepler's laws of planetary motion. Newton explained why planets travel in elliptical paths, speed up when they are closest to the sun, and obey the law of periods concerning the time it takes for a planet to make one revolution.

SKILL 2.3   Solve problems involving force and motion.

The simplest kinds of problems in dynamics are applications of $F = ma$ to a point mass. When two of the three variables are given and you must calculate the third. In the case of the motion of objects near the Earth's surface, the acceleration is always downward at a rate of 9.8 m/s^2.

Problems involving inclined planes require considering the vector nature of force and calculating the components of the force perpendicular to the surface of the plane and parallel to it. This is a simple example of motion in two dimensions because there are two forces, friction and gravity, acting in different directions.

The law governing frictional forces is $F_{\text{friction}} = \mu N$, where μ is the coefficient of friction and N is the normal force, which is generally looked up in tables.

Another example of motion in two dimensions is projectile motion at the surface of the Earth. To solve these problems, the horizontal motion is considered separately from the vertical motion. In the horizontal direction, the acceleration is

0 m/s² and in the vertical direction it is 9.8 m/s². The two separate solutions can be combined to arrive at the result: An object near the Earth's surface moves in a parabola.

To solve the motion of an object not near the surface of Earth means taking into consideration the universal law of gravity, which is not constant but follows the inverse square law. To solve this problem requires a knowledge of calculus and differential equations. The motion is not parabolic, but is elliptical. The elliptical shape of orbits is one of Kepler's laws of planetary motion.

Algebra alone can be used to solve the problem of circular motion, as when an automobile turns a corner. When a force is applied to a moving mass in a direction that is perpendicular to the motion, the object changes direction. The change in direction constitutes an acceleration which is called a centripetal acceleration. It is given by the formula:

$$a_{centripetal} = \frac{v^2}{r}$$

Where *v* is the speed of the object and *r* is the radius of curvature of the motion.

An example of the conservation of mechanical energy is the pendulum. The falling motion of the bob is accompanied by an increase in speed. As the bob loses height and potential energy, it gains speed and kinetic energy. The sum of potential energy and kinetic energy remains constant; the total of the two forms of mechanical energy is conserved.

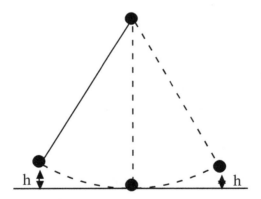

A pendulum can also be considered a case of simple harmonic motion, which occurs when the force is proportional to the displacement. While the gravitational force on the bob is constant, what is relevant is the component of the force in the direction of motion. This component is proportional to the displacement (*h*). This occurs also with springs and is known as Hooke's law: $F_{elastic} = kx$.

SKILL 2.4   Identify types, characteristics, and properties of waves

A **mechanical wave** is a disturbance that propagates through a medium at a speed characteristic of the medium. There is a transfer of energy, but there is not a bulk transfer of matter. In the case of sound, for example, the medium is air and the disturbance is produced by perhaps a tuning fork that vibrates at a fixed rate. Each single disturbance produces a pulse.

The **speed of a wave** is the speed the disturbance propagates through the medium. The **period** of a wave is the time between disturbances and the **frequency** is the inverse of the period. The unit of measure for frequencies is the hertz which is 1/second. The **amplitude** of a wave is a measure of how much the medium is being distorted. In the case of water waves, the amplitude is the height of the wave. The **wavelength** of a wave is the distance between the pulses or individual disturbances. The wave equation relates the frequency (f), wavelength (λ), and speed (v) of a wave: $v = \lambda f$.

Waves are also longitudinal or transverse. In transverse waves, the disturbance of the medium is perpendicular to the direction of motion of the disturbance. In longitudinal waves, the disturbance is parallel to the direction of motion. Water waves are an example of transverse waves. Sound is a longitudinal wave. A tuning fork, for example, creates alternate areas of compression of the air and rarefaction of the air.

In the case of sound waves, the frequency produces the sensation of **pitch** when you hear it and the amplitude produces the sensation of loudness. The pitch used for tuning in Western music is 440 Hz. The intensity of a sound wave is measured in decibels.

Visible light, radio waves, X-rays, microwaves, gamma rays, and radar consist of vibrating electric and magnetic fields. They are waves, but not mechanical waves because they travel through a vacuum. The speed of this radiation is 186,000 miles per second or 3×10^8 meters per second. Clerk Maxwell derived the speed of light in the 19th century from measurement in electricity and magnetism.

The electric and magnetic fields are perpendicular to each other and to the direction of propagation of the wave. Hence, **electromagnetic radiation** is a transverse wave. A look at a chart of electromagnetic radiation will show the different types of radiation and their wavelength and frequency. AM radio waves have a wavelength of 100 meters and a frequency of 10^6 Hz. High-energy gamma rays have a wavelength of 10^{24} Hz and a correspondingly small wavelength.

Seismic waves are elastic waves that travel through the Earth when there are earthquakes. There are also induced seismic waves produced by dynamite for exploratory purposes. Primary waves (P waves) are longitudinal waves and the fastest traveling. Secondary waves (S waves) are transverse waves and slower than P waves. S waves do not travel through liquids.

Everything from earthquakes to ship wakes creates **water waves**; however, the most common cause is wind. As wind passes over the water's surface, friction forces it to ripple. The strength of the wind, the distance the wind blows (fetch) and the length of the gust (duration) determine how big the ripples will become. Waves are divided into several parts. The crest is the highest point on a wave, while the trough or valley between two waves is the lowest point. Wavelength is the horizontal distance, either between the crests or troughs, of two consecutive waves. Wave height is a vertical distance between a wave's crest and the next trough. The wave period can be measured by picking a stationary point and counting the seconds it takes for two consecutive crests or troughs to pass it.

If we followed a single drop of water during a passing wave, we would see it move in a vertical circle, returning to a point near its original position at the wave's end. These vertical circles are more obvious at the surface. As depth increases, their effects slowly decrease until completely disappearing about half a wavelength below the surface.

SKILL 2.5   **Analyze characteristics of wave phenomena (e.g., intensity, refraction, interference, Doppler effect, wave-particle duality) as they apply to real-world situations.**

Superposition means that two or more different waves can be in the same medium and the same time. In **constructive interference**, the amplitudes of the different waves reinforce one another and the resulting wave has a greater amplitude that the superposed waves. In **destructive interference**, the amplitudes cancel out to a certain degree.

An example of interference is the phenomena of **beats** in the case of sound waves. If you superpose two sounds with frequencies that are close in value, say 400 Hz and 410 Hz, there will be a variation in loudness that depends on the difference between the two frequencies.

Another phenomena common to all waves is the **Doppler effect**. If the source of the wave is moving towards the observer the wavelength is shorter than it would be if the source was stationary. Likewise, if the source is moving away from the observer, the wavelength is longer. The Doppler effect is used to measure the speed of baseball and automobiles. In these devices, radar is used to produce a series of pulses with a definite wavelength and frequency. When the radar pulses hits the moving object they are **reflected**. The radar gun measures the frequency of the reflected beam and thereby measures the speed of the object.

When a wave is incident upon a boundary between two different media (for example, light in a vacuum incident upon glass) part of the wave is reflected, and part of the wave is **refracted**. The refracted wave continues to propagate in the new medium. The less the difference between the two media is, the greater the amount of refracted wave. When sound traveling in air hits a brick wall, the intensity of the reflected sound will be much greater than the intensity of the sound wave propagated inside the wall. The **intensity** of a wave is a measure of how much energy is being transported by the wave.

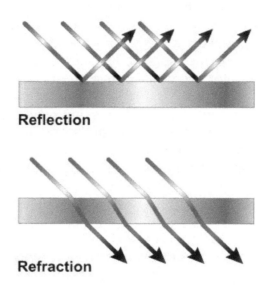

Reflection

Refraction

Fouad A. Saad/Shutterstock.com

Diffraction refers to the fact that waves have a tendency to spread out in a medium. This is because a wave is a disturbance in a medium and each point of disturbance is a source of further disturbances. This means waves can travel around barriers placed in the medium.

The wavelength of light can be measured by combining the phenomena of diffraction and interference. When light is incident upon a double slit, each slit will become a new source of light because of diffraction. The two beams will then superimpose and interfere. There will be constructive and destructive interference, which will produce dark and bright lines on a screen. From the distance between the dark lines, the wavelength of the incident light can be measured.

You can demonstrate the phenomena of diffraction and interference with a single slit by yourself. Press your thumb and forefinger together, making a very thin slit between them. Hold the slit about 8 cm from your eye and look at a distant source of light. The dark and light pattern you observe is caused by the diffraction and interference of light.

Before the discovery of the diffraction of light, it was believed that light was made of particles that traveled in a straight line and produced sharp shadows. Because light has such a small wavelength, it can be assumed light consists of rays traveling in a straight line. Scientists do this in the branch of physics called optics.

When a light ray is incident upon a smooth glass surface at an angle, there is a reflected ray and a refracted ray. The refracted ray changes direction because the speed of light in glass is less than the speed of light in a vacuum. If the ray hits the surface of the glass perpendicularly, there will be no change in direction. This phenomena is described by Snell's law. The reflected ray leaves the surface of the glass at the angle of incidence.

Wave-particle duality is the exhibition of both wavelike and particle-like properties by photons (particles of light), electrons, protons, and neutrons. All objects exhibit wave-particle duality to some extent, but for macroscopic objects the quantum mechanical wavelength is so small it can't be observed.

The existence of shells and energy levels in atoms can be understood from the phenomena of standing waves. Standing waves occur from the interference of waves traveling in opposite directs but having the same frequency and wavelength. There is no net propagation of energy, but interference creates nodes and anti-nodes. Shells are created in atoms because the wavelength of the electron has to be some multiple of the orbit size. In the lowest energy level, the wavelength of the electron is exactly equal to the circumference of the orbit.

The particle-like property of electromagnetic radiation was discovered with the photoelectric effect. In this phenomenon, light striking a metal surface causes electrons to be emitted from the metal. This can only be understood if light is considered to be a particle with momentum and energy but without mass, that is, a photon. For photons/electromagnetic radiation, radio waves behave more like waves than particles and gamma rays behave more like particles than waves.

SKILL 2.6   Identify causes, characteristics, and examples of electricity

Electrostatics is the study of stationary electric charges. A plastic rod that is rubbed with fur or a glass rod that is rubbed with silk will become electrically charged. The charge on the plastic rod is negative because electrons from the fur transfer to the plastic rod.

A simple device used to indicate the existence of a positive or negative charge is called an **electroscope**. An electroscope is made up of a metal knob with very lightweight leaves of aluminum foil attached to it. When a charged object touches the knob, the leaves push away from each other because like charges repel. It is not possible to tell whether if the charge is positive or negative. If the charged object is positive, electrons will flow from the electroscope into the charged object, making the leaves and the knob positive.

An electroscope can also be charge by induction. In this case, the charged object is brought close to the knob but does not touch it. If the charged object is positively charged, it will attract electrons to the knob. This will make the knob negatively charged and the leaves positively charged. Charge can be removed from an object by connecting it to the Earth through a conductor. The removal of static electricity by conduction is called **grounding**.

A metal rod can be given a charge by placing it in water. Water molecules are polar, that is, they have a positive side and a negative side. A metal consists of a lattice of positively charged nuclei in a sea of electrons. Water molecules will surround a metallic nuclei and cause it to go into solution, leaving behind a negative charge on the metal rod. The concentration of charge on the metal, or **voltage**, is determined by the properties of the metal. A battery is constructed by placing two different types of metals (terminals) in water, thereby producing a voltage difference. Voltage is measured in units called volts.

A battery produces an **electric current** when a wire connects the two terminals of the battery. The voltage difference will cause electrons to flow at a slow drift velocity from one terminal to the other. At the same time, metal ions will reattach to one terminal and be removed from the other until the battery goes dead. The unit of measurement for current is the ampere (amp).

SKILL 2.7 Identify types of magnets and characteristics of magnetic fields.

Magnets are objects with a north pole and a south pole. Like poles repel and unlike poles attract. Magnets exert a force on other magnets and on moving electric charges. A magnet creates a **magnetic field** is the space around it, and it is the magnetic field that exerts the force.

Magnetic fields are created by moving charges. A current flowing in a straight wire produces a circular magnetic field pointing in a direction determined by the direction of current flow. There is no north pole or south pole. However, if the wire forms a loop or circle, the magnetic field lines will enter one side of the loop and exit the other side. The side they exit is the north pole and the side the enter is the south pole. By wrapping wire around a pole, you can stack these current loops and produce a very strong magnet. Such a device is called an **electromagnet**.

MAGNETIC FIELD

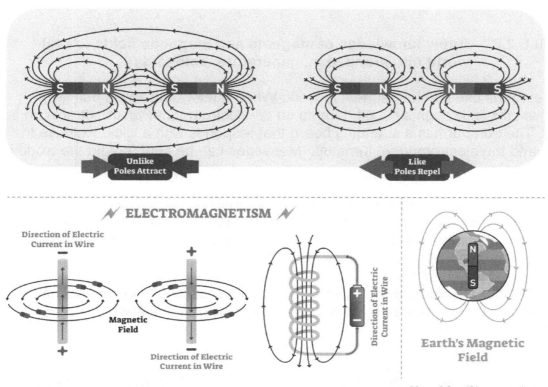

VectorMine/Shutterstock.com

Electrons behave like tiny magnets because they are rotating about their own axis. Electrons in an atom are also rotating around the nucleus and are creating a magnetic field in this way as well. Protons also produce a magnetic field. Most substances are not magnetized because the magnetic fields produced by electrons, atoms, and protons cancel out.

When an object is brought close to a magnet, the object will become magnetized. In other words, a north pole and south pole will be induced on the object. A few substances are diamagnetic, but all other substances are paramagnetic. With paramagnetic substances a north pole induces a south pole and the paramagnet is attracted to the magnet.

Ferromagnetism is a special case of paramagnetism. The main ferromagnetic materials are iron, nickel, and cobalt. The nuclei of these substances are connected is such a way that small magnetic domains are created where the magnetic poles of the atoms are all aligned. The north and south poles of the domains are random within the substance, but an external magnetic field will line them up and a permanent magnet can be created.

The Earth produces a magnetic field. The field is directed away from the geographic south pole, circles the globe, and enters the geographic north pole. In a compass, a tiny, lightweight magnet is suspended and will line up with Earth's magnetic field. The cause of the Earth's magnetic field is only partially understood.

SKILL 2.8   Apply knowledge of magnets and magnetic fields to real-world situations (e.g., generators, solenoids).

Telegraphs use electromagnets to work. When a telegraph key is pushed, current flows through a circuit, turning on an electromagnet which attracts an iron bar. The iron bar hits a sounding board that responds with a click. Release the key and the electromagnet turns off. Messages can be sent around the world in this way.

Scrap metal can be removed from waste materials by the use of a large electromagnet that is suspended from a crane. When the electromagnet is turned on, the metal in the pile of waste will be attracted to it. All other materials will stay on the ground.

Air conditioners, vacuum cleaners, and washing machines use electric motors. An electric motor uses an electromagnet to change electric energy into mechanical energy.

SKILL 2.9   Identify characteristics of motion as they apply to real-world situations (e.g., speed, velocity, acceleration, linear and angular momentum).

Dynamics is the study of forces and how forces produce motion. Kinematics is the study of motion without regard to the cause of motion. Suppose someone travels in a car from Miami to Jacksonville, a distance of 400 miles, and it takes 10 hours. The average speed of the car was 40 miles per hour:

$$\bar{v} = \frac{s_1 - s_2}{t} = \frac{400 \text{ miles}}{10 \text{ hours}} = 40 \text{ mph}$$

The instantaneous speed (v) is the speed at each instant in time and is determined by looking at the car's speedometer. It can be understood mathematically as the average speed over a very small time interval.

The average acceleration over a period of time (t) is

$$a = \frac{v_1 - v_2}{t} \text{ or } v_2 = v_1 + at$$

In kinematics, we generally assume that the acceleration of an object is constant in time, that is, it is either zero or not zero. For example, all objects near the surface of Earth accelerate at 9.8 m/s². Actually, as a falling object moves closer to the center of Earth, which is 4,000 miles away, its acceleration increases slightly since the force of gravity increases slightly. For this reason, we leave out the horizontal bar which indicates an average value.

Since the acceleration is always constant, there is another equation for the average speed:

$$\overline{v} = \frac{v_1 + v_2}{2}$$

Thus, in kinematics we have a set of three equations with seven variables. Kinematic problems use two more equations that are obtained from these three:

$$s_2 = s_1 + v_1 t + \frac{1}{2} a t^2$$

$$v_2^2 = v_1^2 + 2a(s_2 - s_1)$$

COMPETENCY 3.0   CONCEPTUAL AND QUANTITATIVE KNOWLEDGE OF ENERGY AND ITS EFFECTS

SKILL 3.1 Differentiate between forms of energy and their transformations.

Work is performed whenever a force acts through a distance. Energy is defined as the ability to do work and there are many kinds of energy. Kinetic energy is the energy of motion. An object located on the top of a building has gravitational potential energy because it will acquire kinetic energy if it falls. In general, mechanical potential energy is stored or future energy. A coiled spring has elastic potential energy. The force of friction will cause an object's kinetic energy to transform into internal energy or heat energy. Chemical energy is the energy stored in atoms and molecules and can be transformed into heat energy by various chemical reactions. Nuclear energy is stored in the nuclei of atoms and is released in nuclear reactors in the form of heat and radiation. The law of conservation of energy is that energy never disappears, it just transforms from one form to another.

SKILL 3.2   Relate energy to transitions between states of matter.

The kinetic theory states that matter consists of molecules in continual random motion. The state of matter (solid, liquid, or gas) depends on the amount of kinetic energy the molecules possess. The molecules of solid matter vibrate because strong intermolecular forces hold the molecules in place. The molecules of liquid matter move more freely and throughout the body, and the molecules of gaseous matter move randomly and at high speeds.

Matter changes state when energy is added or taken away. The addition of energy, in the form of heat or mechanical energy (work), increases the kinetic energy of the component molecules. Faster moving molecules more readily overcome the intermolecular attractions that maintain the form of solids and liquids. As the speed of molecules increases, matter changes its state from solid to liquid to gas (melting and evaporation).

SKILL 3.3 Distinguish between temperature, heat, and thermal energy.

Water, like most substances, can exist in all three phases. The phase changes melting and freezing refer to changes between the solid and liquid phase. The phase changes between liquid and gas are called condensation and evaporation. Carbon dioxide in the solid phase is called dry ice. As is well known, when heat is added to dry ice, it converts to carbon dioxide gas without becoming a liquid. This process is called sublimation. The freezing point and melting point of substances are physical properties.

It takes energy to change the phase of a substance. If heat is added to ice that is at a temperature of –20 C°, for example, the temperature will rise. When the melting point is reached (0 C°), the ice will convert to liquid water. During this phase change, the temperature of the ice and liquid water will stay at 0 C° because the heat energy is being used to change the phase of the water.

Temperature is measured with a thermometer and is directly related to the sensation of hot and cold. The units of temperature are Fahrenheit or Celsius degrees. If the temperature of 1 gram of water increases by 1 degree Celsius, we say that 1 calorie of heat has been added to the water. (The units used by dieters are 1000 times bigger and spelled with a capital C).

Heat is a form of thermal energy. It is called thermal energy to distinguish from mechanical energy. Another form of thermal energy is internal energy which is the mechanical energy possessed by the atoms and molecules in an object. Thus, when we add heat to an object, its internal energy increases.

When a hot object comes into thermal contact with a cold object, the temperature of one will decrease and the temperature of the other will increase until the temperatures are the same. Heat will flow from the hot object to the cold object. Eventually, they will have the same temperature. When this happens, they are in **thermal equilibrium.**

We cannot rely on our sense of touch to determine temperature because the heat from a hand may be conducted more efficiently by certain objects, making them feel colder. This is why thermometers are used to measure temperature. A small amount of mercury in a capillary tube will expand when heated. In the Celsius scale, the freezing point of water is defined to be 0 °C and the boiling point of water is 100 °C. In the Fahrenheit scale, these points are 32 °F and 212 °F. The Fahrenheit scale was initially based on the freezing point of salt water and the body temperature of human beings.

The Kelvin scale is based on measurements of the temperatures of gases and their volumes. These experiment show that the lowest possible temperature is –273.15 °C. Kelvin degrees add this number to the Celsius scale so that all temperatures are positive. No degree sign is used with Kelvin temperatures.

The specific heat capacity (*c*) of water is defined as

$$\frac{1\ \text{calorie}}{(1\ \text{gram})(1\ \text{C}°)}$$

If you add one calorie of heat to a gram of lead, the temperature will increase 32 °C. This means the specific heat capacity of lead is 32 times smaller. Liquid water has a very high specific heat, in fact, it is twice the specific heat of ice. The equation connecting heat flow and change of temperature for an object of mass *m* is

$$Q = mc\Delta T$$

where *c* is the specific heat of the substance the object is made of.

SKILL 3.4 **Distinguish between the types of thermal energy transfer (e.g., radiation, conduction, convection).**

Conduction occurs when two objects are in thermal contact and heat from the hotter object flows into the cooler object. **Convection** occurs when heat is transported by the movement of a heated substance. Warmed air rising from a heat source such as a fire or electric heater is a common example of convection. Convection ovens make use of circulating air to more efficiently cook food.

A hot object emits infrared radiation. This can be seen by placing your hand one or two inches from the red-hot wires in an electric heater. It will be too hot to keep your hand there more than a second. However, if you place a piece of paper between your hand and the heater, there will be no pain at all. The heater is emitting infrared radiation that is being absorbed by your hand and/or the piece of paper. The heater also heads by convection because air right next to the hot wires will heat up and move around the room.

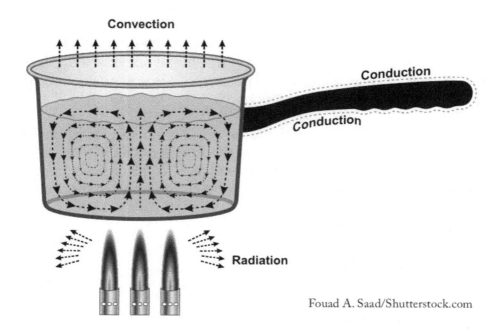

Fouad A. Saad/Shutterstock.com

An example of all three methods of heat transfer occurs in the thermos bottle or Dewar flask. The bottle is constructed of double walls of Pyrex glass that have a space in between. Air is evacuated from the space between the walls and the inner wall is silvered. The lack of air between the walls lessens heat loss by convection and conduction. The heat inside is reflected by the silver, cutting down heat transfer by radiation. Hot liquids remain hotter and cold liquids remain colder for longer periods of time.

SKILL 3.5   Apply the laws of thermodynamics to real-world situations.

In mechanics, energy is the ability to do work, which is force times distance. The units of work and energy are joules: 1 joule = 1 newton × 1 meter. Internal energy and heat are also forms of energy because they have the ability to do work. Steam engines and combustion engines use hot expanding gas to drive pistons. The **mechanical equivalent of heat** is 4.186 joules = 1 calorie. If you stir up a quantity of water until the temperature rises by 1 C°, you will find that it required 4.186 joules of mechanical energy.

It is apparent that mechanical energy is not conserved because of the force of friction. A pendulum will eventually stop because the mechanical energy is converted into the internal energy of the air the bob is moving through and the pivot point. The **first law of thermodynamics** states that mechanical energy and internal energy are conserved:

$$\Delta U = \Delta Q + \Delta W$$

This states the increase of the internal energy of a system is equal to the heat added to the system minus the work done by the system. The law is used to understand the thermodynamics of a simple engine made with a gas and a movable piston. You heat up or cool down the gas by conduction. The gas does work when the volume of the gas increases, and work is done on the gas when the volume of the gas decreases. The law of conservation of energy is frequently stated to be: Energy can be transformed, but it can neither be created nor destroyed.

The **zeroth law of thermodynamics** states, in effect, that you can measure the temperature of a substance with a thermometer. The **third law of thermodynamics** is that a temperature of absolute zero can never be reached. The **second law of thermodynamics** can be formulated a number of different ways:

1. Heat cannot flow from a colder to a hotter object. Heat always flows from the hotter to the colder object until the temperatures are the same.
2. A gas will always occupy the entire vessel containing it in a uniform way. There are no parts of the vessel where the density is zero or very low.
3. The amount of disorder in a system is called entropy: the entropy of a closed system always increases. (Explanation: If you compress a gas to half its volume, there is a decrease in the entropy of the gas because there is twice as much knowledge about the location of all the atoms. There is more order, not less order. However, this is not a closed system. A force outside of the system increased the entropy of the gas.)
4. No machine can be imagined that converts heat energy to work energy with 100% efficiency. (Explanation: There is always a loss of heat to the environment because a machine always operates between two temperatures, a high temperature and a low temperature. The low temperature can never be absolute zero because of the third law of thermodynamics.)

SKILL 3.6   Differentiate between potential and kinetic energy.

Energy the ability to do work and the two concepts are rooted in personal experience. We need to exert our *muscle-force* over a *distance* to get out of bed in the morning and we can only do this if we have enough *energy*. However, there is no definition of energy in science, there are only definitions of particular kinds of energy. For this reason, there is no law that energy is conserved. There are laws saying momentum is conserved and mass is conserved. The law of conservation of momentum is an absolute truth and comes from $F = ma$. There is also a law saying mass is conserved, but it is understood to be only an approximation.

What is true, however, is that whenever physicists have discovered energy not being conserved they have been able to define a new energy that would save the principle. Kinetic energy is obviously not constant in the motion of the pendulum. But when you define potential energy in terms of the height of the bob ($PE = mgh$), the sum of kinetic and potential energy is a constant. Gravity is a conservative force because a potential energy can be defined. The other conservative forces are electrical, magnetic, and elastic. Thus we have the conservation of mechanical energy.

The first law of thermodynamics is an example of inventing a new energy called *internal energy.* Internal energy explains what happens to mechanical energy when it disappears. Mechanical energy is transformed into the internal energy of the objects exerting the forces that produce mechanical energy.

The photoelectric effect refers to the phenomena of light causing electrons to be ejected from a metal. Energy is conserved if you assume light is composed of photons and each photon has the energy expressed In terms of Plank's constant and the frequency of the light: $E = hf$.

The other form of energy is the energy associated with mass: $E = mc^2$. This conversion between mass and energy can be seen in two ways. The forces binding neutrons and protons together are called nuclear forces or strong forces. The potential energy associated with these forces is called nuclear binding energy. When neutrons and protons become bound in a nucleus, the mass decreases but there is an increase in the binding energy. Also, protons are not the only positively charged particles. There are positrons, which have the same mass as an electron. In positron-electron annihilation, the mass of the particles is converted into the energy of a photon.

SKILL 3.7   Identify characteristics of nuclear reactions.

The most common nuclear reaction is radioactive decay, which occurs when a nucleus is unstable. There are no stable nuclides with atomic numbers greater than 83 (bismuth). Also, many isotopes with smaller atomic numbers are unstable. Nuclides decay by emitting alpha particle (nucleus of a helium atom), beat particles (electrons), positrons (elementary particle with the same mass as an electron, but with a positive charge), and gamma rays (photons). There is also decay by capturing an electron from one of the inner shells. The new nuclide created by the decay may also be unstable.

Nuclei decay at different rates. The half-life of radium-226 is 1620 years and the half-life of technetium-99 is 6 hours. Radium-226 decays into radon-222. This means that if you start with 10 grams of radium-226, in 1620 years you will have 5 grams of radium-226 and 5 grams of radon-222 and a lot of helium

An important quantity in nuclear physics is the binding energy per nucleon. The binding energy of a nucleus is the sum of the masses of the neutrons and protons minus the mass of the nucleus. There is a decrease in mass because the mass is converted into binding energy according to the equation $E = \Delta mc^2$.

The nuclei with the greatest binding energy per nucleon is helium, which is why alpha particles are frequently emitted when nuclei decay. It is the decrease in binding energy per nucleon that causes the lack of stability in bigger nuclides.

Nuclear fission is used in nuclear power plants and atomic bombs. Uranium-235, which is only 0.7% of the uranium found in nature, splits into krypton-92 and barium-141 plus three neutrons when it absorbs a neutron. If there is enough fissionable uranium, a chain reaction can occur. In a nuclear power plant, the chair reaction is controlled with chromium and carbon rods. The fragments have a tremendous amount of kinetic energy, which is used to heat up water for steam turbines.

Nuclear fusion occurs on the sun and in hydrogen bombs when hydrogen isotopes combine to form helium. In both fission and fusion there is a decrease in binding energy and a corresponding release of energy. The radiation released in solar fusion is what supplies Earth with sunlight. Scientists estimate that the sun has enough hydrogen to keep it glowing for another four billion years.

Radioactive nuclides are used in the treatment of cancer because the radiation produced can kill cancer cells. Healthy cells are damaged too in these treatments, but healthy cells are better able to repair the damage done. People working around such substances must protect themselves with the correct clothing, equipment, and procedures.

SKILL 3.8   Identify the regions of the electromagnetic spectrum and energy associated with each.

Visible light is part of the electromagnetic spectrum and consists of photons, which have both wave properties and particle properties. Color is the sensation we feel when light enters our eyes. Black, the absence of light, is considered a color. White is the color we sense when light of all wavelengths enters our eyes. Red light has a wavelength of $620-750 \times 10^{-9}$ meters and travels at a speed of 3.0×10^9 meters per second. From the wave equation ($v = \lambda f$) the frequency can be calculated. The wavelength of violet light is $380-450 \times 10^{-9}$ meters. The energy of a photon is found by the equation $E = hf$, where $h = 6.6 \times 10^{-34}$ joules per hertz. The energy of the lowest energy visible photon is 3.2×10^{-19} joules. The types of radiation and their size are given in the following table:

Type of radiation	Size
radio waves	football field
microwaves	insects
infrared radiation	point of a needle
visible light	protozoa
ultraviolet radiation	molecule
X-rays	atoms
gamma rays	nuclei

SKILL 3.9 Identify the use of light and optics in real-world applications (e.g., optical instruments, communication).

Visible light and other electromagnetic radiation can be polarized because the electric and magnetic fields are perpendicular to the direction of the motion of the wave. Polarized light has vibrations confined to a single plane. Light can be polarized by passing it through Polaroid sheets that block all vibrations except those in a single plane. Polaroid sheets are made up of long molecules that are aligned in one direction. Only light waves parallel to the molecules passes through. By blocking out all but one plane of vibration, polarized sunglasses cut down on glare.

When a ray of light inside glass is incident upon the glass-to-air surface, there will be a reflected and a refracted ray, as in the case of a ray of light in air striking a glass surface. However, if the angle of incidence is too small, there will be no refracted ray. This phenomenon is total internal reflection. This is why fiber cables are used to communicate information. Light on the inside of these fibers is internally reflected so that it stays inside the fiber until it reaches its destination the other end. Fiber optics is used to carry telephone messages. Sound waves are converted to electric signals that are coded into a series of light pulses that move through the optical fiber until they reach the other end. At that time, they are converted back into sound.

Cameras, microscopes, and telescopes use spherically shaped lenses to produce images. A **convex lens** is thicker in the middle than at the edges and causes parallel beams of light to converge at a point called the *focal point*. Such a lens can create small inverted images of objects at a point near the lens.

Eyeglasses can help correct deficiencies of sight by changing where the image is focused on the retina of the eye. If a person is nearsighted, the lens of his eye focuses images in front of the retina. In this case, the corrective lens placed in the eyeglasses will be concave so that the image will reach the retina. In the case of farsightedness, the lens of the eye focuses the image behind the retina. The correction will call for a convex lens to be fitted into the glass frames so that the image is brought forward into sharper focus.

SKILL 3.10 Solve problems involving energy, work, power, mechanical advantage, and efficiency.

Newton's second law defines the force as $F = ma$ and a newton is the unit of force in SI units. The unit of force in the English system is the pound, and one pound is equal to 4.4 newtons. Work is defined by the equation $W = Fs$ and a joule is the unit of work in SI units. The foot-pound is the corresponding English unit. Energy is the ability to do work and includes kinetic energy and potential energy. Power is defined by the equation $P = W/t$ and is the rate at which work is done. The unit of power is the watt in SI units and horsepower in English units. A watt is one joule per second and a horsepower is 550 foot-pounds per second. One horsepower is equal to 746 watts.

A machine is a device that makes it easier for human beings to do work. Suppose a man weighing 200 pounds wants to get to a scaffold 10 feet high. He must do 2000 foot-pounds of work. A grasshopper would do that amount of work by jumping up. But a human being uses a device called a ramp. The ramp means there is a longer distance to travel, but less force is needed.

A lever enables a human to lift very heavy objects by doing the same thing: transferring a small force exerted for big distance to a large force exerted for a small distance. In the case of rowing a boat, the opposite is desired. A big force over a short distance produces a smaller force over a greater distance. The other simple machine is the pulley. Applying the conservation of energy to simple machines when there is no friction give us:

$$F_{in}D_{in} = F_{out}D_{out}$$

The mechanical advantage is the ratio of the input force to the output force or the output distance to the input distance. This is called the ideal mechanical advantage when friction is ignored. For example, lifting a box straight up to get it on the table involves very little friction compared to sliding it up a ramp. Using the ramp involves overcoming the force of friction, so the actual mechanical advantage is less than the ideal mechanical advantage.

The **efficiency** of a simple machine without friction is 100%. Friction reduces the efficiency and is defined as the work output divided by the work input. The more efficient a system is, the less energy that is lost within that system

SKILL 3.11   Apply the law of conservation of mass and energy to chemical reactions, nuclear reactions, physical processes, and biological processes.

Chemical reactions are the interactions of substances resulting in the chemical change of the substances. Chemical reactions involve the breaking and forming of chemical bonds. Reactants are the original substances that interact to form the resulting products. Endothermic chemical reactions require the input of energy while exothermic chemical reactions release energy with product formation. Chemical reactions occur continually in nature and are also induced by man for many purposes. Mass is conserved in chemical reactions because the energies of chemical bonds are so small that the change is mass is negligible.

Nuclear reactions, or **atomic reactions**, are reactions that change the composition or structure of atomic nuclei. Nuclear reactions change the number of protons and neutrons in the nucleus. The two main types of nuclear reactions are fission (splitting of nuclei) and fusion (joining of nuclei). Fusion and fission reactions are both exothermic. In nuclear reactions, the binding energies are so great that the change in masses is measurable.

Nuclear reactions are also produced in laboratories for the sake of research. Particle accelerators bombard various target nuclei with particles such as electrons, protons, alpha particles, neutrons, etc. Knowledge about nuclear forces is gained by such experiments.

The laws of physics and chemistry are used to understand geology and biology. Biology is the study of living organisms and geology is the study of Earth and how it has changed since its formation.

SKILL 3.12   Identify types, characteristics, and measurement of electrical quantities.

The basic unit of charge in electricity in the SI system of units is the ampere (amp). When two parallel wires, 1 meter long 1 meter apart, have currents of 1 amp flowing through each of them, the force between the wires will be 2×10^{-7} newtons. The force arises because a current carrying wire produces circular magnetic fields and magnetic fields exert a force on a current carrying wire. A coulomb is defined as the amount of charge transported by 1 amp of current in one second: 1 coulomb = 1 amp $\times$ 1 second.

In 1909, the Millikan oil-drop experiment determined that the charge on an electron was -1.6×10^{-19} coulombs. The charge was measured by measuring the acceleration of tiny oil drops that picked up extra electrons in an electric field.

In a battery, the positive terminal will have a lower density of electrons on it than the negative terminal. This means the potential energy of the electrons on one terminal will be greater than the potential energy of the electrons on the other terminal. Potential is a property of space in the vicinity of charges. It is the potential energy of a charge at some point in space divided by the charge. It is measured in volts, which is a unit equal to one joule divided by one coulomb. Thus, the two terminals of a battery produce a potential difference (V). When a wire is connected to the two terminals a current (I) will flow in the wires because the potential difference produces an electric field in the wire and the electric field exerts a force on the electrons, which are free to move in a conductor. They move very slowly (1 to 2 centimeters per hour) because they bump into the positively charged nuclei of the metal. If you double the length of the wire, the electric field will reduced by ½ , the average speed of the electrons will be reduced by ½ , and the current will be reduced by ½. If you double the diameter of the wire, the current will increase by a factor of four because there will be four times as many electrons drifting in the wire. The resistance of the wire is the ratio of the voltage difference defined by Ohm's law and an ohm is defined as one volt divided by one amp.

The power is measured in watts, which is one joule per second. This definition applies to electric circuits as well:

$$\text{watt} = \frac{\text{joule}}{\text{second}} = \frac{\text{joule}}{\text{coulomb}} \times \frac{\text{coulomb}}{\text{second}} = \text{volt} \times \text{ampere}$$

SKILL 3.13 Apply knowledge of currents, circuits, conductors, insulators, and resistors to real-world situations.

Electricity can be used to change the chemical composition of a material. For instance, when electricity is passed through water, it breaks the water down into hydrogen gas and oxygen gas.

Circuit breakers and fuses in a home monitor the electric current. If there is an overload, the circuit breaker will create an open circuit. This stops the flow of electricity in the fuse box, where no fire can start.

Computers can be made small enough to fit inside a plastic credit card by creating what is known as a solid-state device. In this device, electrons flow through solid material such as silicon.

Resistors are used to regulate volume on a television or radio or through a dimmer switch for lights.

A bird can sit on an electrical wire without being electrocuted because the bird and the wire have about the same potential. However, if that same bird would touch two wires at the same time he would not have to worry about flying south next year.

When caught in an electrical storm, a car is a relatively safe place from lightening because of the resistance of the rubber tires. A metal building would not be safe unless there was a lightning rod that would attract the lightening and conduct it into the ground.

SKILL 3.14   Solve mathematical problems involving current, voltage, power, and energy in direct current (DC) circuits.

The current (*I*) that flows in the wire for a given voltage difference (*V*) depends only on the length of the wire, its area, and the type of metal. Copper, for example, is a better conductor than iron. Also the current is directly proportional to the voltage. Ohm's law states: $V = IR$

R is the **resistance** of the wire and is measured in units called ohms. If a wire has a resistance of 5 ohms and is connected to a battery whose terminals have a potential difference of of 75 volts, the current produced is is across th, you can calculate the current by

$$I = \frac{V}{R} = \frac{75 \text{ volts}}{5 \text{ ohms}} = 15 \text{ amps}$$

Materials through which electric charges can easily flow are called conductors. On the other hand, an **insulator** is a material through which electric charges do not move easily, if at all.

An **electric circuit** is a path along which electrons flow. A simple circuit can be created with a dry cell, a light bulb, a switch, and connecting wires. When all are connected, the electrons flow from the negative terminal through the wire to the light bulb and back to the positive terminal of the dry cell. If there are no breaks in the circuit, the device will work. The circuit is closed. Any break in the flow will create an open circuit and cause the device to shut off.

A **series circuit** is one where the electrons have only one path along which they can move. When one load in a series circuit goes out, the circuit is open. An example of this is a set of Christmas tree lights that is missing a bulb. None of the bulbs will work.

A **parallel circuit** is one where the electrons have more than one path to move along. If a load goes out in a parallel circuit, the other load will still work because the electrons can still find a way to continue moving along the path.

When an electron goes through a load, it heats up the wire or does work, and therefore loses some of its potential energy. The potential of a point on an electric circuit is measured by a device called a voltmeter. To use a voltmeter, place it in a circuit parallel to the two points you are measuring. Current is measured with a device called an ammeter. To use an ammeter, put it in series with the load you are measuring.

COMPETENCY 4.0   KNOWLEDGE OF EARTH AND THE PROCESSES THAT AFFECT IT

SKILL 4.1   Relate geologic surface and subsurface processes to the movement of tectonic plates.

Data obtained from many sources led scientists to develop the theory of plate tectonics. This theory is the most current model that explains not only the movement of the continents, but also the changes in the Earth's crust caused by internal forces.

Plates are rigid blocks of Earth's crust and upper mantle. These rigid solid blocks make up the lithosphere. The Earth's lithosphere is broken into nine large sections and several small ones. These moving slabs are called plates. The major plates are named after the continents they are "transporting."

The plates float on and move with a layer of hot, plastic-like rock in the upper mantle. Geologists believe that the heat currents circulating within the mantle cause this plastic zone of rock to slowly flow, carrying along the overlying crustal plates.

Movement of these crustal plates creates areas where the plates diverge as well as areas where the plates converge. A major area of divergence is located in the Mid-Atlantic. Currents of hot mantle rock rise and separate at this point of divergence creating new oceanic crust at the rate of 2 to 10 centimeters per year. Convergence is when the oceanic crust collides with either another oceanic plate or a continental plate. The oceanic crust sinks forming an enormous trench and generating volcanic activity. Convergence also includes continent to continent plate collisions. When two plates slide past one another a transform fault is created.

These movements produce many major features of the Earth's surface, such as mountain ranges, volcanoes, and earthquake zones. Most of these features are located at plate boundaries, where the plates interact by spreading apart, pressing together, or sliding past each other. These movements are very slow, averaging only a few centimeters a year.

Boundaries form between spreading plates where the crust is forced apart in a process called rifting. Rifting generally occurs at mid-oceanic ridges. Rifting can also take place within a continent, splitting the continent into smaller land masses that drift away from each other, thereby forming an ocean basin between them. The Red Sea is a product of rifting. As the seafloor spreading takes place, new material is added to the inner edges of the separating plates. In this way the plates grow larger, and the ocean basin widens. This is the process that broke up the super continent Pangaea and created the Atlantic Ocean.

CONTINENTAL DRIFT

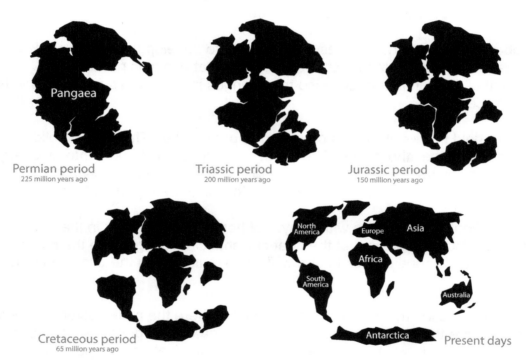

Tinkivinki/Shutterstock.com

Boundaries between plates that are colliding are zones of intense crustal activity. When a plate of ocean crust collides with a plate of continental crust, the more dense oceanic plate slides under the lighter continental plate and plunges into the mantle. This process is called **subduction**, and the site where it takes place is called a subduction zone. A subduction zone is usually seen on the sea-floor as a deep depression called a trench.

The crustal movement which is identified by plates sliding sideways past each other produces a plate boundary characterized by major faults that are capable of unleashing powerful earthquakes. The San Andreas Fault forms such a boundary between the Pacific Plate and the North American Plate.

SKILL 4.2   Trace the development of the theory of continental drift to the current theory of plate tectonics.

Early in the 20th century, geologists believed that mountains were caused by the contraction of Earth as its molten center cooled down. The Earth's crust was thought to be like a skin that became wrinkled, just like the skin of fruit when it dries out. It was not until the 1960s that evidence accumulated in support of plate tectonics. The evidence includes the fit of continents, fossils, similarities of rock type and rock structure, and Earth's magnetism.

In 1915 Alfred Wegener advanced the theory of continental drift and suggested that 200 million years ago there was a supercontinent called Pangaea. All the present continents broke into the smaller continents we have today. The fit between the east coast of South America and the west coast of Africa is evidence of this.

An example of the fossil evidence is the mesosaur, a reptile whose fossils are found only in eastern South America and southern Africa. If the mesosaur could have swum across an ocean, it would be more widely dispersed. The mesosaur fossils are in these two locations because the locations were once connected. There is good correlation between rocks in eastern Brazil and rocks found in northwestern Africa. In both regions, 440 million-year-old rocks lie adjacent to 2 billion-year-old rocks in continuous lines that fit together. Another example is the similarity between the Appalachians in the U.S. and mountain ranges in Europe.

The Earth behaves like a giant bar magnet with magnetic field lines entering Earth's crust at a point near the North Pole and exiting at a point near the South Pole. While there has been some movement in the axis of rotation and the magnetic poles, they have been relatively stable. When iron-rich lava cools, the minerals become magnetized and point in the direction of the Earth's magnetic field. A study of the direction of the magnetic fields produced by rocks over the last 500 million years shows a correlation between the rocks in North America and the rocks in Eurasia.

SKILL 4.3   Relate the characteristics of geologic structures to the mechanisms by which they were formed.

Mountain Building

Orogeny is the term given to natural mountain building. A mountain is terrain that has been raised high above the surrounding landscape by volcanic action, or some form of tectonic plate collisions. The plate collisions could be intercontinental or ocean floor collisions with a continental crust (subduction). The physical composition of mountains would include igneous, metamorphic, or sedimentary rocks; some may have rock layers that are tilted or distorted by plate collision forces.

There are many different types of mountains. The physical attributes of a mountain range depends upon the angle at which plate movement thrust layers of rock to the surface. Many mountains (Adirondacks, Southern Rockies) were formed along high angle faults.

Folded mountains (Alps, Himalayas) are produced by the folding of rock layers during their formation. The Himalayas are the highest mountains in the world and contain Mount Everest which rises almost 9 km above sea level. The Himalayas were formed when India collided with Asia. The movement which created this collision is still in process at the rate of a few centimeters per year.

Fault-block mountains (Utah, Arizona, and New Mexico) are created when plate movement produces tension forces instead of compression forces. The area under tension produces normal faults and rock along these faults is displaced upward.

Dome mountains are formed as magma tries to push up through the crust but fails to break the surface. Dome mountains resemble a huge blister on the Earth's surface.

Upwarped mountains (Black Hills of South Dakota) are created in association with a broad arching of the crust. They can also be formed by rock thrust upward along high angle faults.

Volcanism is the term given to the movement of magma through the crust and its emergence as lava onto the Earth's surface. Volcanic mountains are built up by successive deposits of volcanic materials.

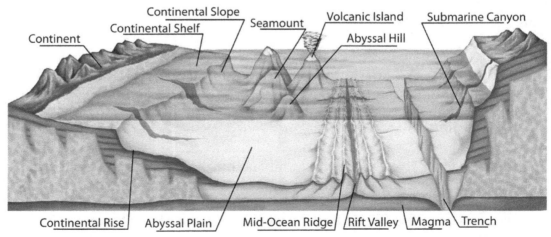

Stihii/Shutterstock.com

An active volcano is one that is presently erupting or building to an eruption. A dormant volcano is one that is between eruptions but still shows signs of internal activity that might lead to an eruption in the future. An extinct volcano is said to be no longer capable of erupting. Most of the world's active volcanoes are found along the rim of the Pacific Ocean, which is also a major earthquake zone. This curving belt of active faults and volcanoes is often called the Ring of Fire. The world's best known volcanic mountains include: Mount Etna in Italy and Mount Kilimanjaro in Africa. The Hawaiian Islands are actually the tops of a chain of volcanic mountains that rise from the ocean floor.

Types of Volcanic Mountains

Shield volcanoes are associated with quiet eruptions. Lava emerges from the vent or opening in the crater and flows freely out over the Earth's surface until it cools and hardens into a layer of igneous rock. A repeated lava flow builds this type of volcano into the largest volcanic mountain. Mauna Loa found in Hawaii, is the largest volcano on Earth.

Cinder cone volcanoes are associated with explosive eruptions as lava is hurled high into the air in a spray of droplets of various sizes. These droplets cool and harden into cinders and particles of ash before falling to the ground. The ash and cinder pile up around the vent to form a steep, cone-shaped hill called the cinder cone. Cinder cone volcanoes are relatively small but may form quite rapidly.

Composite volcanoes are described as being built by both lava flows and layers of ash and cinders. Mount Fuji in Japan, Mount St. Helens in Washington, USA and Mount Vesuvius in Italy are all famous composite volcanoes.

Mechanisms of Producing Mountains

Mountains are produced by different types of mountain-building processes. Most major mountain ranges are formed by the processes of folding and faulting.

Folded mountains are produced by the folding of rock layers. Crustal movements may press horizontal layers of sedimentary rock together from the sides, squeezing them into wavelike folds. Up-folded sections of rock are called anticlines; down-folded sections of rock are called synclines. The Appalachian Mountains are an example of folded mountains with long ridges and valleys in a series of anticlines and synclines formed by folded rock layers.

Faults are fractures in the Earth's crust which have been created by either tension or compression forces transmitted through the crust. These forces are produced by the movement of separate blocks of crust. Faultings are categorized on the basis of the relative movement between the blocks on both sides of the fault plane. The movement can be horizontal, vertical or oblique.

A dip-slip fault occurs when the movement of the plates is vertical and opposite. The displacement is in the direction of the inclination, or dip, of the fault. Dip-slip faults are classified as normal faults when the rock above the fault plane moves down relative to the rock below.

Reverse faults are created when the rock above the fault plane moves up relative to the rock below. Reverse faults having a very low angle to the horizontal are also referred to as thrust faults.

Faults in which the dominant displacement is horizontal movement along the trend or strike (length) of the fault are called **strike-slip faults**. When a large strike-slip fault is associated with plate boundaries it is called a **transform fault**. The San Andreas Fault in California is a well-known transform fault.

Faults that have both vertical and horizontal movement are called **oblique-slip faults**.

When lava cools, **igneous rock** is formed. This formation can occur either above ground or below ground.

Intrusive rock includes any igneous rock that was formed below the Earth's surface. Batholiths are the largest structures of intrusive-type rock and are composed of near granite materials; they are the core of the Sierra Nevada Mountains.

Extrusive rock includes any igneous rock that was formed at the Earth's surface.

Dikes are old lava tubes formed when magma entered a vertical fracture and hardened. Sometimes magma squeezes between two rock layers and hardens into a thin horizontal sheet called a **sill**. A **laccolith** is formed in much the same way as a sill, but the magma that creates a laccolith is very thick and does not flow easily. It pools and forces the overlying strata creating an obvious surface dome.

A **caldera** is normally formed by the collapse of the top of a volcano. This collapse can be caused by a massive explosion that destroys the cone and empties most if not all of the magma chamber below the volcano. The cone collapses into the empty magma chamber forming a caldera.

An inactive volcano may have magma solidified in its pipe. This structure, called a volcanic neck, is resistant to erosion and today may be the only visible evidence of the past presence of an active volcano.

Glaciation

A continental glacier covered a large part of North America during the most recent ice age. Evidence of this glacial coverage remains as abrasive grooves, large boulders from northern environments dropped in southerly locations, glacial troughs created by the rounding out of steep valleys by glacial scouring, and the remains of glacial sources called **cirques** that were created by frost wedging the rock at the bottom of the glacier. Remains of plants and animals found in warm climate have been discovered in the moraines and out wash plains help to support the theory of periods of warmth during the past ice ages.

The Ice Age began about 2–3 million years ago. This age saw the advancement and retreat of glacial ice over millions of years. Theories relating to the origin of glacial activity include plate tectonics, where it can be demonstrated that some continental masses, now in temperate climates, were at one time blanketed by ice and snow. Another theory involves changes in the Earth's orbit around the sun, changes in the angle of the Earth's axis, and the wobbling of the Earth's axis. Support for the validity of this theory has come from deep ocean research that indicates a correlation between climatic sensitive microorganisms and the changes in the Earth's orbital status.

About 12,000 years ago, a vast sheet of ice covered a large part of the northern United States. This huge, frozen mass had moved southward from the northern regions of Canada as several large bodies of slow-moving ice, or glaciers. A time period in which glaciers advance over a large portion of a continent is called an ice age. A glacier is a large mass of ice that moves or flows over the land in response to gravity. Glaciers form among high mountains and in other cold regions.

There are two main types of glaciers: **valley glaciers** and **continental glaciers**. Erosion by valley glaciers is characteristic of U-shaped erosion. They produce sharp peaked mountains such as the Matterhorn in Switzerland. Erosion by continental glaciers often rides over mountains in their paths leaving smoothed, rounded mountains and ridges.

SKILL 4.4   Identify the evidence used to define geologic eras (e.g., geologic events, biotic factors, abiotic factors).

The biological history of the Earth is partitioned into four major **eons**. The most recent eon is the **Phanerozoic eon,** which marks the beginning of life 570 million years ago. The other three eons are part of Precambrian time and go back to Earth's formation 4.6 billion years ago.

The four eons are broken up into 10 eras, with the current eon having eras named: **Cenozoic** (age of recent life), **Mesozoic** (age of middle life), and **Paleozoic** (age of ancient life)

Each era is subdivided into **periods**. The Cenozoic era has two periods (Quarternary and Tertiary). The Mesozoic era has three periods, the most familiar one being the Jurassic period, which covers 208–144 million years ago. The Paleozoic era has seven periods. Each of the 12 periods is broken up into epochs, usually described as *early*, *middle*, and *late.* Only the Cenozoic epochs have names: Holocene, Pleistocene, Pliocene, Miocene, Oligocene, Eocene, and Paleocene.

The end of an era is most often characterized by (1) a general uplifting of the crust, (2) the extinction of the dominant plants or animals, and (3) the appearance of new life-forms.

Era	Period	Time	Characteristics
Cenozoic	Quaternary	1.6 million years ago to the present.	The Ice Age occurred, and human beings evolved.
	Tertiary	66–1.6 million years ago.	Mammals and birds evolved to replace the great reptiles and dinosaurs that had just become extinct. Forests gave way to grasslands, and the climate become cooler.
Mesozoic	Cretaceous	144–66 million years ago.	Reptiles and dinosaurs roamed the Earth. Most of the modern continents had split away from the large landmass, Pangaea, and many were flooded by shallow chalk seas.
	Jurassic	245–144 million years ago.	Reptiles were beginning to evolve. Pangaea started to break up. Deserts gave way to forests and swamps.
	Triassic		

Era	Period	Time	Characteristics
Paleozoic	Permian Carboniferous	360–245 million years ago.	Continents came together to form one big landmass, Pangaea. Forests (that formed today's coal) grew on deltas around the new mountains, and deserts formed.
	Devonian	408–360 million years ago.	Continents started moving toward each other. The first land animals, such as insects and amphibians, existed. Many fish swam in the seas.
	Silurian Ordovician	505–408 million years ago.	Sea life flourished, and the first fish evolved. The earliest land plants began to grow around shorelines and estuaries.
	Cambrian	570–505 million years ago.	No life on land, but all kinds of sea animals existed.

The History of an Area Using Geologic Evidence

The determination of the age of rocks by cataloging their composition has been outmoded since the middle 1800s. Today a sequential history can be determined by the fossil content (principle of fossil succession) of a rock system as well as its superposition within a range of systems. This classification process was termed **stratigraphy** and permitted the construction of a geologic column in which rock systems are arranged in their correct chronological order.

Uniformitarianism is a fundamental concept in modern geology. It simply states that the physical, chemical, and biological laws that operated in the geologic past operate in the same way today. The forces and processes that we observe presently shaping our planet have been at work for a very long time. This idea is commonly stated as "the present is the key to the past." **Catastrophism** is the concept that the Earth was shaped by catastrophic events of a short term nature.

SKILL 4.5   **Apply methods for determining geologic age (e.g., lat of superposition, radioactive decay, relative dating).**

Estimates of the Earth's age have been made possible with the discovery of **radioactivity** and the invention of instruments that can measure the amount of radioactivity in rocks. The use of radioactivity to make accurate determinations of Earth's age is called Absolute Dating. This process depends upon comparing the amount of radioactive material in a rock with the amount that has decayed into another element. Studying the radiation given off by atoms of radioactive elements is the most accurate method of measuring the Earth's age. These atoms are unstable and are continuously breaking down or undergoing decay. The radioactive element that decays is called the parent element. The new element that results from the radioactive decay of the parent element is called the daughter element. The time required for one half of a given amount of a radioactive element to decay is called the half-life of that element or compound. Geologists commonly use Carbon Dating to calculate the age of a fossil substance.

Before the discovery of dating from radioactivity, a geological time scale was developed using relative dating and the law of superposition. Relative dating means that events are placed in their proper sequence or order without knowing their absolute age in years. The law of superposition states in an undeformed sequence of sedimentary rocks each layer is older than the one above it and younger than the one below it.

SKILL 4.6 Interpret various charts and models (e.g., topographic, geologic, weather).

Decode Map Symbols

A system of imaginary lines has been developed that helps people describe exact locations on Earth. Looking at a globe of Earth, you will see lines drawn on it. The equator is drawn around Earth halfway between the North and South Poles. Latitude is a term used to describe distance in degrees north or south of the equator. Lines of latitude are drawn east and west parallel to the equator. Degrees of latitude range from 0 at the equator to 90 at either the North Pole or South Pole. Lines of latitude are also called parallels.

Lines drawn north and south at right angles to the equator and from pole to pole are called meridians. Longitude is a term used to describe distances in degrees east or west of a 0° meridian. The prime meridian is the 0° meridian and it passes through Greenwich, England.

Time zones are determined by longitudinal lines. Each time zone represents one hour. Since there are 24 hours in one complete rotation of the Earth, there are 24 international time zones. Each time zone is roughly 15° wide. While time zones are based on meridians, they do not strictly follow lines of longitude. Time zone boundaries are subject to political decisions and have been moved around cities and other areas at the whim of the electorate.

The International Date Line is the 180° meridian and it is on the opposite side of the world from the prime meridian. The International Date Line is one-half of one day or 12 time zones from the prime meridian. If you were traveling west across the International Date Line, you would lose one day. If you were traveling east across the International Date Line, you would gain one day.

Principles of Contouring

A contour line is a line on a map representing an imaginary line on the ground that has the same elevation above sea level along its entire length. Contour intervals usually are given in even numbers or as a multiple of five. In mapping mountains, a large contour interval is used. Small contour intervals may be used where there are small differences in elevation.

Relief describes how much variation in elevation an area has. Rugged or high relief, describes an area of many hills and valleys. Gentle or low relief describes a plain area or a coastal region. Five general rules should be remembered in studying contour lines on a map.

1. Contour lines close around hills and basins or depressions. Hachure lines are used to show depressions. Hachures are short lines placed at right angles to the contour line and they always point toward the lower elevation. A contour line that has hachures is called a depression contour.
2. Contours lines never cross. Contour lines are sometimes very close together. Each contour line represents a certain height above sea level.
3. Contour lines appear on both sides of an area where the slope reverses direction. Contour lines show where an imaginary horizontal plane would slice through a hillside or cut both sides of a valley.
4. Contours lines form V's that point upstream when they cross streams. Streams cut beneath the general elevation of the land surface, and contour lines follow a valley.
5. All contours lines either close (connect) or extend to the edge of the map. No map is large enough to have all its contour lines close.

Interpret maps and imagery

Like photographs, maps readily display information that would be impractical to express in words. Maps that show the shape of the land are called topographic maps. Topographic maps, which are also referred to as quadrangles, are generally classified according to publication scale. Relief refers to the difference in elevation between any two points. Maximum relief refers to the difference in elevation between the high and low points in the area being considered. Relief determines the contour interval, which is the difference in elevation between succeeding contour lines that are used on topographic maps.

Map scales express the relationship between distance or area on the map to the true distance or area on the Earth's surface. It is expressed as so many feet (miles, meters, km, or degrees) per inch (cm) of map.

SKILL 4.7   Identify characteristics of ocean currents and how they influence weather patterns.

World weather patterns are greatly influenced by ocean surface currents in the upper layer of the ocean. These currents continuously move along the ocean surface in specific directions. Ocean currents that flow deep below the surface are called sub-surface currents. These currents are influenced by such factors as the location of landmasses in the current's path and the Earth's rotation.

Surface currents are caused by winds and are classified by temperature. Cold currents originate in the Polar regions and flow through surrounding water that is measurably warmer. Those currents with a higher temperature than the surrounding water are called warm currents and can be found near the equator. These currents follow swirling routes around the ocean basins and the equator.

The Gulf Stream and the California Current are the two main surface currents that flow along the coastlines of the United States. The Gulf Stream is a warm current in the Atlantic Ocean that carries warm water from the equator to the northern parts of the Atlantic Ocean. Benjamin Franklin studied and named the Gulf Stream. The California Current is a cold current that originates in the Arctic regions and flows southward along the west coast of the United States.

Differences in water density also create ocean currents. Water found near the bottom of oceans is the coldest and the densest. Water tends to flow from a denser area to a less dense area. Currents that flow because of a difference in the density of the ocean water are called density currents. Water with a higher salinity is denser than water with a lower salinity. Water that has salinity different from the surrounding water may form a density current.

Causes and Effects of Waves

The movement of ocean water is caused by the wind, the sun's heat energy, the Earth's rotation, the moon's gravitational pull on Earth, and by underwater earthquakes. Most ocean waves are caused by the impact of winds. Wind blowing over the surface of the ocean transfers energy (friction) to the water and causes waves to form. Waves are also formed by seismic activity on the ocean floor. A wave formed by an earthquake is called a seismic sea wave. These powerful waves can be very destructive, with wave heights increasing to 30 m or more near the shore. The crest of a wave is its highest point. The trough of a wave is its lowest point. The distance from wave top to wave top is the wavelength. The wave period is the time between the passing of two successive waves.

SKILL 4.8   Identify characteristics of Florida's geology and its formation.

The Florida peninsula is a porous plateau of limestone on top of bedrock. There are many underwater caves, sinkholes, and springs found throughout the state. The limestone is topped with sandy soils, which were deposited over millions of years as global sea levels rose and fell. During the last glacial period, there was a much wider peninsula, mostly made up of grassy plains with few trees.

Florida's Everglades is the largest wetland—marshes, swamps, bogs— system in the United States. A wetland is an area of land whose soil is saturated with moisture either permanently or seasonally. The system begins near Orlando with the Kissimmee River, which discharges into the vast but shallow Lake Okeechobee. Water leaving the lake in the wet season forms a slow-moving river 60 miles (97 km) wide and over 100 miles (160 km) long, flowing southward across a limestone shelf to Florida Bay at the southern end of the state.

Because Florida is not located near any tectonic plate boundaries, earthquakes are very rare, but not totally unknown. In 2006, a magnitude 6.0 earthquake centered about 260 miles (420 km) southwest of Tampa in the Gulf of Mexico sent shock waves through southwest and central Florida. The earthquake was too small to trigger a tsunami and no damage was reported

SKILL 4.9   Identify the major processes of formation and properties of rocks, minerals, and fossils

A fossil is the remains or trace of an ancient organism that has been preserved naturally in the Earth's crust. Sedimentary rocks usually are rich sources of fossil remains. Those fossils found in layers of sediment were embedded in the slowly forming sedimentary rock strata. The oldest fossils known are the traces of 3.5 billion year old bacteria found in sedimentary rocks. Few fossils are found in metamorphic rock and virtually none found in igneous rocks. The magma is so hot that any organism trapped in the magma is destroyed.

The fossil remains of a woolly mammoth embedded in ice were found by a group of Russian explorers. However, the best-preserved animal remains have been discovered in natural tar pits. When an animal accidentally fell into the tar, it became trapped, sinking to the bottom. Preserved bones of the saber-toothed cat have been found in tar pits. Prehistoric insects have been found trapped in ancient amber or fossil resin that was excreted by some extinct species of pine trees.

Fossil molds are the hollow spaces in a rock previously occupied by bones or shells. A fossil cast is a fossil mold that fills with sediments or minerals that later hardens forming a cast. Fossil tracks are the imprints in hardened mud left behind by birds or animals.

Sedimentary, Metamorphic, and Igneous Rocks

When fluid sediments are transformed into solid sedimentary rocks, the process is known as **lithification**. One very common process affecting sediments is compaction where the weights of overlying materials compress and compact the deeper sediments. The compaction process leads to cementation. **Cementation** is when sediments are converted to sedimentary rock.

Igneous rocks can be classified according to their texture, their composition, and the way they formed. Molten rock is called magma. When molten rock pours out onto the surface of Earth, it is called lava. As magma cools, the elements and compounds begin to form crystals. The slower the magma cools, the larger the crystals grow. Rocks with large crystals are said to have a coarse-grained texture. Granite is an example of a coarse grained rock. Rocks that cool rapidly before any crystals can form have a glassy texture such as obsidian, also commonly known as volcanic glass.

Metamorphic rocks are formed by high temperatures and great pressures. The process by which the rocks undergo these changes is called metamorphism. The outcome of metamorphic changes include deformation by extreme heat and pressure, compaction, destruction of the original characteristics of the parent rock, bending and folding while in a plastic stage, and the emergence of completely new and different minerals due to chemical reactions with heated water and dissolved minerals.

Metamorphic rocks are classified into two groups, foliated (leaflike) rocks and unfoliated rocks. Foliated rocks consist of compressed, parallel bands of minerals, which give the rocks a striped appearance. Examples of such rocks include slate, schist, and gneiss. Unfoliated rocks are not banded and examples of such include quartzite, marble, and anthracite rocks.

Minerals are natural, non-living solids with a definite chemical composition and a crystalline structure. **Ores** are minerals or rock deposits that can be mined for a profit. **Rocks** are Earth materials made of one or more minerals. A **Rock Facies** is a rock group that differs from comparable rocks (as in composition, age or fossil content).

Minerals must adhere to five criteria. They must be (1) non-living, (2) formed in nature, (3) solid in form, (4) their atoms form a crystalline pattern, (5) its chemical composition is fixed within narrow limits. There are over 3000 minerals in Earth's crust. Minerals are classified by composition. The major groups of minerals are silicates, carbonates, oxides, sulfides, sulfates, and halides. The largest group of minerals is the silicates. Silicates are made of silicon, oxygen, and one or more other elements.

Minerals

Minerals are natural inorganic compounds. They are solid with homogenous crystal structures. Crystal structures are the 3-D geometric arrangements of atoms within minerals. Though these mineral grains are often too small to see, they can be visualized by X-ray diffraction. Both chemical composition and crystal structure determine mineral type. The chemical composition of minerals can vary from purely elemental to simple salts to complex compounds. However, it is possible for two or more minerals to have identical chemical composition, but varied crystal structure. Such minerals are known as polymorphs. One example of polymorphs demonstrates how crystal structures influence the physical properties of minerals with the same chemical composition: diamonds and graphite. Both are made from carbon, but diamonds are extremely hard because the carbon atoms are arranged in a strong 3-D network while graphite is soft because the carbon atoms are present in sheets that slide past one another. There are over 4,400 minerals on Earth, which are organized into the following classes:

- Silicate minerals are composed mostly of silicon and oxygen. This is the most abundant class of minerals on Earth and includes quartz, garnets, micas, and feldspars.
- Carbonate class minerals are formed from compounds including carbonate ions (including calcium carbonate, magnesium carbonate, and iron carbonate). They are common in marine environments, in caves (stalactite and stalagmites), and anywhere minerals can form via dissolution and precipitation. Nitrate and borate minerals are also in this class.
- Sulfate minerals contain sulfate ions and are formed near bodies of water where slow evaporation allows precipitation of sulfates and halides. Sulfates include celestite, barite, and gypsum.
- Halide minerals include all minerals formed from natural salts including calcium fluoride, sodium chloride, and ammonium chloride. Like the sulfides, these minerals are typically formed in evaporative settings. Minerals in this class include fluorite, halite, and sylvite.
- Oxide class minerals contain oxide compounds including iron oxide, magnetite oxide, and chromium oxide. They are formed by various processes including precipitation and oxidation of other minerals. These minerals form many ores and are important in mining. Hematite, chromite, rutile, and magnetite are all examples of oxide minerals.
- Sulfide minerals are formed from sulfide compounds such as iron sulfide, nickel iron sulfide and lead sulfide. Several important metal ores are members of this class. Minerals in this class include pyrite (fool's gold) and galena.

- Phosphate class minerals includes not only those containing phosphate ions, but any mineral with a tetrahedral molecular geometry in which an element is surrounded by four oxygen atoms. This can include elements such as phosphorous, arsenic, and antimony. Minerals in this class are important biologically, as they are common in teeth and bones. Phosphate, arsenate, vanadate, and antimonite minerals are all in this class.
- Element class minerals are formed from pure elements, whether they are metallic, semi-metallic or non-metallic. Accordingly, minerals in this class include gold, silver, copper, bismuth, and graphite as well as natural alloys such as electrum and carbides.

SKILL 4.10 Distinguish between the processes of weathering, erosion, and deposition and their products.

Erosion is the inclusion and transportation of surface materials by another moveable material, usually water, wind, or ice. The most important cause of erosion is running water. Streams, rivers, and tides are constantly at work removing weathered fragments of bedrock and carrying them away from their original location.

A stream erodes bedrock by the grinding action of the sand, pebbles and other rock fragments. This grinding against each other is called abrasion. Streams also erode rocks by dissolving or absorbing their minerals. Limestone and marble are readily dissolved by streams.

The breaking down of rocks at or near to the Earth's surface is known as **weathering**. Weathering breaks down these rocks into smaller and smaller pieces. There are two types of weathering: physical weathering and chemical weathering.

Physical weathering is the process by which rocks are broken down into smaller fragments without undergoing any change in chemical composition. Physical weathering is mainly caused by the freezing of water, the expansion of rock, and the activities of plants and animals.

Frost wedging is the cycle of daytime thawing and refreezing at night. This cycle causes large rock masses, especially the rocks exposed on mountain tops, to be broken into smaller pieces.

The peeling away of the outer layers from a rock is called exfoliation. Rounded mountain tops are called exfoliation domes and have been formed in this way. Chemical weathering is the breaking down of rocks through changes in their chemical composition. An example would be the change of feldspar in granite to clay. Water, oxygen, and carbon dioxide are the main agents of chemical weathering. When water and carbon dioxide combine chemically, they produce a weak acid that breaks down rocks.

Deposition, also known as sedimentation, is the term for the process by which material from one area is slowly deposited into another area. This is usually due to the movement of wind, water, or ice containing particles of matter. When the rate of movement slows down, particles filter out and remain behind, causing a buildup of matter. Note that this is a result of matter being eroded and removed from another site.

Soil

Soils are composed of particles of sand, clay, various minerals, tiny living organisms, and humus, plus the decayed remains of plants and animals. Soils are divided into three classes according to their texture. These classes are sandy soils, clay soils, and loamy soils.

Sandy soils are gritty, and their particles do not bind together firmly. Sandy soils are porous—water passes through them rapidly. Sandy soils do not hold much water.

Clay soils are smooth and greasy; their particles bind together firmly. Clay soils are moist and usually do not allow water to pass through easily.

Loamy soils feel somewhat like velvet and their particles clump together. Loamy soils are made up of sand, clay, and silt. Loamy soils holds water but some water can pass through.

In addition to three main classes, soils are further grouped into three major types based upon their composition. These groups are pedalfers, pedocals, and laterites.

Pedalfers form in the humid, temperate climate of the eastern United States.

Pedalfer soils contain large amounts of iron oxide and aluminum-rich clays, making the soil a brown to reddish brown color. This soil supports forest type vegetation.

Pedocals are found in the western United States where the climate is dry and temperate. These soils are rich in calcium carbonate. This type of soil supports grasslands and brush vegetation.

Laterites are found where the climate is wet and tropical. Large amounts of water flow through this soil. Laterites are red-orange soils rich in iron and aluminum oxides. There is little humus and this soil is not very fertile.--

SKILL 4.11   Identify the characteristics and functions of the atmospheric layers

Dry air is composed of three basic components; dry gas, water vapor, and solid particles (dust from soil, etc.). The most abundant dry gases in the atmosphere are in the table below.

Name	Formula	Percent
nitrogen	N_2	78.09
oxygen	O_2	20.95
argon	Ar	0.93
carbon dioxide	CO_2	0.03

Layers of Atmosphere

Troposphere is the layer closest to the Earth's surface and all weather phenomena occurs here as it is the layer with the most water vapor and dust. Air temperature decreases with increasing altitude. The average thickness of the Troposphere is 7 miles (11 km).

The **stratosphere** contains very little water, clouds within this layer are extremely rare. The ozone layer is located in the upper portions of the stratosphere. Air temperature is fairly constant but does increase somewhat with height due to the absorption of solar energy and ultra violet rays from the ozone layer.

For the **mesosphere** layer, air temperature also decreases with height. It is the coldest layer with temperatures in the range of −100° C at the top.

The **thermosphere** extends upward into space. Oxygen molecules in this layer absorb energy from the sun, causing temperatures to increase with height. The lower part of the thermosphere is called the ionosphere. Here charged particles or ions and free electrons can be found. When gases in the ionosphere are excited by solar radiation, the gases give off light and glow in the sky. These glowing lights are called the Aurora Borealis in the northern hemisphere and Aurora Australis in southern hemisphere. The upper portion of the thermosphere is called the exosphere. Gas molecules are very far apart in this layer. The exosphere includes the Van Allen belts, which are energetic charged particles held together by Earth's magnetic field.

Types of Clouds

Clouds form when air above the surface cools below the point when liquid water forms. The shape of a cloud depends on the air movement that forms it. **Stratiform clouds** are formed by horizontal air movement and **cumuliform clouds** are formed by vertical air movements. Clouds are also categorized by their height.

Cirrus clouds are white and feathery. **Cumulus clouds** are thick, white, and fluffy. **Stratus clouds** are low sheets or layers of cloud. **Nimbus clouds** are heavy, dark clouds that cause thunderstorms. Variations on the clouds are cumulonimbus and stratocumulus.

SKILL 4.12   Relate atmospheric conditions to weather.

El Niño refers to a sequence of changes in the ocean and atmospheric circulation across the Pacific Ocean. The water around the equator is unusually hot every two to seven years. Trade winds normally blow east to west across the equatorial latitudes, piling warm water into the western Pacific. A huge mass of heavy thunderstorms usually forms in the area and produces vast currents of rising air that displace heat poleward. This helps create the strong mid-latitude jet streams. The world's climate patterns are disrupted by this change in location of thunderstorm activity.

Air masses moving toward or away from the Earth's surface are called air currents. Air moving parallel to Earth's surface is called **wind**. Weather conditions are generated by winds and air currents carrying large amounts of heat and moisture from one part of the atmosphere to another. Wind speeds are measured by instruments called anemometers.

The wind belts in each hemisphere consist of convection cells that encircle Earth like belts. There are three major wind belts on Earth: (1) trade winds (2) prevailing westerlies, and (3) polar easterlies. Wind belt formation depends on the differences in air pressures that develop in the doldrums, the horse latitudes, and the polar regions. The Doldrums surround the equator. Within this belt heated air usually rises straight up into Earth's atmosphere. The Horse latitudes are regions of high barometric pressure with calm and light winds and the Polar regions contain cold dense air that sinks to the Earth's surface. Winds caused by local temperature changes include sea breezes, and land breezes.

Sea breezes are caused by the unequal heating of the land and an adjacent, large body of water. Land heats up faster than water. The movement of cool ocean air toward the land is called a sea breeze. Sea breezes usually begin blowing about mid-morning; ending about sunset. A breeze that blows from the land to the ocean or a large lake is called a **land breeze.**

Monsoons are huge wind systems that cover large geographic areas and that reverse direction seasonally. The monsoons of India and Asia are examples of these seasonal winds. They alternate wet and dry seasons. As denser cooler air over the ocean moves inland, a steady seasonal wind called a summer or wet monsoon is produced.

Relative humidity is the actual amount of water vapor in a certain volume of air compared to the maximum amount of water vapor this air could hold at a given temperature. The air temperature at which water vapor begins to condense is called the **dew point.**

Types of Storms

A **thunderstorm** is a brief, local storm produced by the rapid upward movement of warm, moist air within a cumulonimbus cloud. Thunderstorms always produce lightning and thunder, and are accompanied by strong wind gusts and heavy rain or hail.

A severe storm with swirling winds that may reach speeds of hundreds of km per hour is called a **tornado.** Such a storm is also referred to as a "twister." The sky is covered by large cumulo-nimbus clouds and violent thunderstorms; a funnel-shaped swirling cloud may extend downward from a cumulonimbus cloud and reach the ground. Tornadoes are storms that leave a narrow path of destruction on the ground.

A swirling, funnel-shaped cloud that **extends** downward and touches a body of water is called a **waterspout.**

Hurricanes are storms that develop when warm, moist air carried by trade winds rotate around a low-pressure "eye." A large, rotating, low-pressure system accompanied by heavy precipitation and strong winds is called a tropical cyclone (better known as a hurricane). In the Pacific region, a hurricane is called a typhoon.

Storms that occur only in the winter are known as blizzards or ice storms. A **blizzard** is a storm with strong winds, blowing snow, and frigid temperatures. An **ice storm** consists of falling rain that freezes when it strikes the ground, covering everything with a layer of ice.

SKILL 4.13 Identify the factors that contribute to the climate of a geographic area

Tropical rain forests covered much of the world millions of years ago. Climatic changes currently limit this biome to about six percent of the Earth's land surface. Rain forests are found in South America, Africa, New Guinea, Malaysia, Burma, and Indonesia. The moist conditions and constant heat provide for a great growing environment. Fifty percent of all the species in the world are found in the rain forest. Only about one percent of the available sunlight reaches the forest floor. The climate is hot and humid; therefore the landform is a jungle. You would rule out polar region, too hot for deciduous trees and grasslands, too moist for a desert.

Deserts are hot like the rain forest but have relatively little moisture. Sand accounts for 15 percent of desert terrain. Most deserts are bare rock or pebbles and gravel areas. The landform requires no moisture.

Tundra are vast regions in which the subsoil is permanently frozen. There have been reports of a small number of mankind living at the Poles during the Ice Age. The Indians, Aleuts, and Eskimos had little effect on the tundra's ecosystem. The climate is extremely cold. Moss and lichens exist in this fragile environment of polar ice. More and more scientists are fearful that the polar caps are melting, which not only would change the landform and vegetation at the poles, but also shift the water levels worldwide.

Taiga are swampy and coniferous forests with a hardy type of lumber such as birch, aspen, poplars, or willows. The temperature is mild. In the niche created by the cool shade of the large trees, there are a great variety of plants. They include lots of mosses, lichens, and ferns. The landform is often laced with rivers and streams. The soils of the taiga thaw out completely each summer and are the home to lots of tiny invertebrates and vertebrates. These microscopic organisms help break down the leaves and evergreen needles on the forest floor, enriching the soil. The recycled nutrients are then available for use by the taiga's trees to continue growing and producing for yet another season.

Grasslands have different names in different parts of the world. In North America they are called prairies, in Asia, steppes, in Africa and Australia, savannas. Grasses have deep root systems. Therefore the climate would have to be mild to support it. For thousands of years the growth cycle of the grasslands has created very rich top soil. Farming has converted much of the grasslands into crops. Only 11% of the Earth is suitable for farming. Grasses are pollinated by wind. The animals of this region tend to be fast and have mottled colors to blend in with the dry grass.

SKILL 4.14 Identify the movement of water in the hydrologic cycle, including sources of water, types of precipitation, and causes of condensation.

Water that falls to Earth in the form of rain and snow is called **precipitation**. Precipitation is part of a continuous process in which water at the Earth's surface evaporates, condenses into clouds, and returns to Earth. This process is termed the **water cycle**. The water located below the surface is called groundwater.

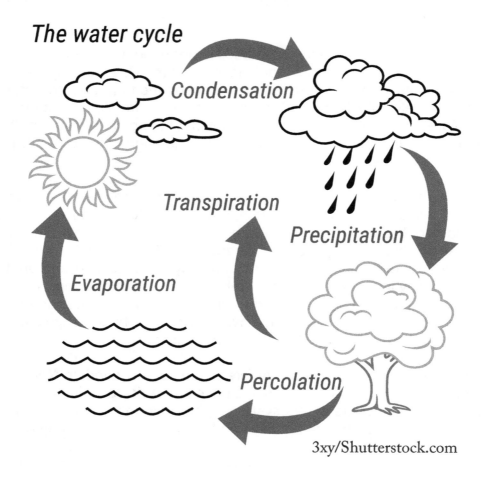

The water cycle

Condensation

Transpiration

Precipitation

Evaporation

Percolation

3xy/Shutterstock.com

The impacts of altitude upon climatic conditions are primarily related to temperature and precipitation. As altitude increases, climatic conditions become increasingly drier and colder. Solar radiation becomes more severe as altitude increases while the effects of convection forces are minimized. Climatic changes as a function of latitude follow a similar pattern (as a reference, latitude moves either north or south from the equator). The climate becomes colder and drier as the distance from the equator increases. Proximity to land or water masses produces climatic conditions based upon the available moisture. Dry and arid climates prevail where moisture is scarce; lush tropical climates can prevail where moisture is abundant. Climate, as described above, depends upon the specific combination of conditions making up an area's environment. Man impacts all environments by producing pollutants in Earth, air, and water. It follows then, that man is a major player in world climatic conditions.

SKILL 4.15   Analyze ways in which Earth and water interact (e.g., soil absorption, runoff, leaching, groundwater, karst topography).

Soils are composed of particles of sand, clay, various minerals, tiny living organisms, and humus, plus the decayed remains of plants and animals. Soils are divided into three classes according to their texture. These classes are sandy soils, clay soils, and loamy soils.

Sandy soils are gritty and their particles do not bind together firmly. Sandy soils are porous; water passes through them rapidly. Therefore, sandy soils do not hold much water and therefore have poor **absorption.**

Clay soils are smooth and greasy; their particles bind together firmly. Clay soils are moist and usually do not allow water to pass through easily. This type of soil has the lowest potential for run off.

Loamy soils feel somewhat like velvet and their particles clump together. Loamy soils are made up of sand, clay, and silt. Loamy soils hold water but some water can pass through. **Percolation** is best in this type of soil.

Large features formed by dissolved limestone (calcium carbonate), include sinkholes, caves, and caverns. **Sinkholes** are funnel-shaped depressions created by dissolved limestone. Many sinkholes started life as a limestone cavern. Erosion weakens the cavern roof causing it to collapse, forming a sinkhole.

Groundwater usually contains large amounts of dissolved minerals, especially if the water flows through limestone. As groundwater drips through the roof of a cave, gases dissolved in the water can escape into the air. A deposit of calcium carbonate is left behind. Stalactites are icicle-like structures of calcium carbonate that hang from the roofs of caves. Water that falls on a constant spot on the cave floor and evaporates leaves a deposit of calcium carbonate and builds a stalagmite.

Groundwater provides drinking water for 53% of the population in the United States. Much groundwater is clean enough to drink without any type of treatment. Impurities in the water are filtered out by the rocks and soil through which it flows. However, many groundwater sources are becoming contaminated. Septic tanks, broken pipes, agriculture fertilizers, garbage dumps, rainwater runoff, leaking underground tanks, all pollute groundwater. Toxic chemicals from farmland mix with groundwater. Removal of large volumes of groundwater can cause collapse of soil and rock underground, causing the ground to sink.

Along shorelines, excessive depletion of underground water supplies allows the intrusion of salt water into the fresh water field. The groundwater supply becomes undrinkable.

Karst topography is a specific type of rock formation with distinctive surface shapes. These structures are formed when mildly acidic water dissolves bedrock (such as limestone or dolostone). The water is made acidic by carbonic acid that forms when water combines with carbon monoxide in the atmosphere. This water then dissolves surface rock and causes fractures. These fractures enlarge over time and as large gaps are formed, underground drainage systems develop which allow even more water to flow in and dissolve the rock. Complex underground drainage systems and caves are important features of karst topography.

Over thousands of years, karsification of a landscape will eventually form features of varied size. Giant spikes, "limestone pavements", and other striking features commonly form on the surface. Sinkholes, springs, and shafts are common below the surface. In the United States, large visible surface structures and complex underground caves formed by karst topography can be found in Missouri and Arkansas.

Surface **run-off** is water that flows over land before reaching a river, lake, or ocean. Run-off occurs when precipitation falls faster than the soil can absorb it and/or when the soil becomes saturated with precipitation. Certain human activities have increased run-off by making surfaces increasingly impervious to precipitation. Water is prevented from flowing in the ground by pavement and buildings in urban areas and by heavily tilled farmland in rural areas. Instead of renewing the ground water supplies, this precipitation is channeled directly to streams and other bodies of water. Not only does this reduce ground water supplies, it can trigger increased erosion, siltation, and flooding. The increased rate of erosion is particularly damaging to agricultural endeavors, since fertile topsoil is carried away at a higher rate.

Another important environmental aspect of the effect of human activity on run-off is the additional contribution to water pollution. As the run-off flows across land, it picks up and carries particulates and soil contaminants. The pollutants, including pesticides and fertilizers used agriculturally, then accumulate in the body of water to which the run-off flows. Increased run-off means even more pollutants in the water supply and that even more fertilizer and pesticides must be applied to grow crops efficiently.

Leaching is the extraction of substances from a solid by a liquid. Leaching includes the natural processes by which water removes soluble nutrients from soil and minerals from rocks. Agriculturally, the process of leaching is often exploited to lower high salt concentrations in soil. The nutrient loss caused by leaching can be mitigated by crop planting and fertilizer application techniques.

Leaching may have negative environmental consequences because it can lead to contamination of soil when water liberates contaminates in buried waste (nuclear waste or that in landfills, etc.). Water can also dissolve agricultural chemicals and carry them to under- and above-ground water sources.

SKILL 4.16 Identify various forms of water storage (e.g., aquifers, reservoirs, water sheds).

Precipitation that soaks into the ground through small pores or openings become groundwater. Gravity causes groundwater to move through interconnected porous rock formations from higher to lower elevations. The upper surface of the zone saturated with groundwater is the water table. A swamp is an area where the water table is at the surface. Sometimes the land dips below the water table and these areas fill with water forming lakes, ponds or streams. Groundwater that flows out from underground onto the surface is called a spring.

There exist well-known systems by which water flows and is collected. In most situations it runs across land and into small streams that feed larger bodies of water. All of the land that acts like a funnel for water flowing into a single larger body of water is known as a watershed or drainage basin. The watershed includes the streams and rivers that bear the water and the surfaces across which the water runs. Thus, the pollution load and general state of all the land within a watershed has an effect on the health and cleanliness of the body of water to which it drains. Large land features, such as mountains, separate watersheds from one another. However, some portion of water from one watershed may enter the groundwater and ultimately flow towards another adjacent watershed.

Not all water flows to the streams, rivers, and lakes that comprise the above ground water supply. Some water remains in the soil as groundwater. Additionally, underground rivers are found in areas of karst topography, though these are relatively rare. It is more common for water to collect in underground aquifers. Aquifers are layers of permeable rock or loose material (gravel, sand, or silt) that hold water. Aquifers may be either confined or unconfined. Confined aquifers are deep in the ground and below the water table. Unconfined aquifers border on the water table. The water table is the level at which ground water exists and is always equal to atmospheric pressure.

To visualize the entire ground water system, we can imagine a hole dug in wet sand at the beach and a small pool of water within the hole. The wet sand corresponds to the aquifer, the hole to a well or lake, and the level of water in the hole to the water table.

In some cases, people have created reservoirs, artificial storage areas that make large amounts of water readily available. Reservoirs are most often created by damming rivers. A dam is built from cement, soil, or rock and the river fills the newly created reservoir. A reservoir may be created by building a dam either across a valley or around the entire perimeter of an artificial lake (a bunded dam). The former technique is more common and relies on natural features to form a watertight reservoir. However, such a feature must exist to allow this type of construction. A fully bunded dam does not require such a natural feature but does necessitate more construction since a waterproof structure must be built all the way around the reservoir. This structure is typically made from clay and/or cement. Since no river feeds such reservoirs, mechanical pumps are used to fill them from nearby water sources. Occasionally, watertight roofs are added to these reservoirs so they can be used to hold treated water. These are known as service reservoirs.

SKILL 4.17 Analyze interactions between the atmosphere, geosphere, hydrosphere, biosphere, and cryosphere and the effects of these interactions.

When we look at the various phenomena in geology and meteorology we can see manifestations of many scientific principles. It is not simply that certain examples exist in the natural world. Rather it is the reverse; scientists observed natural phenomena to formulate and refine the theories and laws of science.

First, there are many simple chemical and physical principles that underlie the various phenomena discussed in this section. For instance, basic principles of radioactive decay are exploited to allow carbon dating. Chemical laws also dictate the dissolution and precipitation that govern the formation of many rocks. Chemical principles are also important in various processes involving water: the dissolution of carbonic acid that causes acid rain; reactions between rock and water lead to karst topography; and solubility rules govern what compounds leach out of soil and into groundwater. The laws of thermodynamics are also extremely important in the natural world since they predict everything from how weather systems move to how water flows to the ultimate heat death of the universe.

Additionally, there are many laws that pertain especially to Earth and atmospheric science. A few are listed below:

The **law of superposition** states that higher layers of sedimentary rock are younger than those beneath it. This is a logical statement, but it means that layers of sedimentary rock can be viewed as a biogeological timeline of sorts.

The **principle of uniformitarianism** states that geological processes took place in the past in the same manner that they take place now. This is an important fact if we are to speculate on past geological events.

Buys-Ballot's law states that wind travels counterclockwise around low-pressure zones in the northern hemisphere and clockwise in the southern hemisphere. This is a consequence of the original observation, that in the northern hemisphere, if you stand with your back to the wind, the low-pressure area will be on your left.

COMPETENCY 5.0   KNOWLEDGE OF SPACE SCIENCE

SKILL 5.1   Identify consequences of Earth's motions and orientation (e.g., seasons, tides, lunar phases).

Earth is the third planet away from the sun in our solar system. Earth's numerous types of motion and states of orientation greatly effect global conditions, such as seasons, tides, and lunar phases. The Earth orbits the Sun in a period of 365 days. During this orbit, the average distance between the Earth and Sun is 93 million miles. The shape of the Earth's orbit around the Sun deviates from the shape of a circle only slightly. This deviation, known as the Earth's eccentricity, has a very small effect on the Earth's climate. The Earth is closest to the Sun at perihelion, occurring around January 2nd of each year, and farthest from the Sun at aphelion, occurring around July 2nd. Because the Earth is closest to the sun in January, the northern winter is slightly warmer than the southern winter.

Seasons

The rotation axis of the Earth is not perpendicular to the orbital (ecliptic) plane. The axis of the Earth is tilted 23.45° from the perpendicular. The tilt of the Earth's axis is known as the obliquity of the ecliptic, and is mainly responsible for the four seasons of the year by influencing the intensity of solar rays received by the northern and southern hemispheres. The four seasons, spring, summer, fall and winter, are extended periods of characteristic average temperature, rainfall, storm frequency, and vegetation growth or dormancy. The effect of the Earth's tilt on climate is best demonstrated at the solstices, the two days of the year when the Sun is farthest from the Earth's equatorial plane. At the summer solstice (June solstice), the Earth's tilt on its axis causes the northern hemisphere to the lean toward the Sun, while the southern hemisphere leans away. Consequently, the northern hemisphere receives more intense rays from the Sun and experiences summer during this time, while the southern hemisphere experiences winter. At the winter solstice (December solstice), it is the southern hemisphere that leans toward the sun and thus experiences summer. Spring and fall are produced by varying degrees of the same leaning toward or away from the Sun.

The orientation of and gravitational interaction between the Earth and the Moon are responsible for the ocean tides that occur on Earth. The term *tide* refers to the cyclic rise and fall of large bodies of water. Gravitational attraction is defined as the force of attraction between all bodies in the universe. At the location on Earth closest to the Moon, the gravitational attraction of the Moon draws seawater toward the Moon in the form of a tidal bulge. Spring tides are especially strong tides that occur when the Earth, Sun, and Moon are in line, allowing both the Sun and the Moon to exert gravitational force on the Earth and increase tidal bulge height. These tides occur during the full moon and the new moon. Neap tides are especially weak tides occurring when the gravitational forces of the Moon and the Sun are perpendicular to one another. These tides occur during quarter moons.

Lunar Phases

The Earth's orientation with respect to the solar system is also responsible for our perception of the phases of the moon. As the Earth orbits the Sun with a period of 365 days, the Moon orbits the Earth every 27 days. As the moon circles the Earth, its shape in the night sky appears to change. The changes in the appearance of the moon from Earth are known as *lunar phases*. These phases vary cyclically according to the relative positions of the Moon, the Earth, and the Sun. At all times, half of the Moon is facing the Sun and is thus illuminated by reflecting the Sun's light. As the Moon orbits the Earth and the Earth orbits the Sun, the half of the moon that faces the Sun changes. However, the Moon is in synchronous rotation around the Earth, which means that the same side of the moon faces the Earth at all times. This side is referred to as the near side of the moon. Lunar phases occur as the Earth and Moon orbit the Sun and the fractional illumination of the Moon's near side changes.

When the Sun and Moon are on opposite sides of the Earth, observers on Earth perceive a full moon, meaning the moon appears circular because the entire illuminated half of the moon is visible. As the Moon orbits the Earth, the Moon wanes as the amount of the illuminated half of the Moon that is visible from Earth decreases. A gibbous moon is between a full moon and a half moon, or between a half moon and a full moon. When the Sun and the Moon are on the same side of Earth, the illuminated half of the moon is facing away from Earth, and the moon appears invisible. This lunar phase is known as the *new moon*. The time between each full moon is approximately 29.53 days.

Viewing the moon from the southern hemisphere would cause the following phases to occur in the opposite order.

Lunar phases	Description
new moon	The moon is invisible.
waxing crescent	The right crescent of the moon is visible.
first quarter	The right quarter of the moon is visible.
waxing gibbous	Only the left crescent is not illuminated.
full moon	The entire illuminated half of the moon is visible.
waning gibbous	Only the right crescent of the moon is not illuminated.
last quarter	The left quarter of the moon is illuminated.
waning crescent	Only the left crescent of the moon is illuminated.

SKILL 5.2   Identify the properties of stars and the factors that affect their evolutionary patterns.

The **sun** is considered the nearest star to Earth that produces solar energy. By the process of nuclear fusion, hydrogen gas is converted to helium gas. Energy flows out of the core to the surface, then radiation escapes into space.

Parts of the sun include: (1) **core:** the inner portion of the sun where fusion takes place, (2) **photosphere:** considered the surface of the sun which produces **sunspots** (cool, dark areas that can be seen on its surface), (3) **chromosphere:** hydrogen gas causes this portion to be red in color (also found here are solar flares (sudden brightness of the chromosphere) and solar prominences (gases that shoot outward from the chromosphere)), and (4) **corona**, the transparent area of sun visible only during a total eclipse.

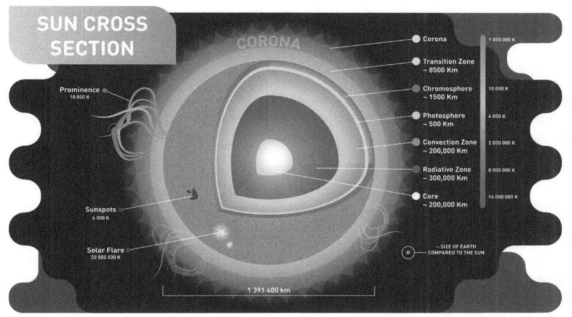

VectorMine/Shutterstock.com

Solar radiation is energy traveling from the sun that radiates into space. **Solar flares** produce excited protons and electrons that shoot outward from the chromosphere at great speeds reaching Earth. These particles disturb radio reception and also affect the magnetic field on Earth.

A star is a ball of hot, glowing gas that is hot enough and dense enough to trigger nuclear reactions, which fuel the star. In comparing the mass, light production, and size of the Sun to other stars, astronomers find that the Sun is a perfectly ordinary star. It behaves exactly the way they would expect a star of its size to behave. The main difference between the Sun and other stars is that the Sun is much closer to Earth.

Most stars have masses similar to that of the Sun. The majority of stars' masses are between 0.3 to 3.0 times the mass of the Sun. Theoretical calculations indicate that in order to trigger nuclear reactions and to create its own energy—that is, to become a star—a body must have a mass greater than 7 percent of the mass of the Sun. Astronomical bodies that are less massive than this become planets or objects called brown dwarfs. The largest accurately determined stellar mass is of a star called V382 Cygni and is 27 times that of the Sun.

The range of brightness among stars is much larger than the range of mass. Astronomers measure the brightness of a star by measuring **its magnitude** and luminosity. Magnitude allows astronomers to rank how bright, comparatively, different stars appear to humans. Because of the way our eyes detect light, a lamp ten times more luminous than a second lamp will appear less than ten times brighter to human eyes. This discrepancy affects the magnitude scale, as does the tradition of giving brighter stars lower magnitudes. The lower a star's magnitude, the brighter it is. Stars with negative magnitudes are the brightest of all.

Magnitude is given in terms of absolute and apparent values. Absolute magnitude is a measurement of how bright a star would appear if viewed from a set distance away. Astronomers also measure a star's brightness in terms of its luminosity. A star's absolute luminosity or intrinsic brightness is the total amount of energy radiated by the star per second. Luminosity is often expressed in units of watts.

SKILL 5.3   Identify devices and techniques for collecting and analyzing data about stars and other celestial objects.

Galileo was the first person to use telescopes to observe the solar system. He invented the first refracting telescope. A **refracting telescope** uses lenses to bend light rays to focus the image.

Sir Isaac Newton invented the **reflecting telescope** using mirrors to gather light rays on a curved mirror which produces a small focused image. The world's largest telescope is located in Mauna Kea, Hawaii. It uses multiple mirrors to gather light rays.

The Hubble Space telescope uses a single-reflector mirror. It provides an opportunity for astronomers to observe objects seven times farther away. Even those objects that are 50 times fainter can be viewed better than by any telescope on Earth. There are future plans to make repairs and install new mirrors and other equipment on the Hubble Space telescope.

Refracting and reflecting telescopes are considered optical telescopes since they gather visible light and focus it to produce images. A different type of telescope that collects invisible radio waves created by the sun and stars is called a *radio telescope*.

Radio telescopes consists of a reflector or dish with special receivers. The reflector collects radio waves that are created by the sun and stars. Using a radio telescope has many advantages. They can receive signals 24 hours a day, can operate in any kind of weather, and dust particles or clouds do not interfere with its performance. The most impressive aspect of the radio telescope is its ability to detect objects from such great distances in space.

The world's largest radio telescope is located in Arecibo, Puerto Rico. It has a collecting dish antenna of more than 300 meters in diameter.

The three formulas astronomers use for calculating distances in space are: (1) the **astronomical unit** (AU), (2) **light year** (ly), and (3) **the parsec** (pc). It is important to remember that these formulas are measures of distance not time. The distance between the Earth and the Sun is about 150×10^6 km. This distance is the astronomical unit. This unit is used to measure distances within the solar system. The distance light travels in one year is a light year (9.5×10^{12} km). Large distances are measured in parsecs. One parsec equals 3.26 light-years. There are approximately 63,000 AUs in one light year.

SKILL 5.4 Explain the role of space exploration and its impact on technological advancements.

Space exploration is the use of astronomy and space technology to explore outer space. The physical exploration of space is conducted both by human spaceflights and by robotic spacecraft.

Weather forecasting, global positioning systems, satellite television, and some long distance communications systems critically rely on space technology. Astronomy and the study of Earth through remote sensing benefit the most from space technology. The hole in the ozone layer was found from an artificial satellite that was exploring Earth's atmosphere.

One of the reasons for going into space includes knowing more about the Sun. Once above Earth's magnetic field and atmosphere, scientists learn more about solar wind and radiation that cannot reach the surface of the Earth. The Sun has an impact on weather on Earth that can affect power generation and transmission systems on Earth and interfere with, and even damage, satellites and space probes.

The exploration of Mars has been an important part of the space exploration programs of the Soviet Union (later Russia), the United States, Europe, and Japan. Dozens of robotic spacecraft, including orbiters, landers, and rovers, have been launched toward Mars since the 1960s. These missions were aimed at gathering data about current conditions and answering questions about the history of Mars.

The exploration of Jupiter and Saturn has consisted solely of a number of automated spacecraft that have visited the planet since 1973. Like all gas giants, there is no solid surface for a probe to land on.

The exploration of Uranus has been solely through the Voyager 2 spacecraft, which was an unmanned space probe. Voyager 2 discovered 10 previously unknown moons, examined its ring system, and studied the planet's unique atmosphere.--

One of the devices used in space is the spectroscope. The **spectroscope** is a device or an attachment for telescopes that is used to separate white light into a series of different colors by wave lengths. This series of colors of light is called a **spectrum**. A **spectrograph** can photograph a spectrum. Wavelengths of light have distinctive colors. The color red has the longest wavelength and violet has the shortest wavelength. Wavelengths are arranged to form an **electromagnetic spectrum**. They range from very long radio waves to very short gamma rays. Visible light covers a small portion of the electromagnetic spectrum. Spectroscopes observe the spectra, temperatures, pressures, and also the movement of stars. The movements of stars indicate if they are moving toward, or away, from Earth.

SKILL 5.5   Identify the components of the solar system (e.g., Kuiper belt, Oort cloud), their individual characteristics, and how they interact (e.g., solar winds, impacts, gravitation attraction) and how they evolve.

Planets

There are eight established planets in our solar system; Mercury, Venus, Earth, Mars, Jupiter, Saturn, Uranus, and Neptune. Pluto was an established planet in our solar system, but as of Summer 2006, its status is being reconsidered. The planets are divided into two groups based on distance from the sun. The inner planets include: Mercury, Venus, Earth, and Mars. The outer planets include: Jupiter, Saturn, Uranus, and Neptune.

Mercury is the closest planet to the sun. Its surface has craters and rocks. The atmosphere is composed of hydrogen, helium, and sodium. Mercury was named after the Roman messenger god.

Venus has a slow rotation when compared to Earth. Venus and Uranus rotate in opposite directions from the other planets. This opposite rotation is called retrograde rotation. The surface of Venus is not visible due to the extensive cloud cover. The atmosphere is composed mostly of carbon dioxide. Sulfuric acid droplets in the dense cloud cover give Venus a yellow appearance. Venus has a greater greenhouse effect than observed on Earth. The dense clouds, combined with carbon dioxide, trap heat. Venus was named after the Roman goddess of love.

Earth is considered a water planet with 70% of its surface covered by water. Gravity holds the masses of water in place. The different temperatures observed on Earth allow for the different states (solid, liquid, gas) of water to exist. The atmosphere is composed mainly of oxygen and nitrogen. Earth is the only planet that is known to support life.

The surface of **Mars** contains numerous craters, active and extinct volcanoes, ridges, and valleys with extremely deep fractures. Iron oxide found in the dusty soil makes the surface seem rust and the skies pink in color. The atmosphere is composed of carbon dioxide, nitrogen, argon, oxygen, and water vapor. Mars has polar regions with ice caps composed of water. Mars has two satellites. Mars was named after the Roman war god.

Jupiter is the largest planet in the solar system. Jupiter has 16 moons. The atmosphere is composed of hydrogen, helium, methane, and ammonia. There are white colored bands of clouds indicating rising gas and dark colored bands of clouds indicating descending gases. The gas movement is caused by heat resulting from the energy of Jupiter's core. Jupiter has a Great Red Spot that is thought to be a hurricane type cloud. Jupiter has a strong magnetic field.

Saturn is the second largest planet in the solar system. Saturn has rings of ice, rock, and dust particles circling it. Saturn's atmosphere is composed of hydrogen, helium, methane, and ammonia. Saturn has over 20 satellites. Saturn was named after the Roman god of agriculture.

Uranus is a gaseous planet. It has 10 dark rings and 15 satellites. Its atmosphere is composed of hydrogen, helium, and methane. Uranus was named after the Greek god of the heavens.

Neptune is another gaseous planet with an atmosphere consisting of hydrogen, helium, and methane. Neptune has 3 rings and 2 satellites. Neptune was named after the Roman sea god because its atmosphere is the same color as the seas.

Pluto was once considered the smallest planet in the solar system; its status as a planet is being reconsidered . Pluto's atmosphere probably contains methane, ammonia, and frozen water. Pluto has 1 satellite. Pluto revolves around the sun every 250 years. Pluto was named after the Roman god of the underworld.

Comets, Asteroids, and Meteors

Astronomers believe that rocky fragments may have been the remains of the birth of the solar system that never formed into a planet. **Asteroids** are found in the region between Mars and Jupiter.

Comets are masses of frozen gases, cosmic dust, and small rocky particles. Astronomers think that most comets originate in a dense comet cloud beyond Pluto. A comet consists of a nucleus, a coma, and a tail. A comet's tail always points away from the sun. The most famous comet, **Halley's Comet,** is named after the person who first discovered. It returns to the skies near Earth every 75 to 76 years.

Meteoroids are composed of particles of rock and metal of various sizes. When a meteoroid travels through the Earth's atmosphere, friction causes its surface to heat up and it begins to burn. The burning meteoroid falling through the Earth's atmosphere is called a **meteor** (also known as a *shooting star*).

Meteorites are meteors that strike the Earth's surface. A physical example of a meteorite's impact on the Earth's surface can be seen in Arizona. The Barringer Crater is a huge meteor crater. There are many other meteor craters throughout the world.

Oort Cloud and Kuiper Belt

The **Oort cloud** is a hypothetical spherical cloud surrounding our solar system. It extends approximately 3 light years or 30 trillion kilometers from the Sun. The cloud is believed to be made up of materials ejected out of the inner solar system because of interaction with Uranus and Neptune, but is gravitationally bound to the Sun. It is named the Oort cloud after Jan Oort who suggested its existence in 1950. Comets from the Oort cloud exhibit a wide range of sizes, inclinations and eccentricities and are often referred to as long-period comets because they have a period of greater than 200 years.

It seems that the Oort cloud objects were formed closer to the Sun than the Kuiper belt objects. Small objects formed near the giant planets would have been ejected from the solar system by gravitational encounters. Those that didn't escape entirely formed the distant Oort cloud. Small objects formed farther out had no such interactions and remained as the Kuiper belt objects.

The **Kuiper belt** is the name given to a vast population of small bodies orbiting the sun beyond Neptune. There are more than 70,000 of these small bodies with diameters larger than 100 km extending outwards from the orbit of Neptune to 50 AU. They exist mostly within a ring or belt surrounding the sun. It is believed that the objects in the Kuiper belt are primitive remnants of the earliest phases of the solar system. It is also believed that the Kuiper belt is the source of many short-period comets (periods of less than 200 years). It is a reservoir for the comets in the same way that the Oort cloud is a reservoir for long-period comets.

Occasionally the orbit of a Kuiper belt object will be disturbed by the interactions of the giant planets in such a way as to cause the object to cross the orbit of Neptune. It will then very likely have a close encounter with Neptune sending it out of the solar system or into an orbit crossing those of the other giant planets or even into the inner solar system. Prevailing theory states that scattered disk objects began as Kuiper belt objects which were scattered through gravitational interactions with the giant planets.

SKILL 5.6 Evaluate celestial objects in order to determine formation, age location, characteristics, and evolution.

Astronomers use groups or patterns of stars called **constellations** as reference points to locate other stars in the sky. Familiar constellations include: Ursa Major (also known as the Big Bear) and Ursa Minor (known as the Little Bear). Within the Ursa Major, the smaller constellation, the Big Dipper is found. Within the Ursa Minor, the smaller constellation, the Little Dipper is found. Different constellations appear as the Earth continues its revolution around the sun with the seasonal changes.

First-magnitude stars are 21 of the brightest stars that can be seen from Earth. These are the first stars noticed at night. In the northern hemisphere there are 15 commonly observed first-magnitude stars.

Vast collections of stars are defined as **galaxies**. Galaxies are classified as irregular, elliptical, and spiral. An irregular galaxy has no real structured appearance; most are in their early stages of life. An elliptical galaxy consists of smooth ellipses, containing little dust and gas, but composed of millions or trillion stars. Spiral galaxies are disk-shaped and have extending arms that rotate around its dense center. Earth's galaxy is found in the Milky Way and it is a spiral galaxy.

A **pulsar** is defined as a variable radio source that emits signals in very short, regular bursts; it is believed to be a rotating neutron star.

A **quasar** is defined as an object that photographs like a star but has an extremely large redshift and a variable energy output; it is believed to be the active core of a very distant galaxy.

Black holes are defined as an object that has collapsed to such a degree that light cannot escape from its surface; light is trapped by the intense gravitational field.

Origin of the Solar System

Two main hypotheses of the origin of the solar system are the (1) the tidal hypothesis and (2) the condensation hypothesis.

The tidal hypothesis proposes that the solar system began with a near collision of the sun and a large star. Some astronomers believe that as these two stars passed each other, the great gravitational pull of the large star extracted hot gases out of the sun. The mass from the hot gases started to orbit the sun, which began to cool then condensing into the nine planets. (Few astronomers support this scenario).

The condensation hypothesis proposes that the solar system began with rotating clouds of dust and gas. Condensation occurred in the center forming the sun and the smaller parts of the cloud formed the nine planets. (This scenario is widely accepted by many astronomers).

Two main theories to explain the origins of the universe include the: (1) Big Bang and (2) Steady-State theory.

The **Big Bang** has been widely accepted by many astronomers. It states that the universe originated from a magnificent explosion spreading of matter and energy into space. The galaxies formed from this material as it cooled during the next half-billion years.

The **Steady-State theory** is the least accepted theory. It states that the universe is a continuously being renewed. Galaxies move outward and new galaxies replace the older galaxies. Astronomers have not found any evidence to prove this theory.

The future of the universe is hypothesized with the oscillating universe model. It states that the universe will oscillate or expand and contract. Galaxies will move away from one another and will in time slow down and stop. Then a gradual moving toward each other will again activate the explosion or a big bang.

The stages of life for a star start with a mass of gas and dust that becomes a nebula, then a main sequence star. Next it becomes a red giant, then a nova, and then, in its final stages, a white dwarf (the dying core of a giant star), a neutron star or a black hole.

The forces of gravity acting on particles of gas and dust in a cloud in an area of space produce stars. This cloud is called a nebula. Particles in this cloud attract each other and, as it grows, its temperature increases. With the increased temperature the star begins to glow. Fusion occurs in the core of the star, releasing radiant energy at the star's surface.

When hydrogen becomes exhausted in a small, or even an average star, its core will collapse and cause its temperature to rise. Stars at this stage are nearing the end of their life. These stars are called red giants or are also called supergiants. A white dwarf is the dying core of a giant star. A nova is an ordinary star that experiences a sudden increase in brightness and then fades back to its original brightness. A supernova radiates even greater light energy. A neutron star is the result of mass left behind after a supernova. A black hole is a star with condensed matter and gravity so intense that light cannot escape.

COMPETENCY 6.0 KNOWLEDGE OF PROCESSES OF LIFE

SKILL 6.1 Identify the relationships between biological processes and the chemical processes (e.g. cellular respiration, ATP energy transfer) necessary for life.

The organization of living systems builds by levels from small to increasingly more large and complex. All aspects, whether it be a cell or an ecosystem, have the same requirements to sustain life. Life is organized from simple to complex. **Organelles** make up **cells** that make up **tissues** that make up **organs**. Groups of organs make up **organ systems**. Organ systems work together to provide life for the **organism.**

Several characteristics have been described to identify living versus non-living substances.

1. Living things are made of cells; they grow, are capable of reproduction and respond to stimuli.
2. Living things must adapt to environmental changes or perish.
3. Living things carry on metabolic processes. They use and make energy.

All organic life has a common element: carbon. Carbon is recycled through the ecosystem through both biotic and abiotic means. It is the link between biological processes and the chemical makeup of life.

SKILL 6.2 Compare prokaryotes and eukaryotes.

The cell is the basic unit of all living things. The two types of cells are prokaryotic and eukaryotic. **Prokaryotic** cells consist only of bacteria and blue-green algae. Bacteria were most likely the first cells and date back in the fossil record to 3.5 billion years ago. The important things that put these cells in their own group are:

1. They have no defined nucleus or nuclear membrane. The DNA and ribosomes float freely within the cell.
2. They have a thick cell wall. This is for protection, to give shape, and to

keep the cell from bursting.

3. The cell walls contain amino sugars (glycoproteins). Penicillin works by
4. disrupting the cell wall, which is bad for the bacteria, but will not harm the host.
5. Some have a capsule made of polysaccharides which make the bacteria sticky.
6. Some have pili, which is a protein strand. This also allows for attachment of the bacteria and may be used for sexual reproduction (conjugation).
7. Some have flagella for movement.

Eukaryotic cells are found in protists, fungi, plants and animals. Some features of eukaryotic cells include:

1. They are usually larger than prokaryotic cells.
2. They contain many organelles, which are membrane bound areas for specific cell functions.
3. They contain a cytoskeleton which provides a protein framework for the cell.
4. They contain cytoplasm to support the organelles and contain the ions and molecules necessary for cell function.

SKILL 6.3   Relate cell organelles to their functions.

1. Nucleus — The brain of the cell. The nucleus contains:

- **chromosomes**—DNA, RNA and proteins tightly coiled to conserve space while providing a large surface area.
- **chromatin**—loose structure of chromosomes. Chromosomes are called chromatin when the cell is not dividing.
- **nucleoli** — where ribosomes are made. These are seen as dark spots in the nucleus.
- **nuclear membrane** — contains pores which let RNA out of the nucleus. The nuclear membrane is continuous with the endoplasmic reticulum which allows the membrane to expand or shrink if needed.

2. Ribosomes—the site of protein synthesis. Ribosomes may be free floating in the cytoplasm or attached to the endoplasmic reticulum. There may be up to a half a million ribosomes in a cell, depending on how much protein is made by the cell.

3. Endoplasmic Reticulum—These are folded and provide a large surface area. They are the "roadway" of the cell and allow for transport of materials. The lumen of the endoplasmic reticulum helps to keep materials out of the cytoplasm and headed in the right direction. The endoplasmic reticulum is capable of building new membrane material. There are two types:

- **Smooth Endoplasmic Reticulum**—contain no ribosomes on their surface.
- **Rough Endoplasmic Reticulum**—contain ribosomes on their surface. This form of ER is abundant in cells that make many proteins, like in the pancreas, which produces many digestive enzymes.

4. Golgi Complex or Golgi Apparatus—This structure is stacked to increase surface area. The Golgi Complex functions to sort, modify and package molecules that are made in other parts of the cell. These molecules are either sent out of the cell or to other organelles within the cell.

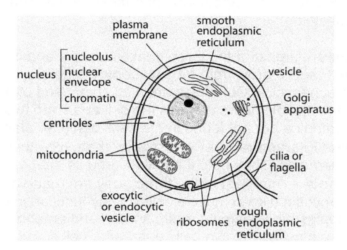

5. Lysosomes—found mainly in animal cells. These contain digestive enzymes that break down food, substances not needed, viruses, damaged cell components, and eventually the cell itself. It is believed that lysosomes are responsible for the aging process.

6. Mitochondria—large organelles that make ATP to supply energy to the cell. Muscle cells have many mitochondria because they use a great deal of energy. The folds inside the mitochondria are called cristae. They provide a large surface where the reactions of cellular respiration occur. Mitochondria have their own DNA and are capable of reproducing themselves if a greater demand is made for additional energy. Mitochondria are found in all cells except bacteria.

- **Chloroplasts**—green, function in photosynthesis. They are capable of trapping sunlight.
- **Chromoplasts**—make and store yellow and orange pigments; they provide color to leaves, flowers and fruits.
- **Amyloplasts**—store starch and are used as a food reserve. They are abundant in roots like potatoes.

7. Cell Wall—found in plant cells only, it is composed of cellulose and fibers. It is thick enough for support and protection, yet porous enough to allow water and dissolved substances to enter. Cell walls are cemented to each other.

8. Vacuoles—hold stored food and pigments. Vacuoles are very large in plants. This is allows them to fill with water in order to provide turgor pressure. Lack of turgor pressure causes a plant to wilt.

9. Cytoskeleton—composed of protein filaments attached to the plasma membrane and organelles. They provide a framework for the cell and aid in cell movement. They constantly change shape and move about. Three types of fibers make up the cytoskeleton:

- **Microtubules**—largest of the three; makes up cilia and flagella for locomotion. Flagella grow from a basal body. Some examples are sperm cells, and tracheal cilia. Centrioles are also composed of microtubules. They form the spindle fibers that pull the cell apart into two cells during cell division. Centrioles are not found in the cells of higher plants.
- **Intermediate Filaments**—they are smaller than microtubules but larger than microfilaments. They help the cell to keep its shape.
- **Microfilaments** — smallest of the three, they are made of actin and small amounts of myosin (like in muscle cells). They function in cell movement such as cytoplasmic streaming, endocytosis, and ameboid movement. This structure pinches the two cells apart after cell division, forming two cells.

SKILL 6.4   **Identify the sequence of events, the significance of the process, and the consequences of irregularities of mitosis and meiosis.**

The purpose of cell division is to provide growth and repair in body (somatic) cells and to replenish or create sex cells for reproduction. There are two forms of cell division. **Mitosis** is the division of somatic cells and **meiosis** is the division of sex cells (eggs and sperm). The table below summarizes the major differences between the two processes.

Mitosis	Meiosis
Division of somatic cell	Division of sex cells
Two cells result from each division.	Four cells or polar bodies result from each division.
Chromosome number is identical to parent cells.	Chromosome number is half the number of parent cells.
For cell growth and repair	Recombinations provide genetic diversity.

Some terms to know:

- **gamete**—sex cell or germ cell; eggs and sperm.
- **chromatin**—loose chromosomes; this state is found when the cell is not dividing.
- **chromosome**—tightly coiled, visible chromatin; this state is found when the cell is dividing.
- **homologues**—chromosomes that contain the same information. They are of the same length and contain the same genes.
- **diploid**—2n number; diploid chromosomes are a pair of chromosomes (somatic cells).
- **haploid**—1n number; haploid chromosomes are a half of a pair (sex cells).

Mitosis and Meiosis

The cell cycle is the life cycle of the cell. It is divided into two stages: **interphase** and the **mitotic division** where the cell is actively dividing. Interphase is divided into three steps; G1 (growth) period, where the cell is growing and metabolizing, S period (synthesis) where new DNA and enzymes are being made and the G2 phase (growth) where new proteins and organelles are being made to prepare for cell division. The mitotic stage consists of the stages of mitosis and the division of the cytoplasm. The stages of mitosis and their events are as follows. Be sure to know the correct order of steps. (IPMAT)

Mitosis

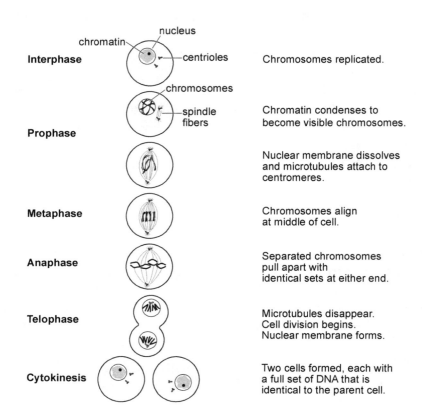

1. Interphase—chromatin is loose, chromosomes are replicated, cell metabolism is occurring. Interphase is technically <u>not</u> a stage of mitosis.

2. Prophase—once the cell enters prophase, it proceeds through the following steps continuously, with no stopping. The chromatin condenses to become visible chromosomes. The nucleolus disappears and the nuclear membrane breaks apart. Mitotic spindles form which will eventually pull the chromosomes apart. They are composed of microtubules. The cytoskeleton breaks down and the spindles are pushed to the poles or opposite ends of the cell by the action of centrioles.

3. Metaphase—kinetechore fibers attach to the chromosomes which causes the chromosomes to line up in the center of the cell (think **m**iddle for **m**etaphase)

4. Anaphase—centromeres split in half and homologous chromosomes separate. The chromosomes are pulled to the poles of the cell, with identical sets at either end.

5. Telophase—two nuclei form with a full set of DNA that is identical to the parent cell. The nucleoli become visible and the nuclear membrane reassembles.

A cell plate is visible in plant cells, whereas a cleavage furrow is formed in animal cells. The cell is pinched into two cells. Cytokinesis, or division, of the cytoplasm and organelles occurs.

Meiosis contains the same five stages as mitosis, but is repeated in order to reduce the chromosome number by one half. This way, when the sperm and egg join during fertilization, the haploid number is reached. In **meiosis I**, the chromosomes are replicated; cells remain diploid. In **meiosis II**, the number of chromosomes is cut in half. The steps of meiosis are as follows:

Prophase I—replicated chromosomes condense and pair with homologues. This forms a tetrad. Crossing over (the exchange of genetic material between homologues to further increase diversity) occurs during Prophase I.

Metaphase I—homologous sets attach to spindle fibers after lining up in the middle of the cell.

Anaphase I—sister chromatids remain joined and move to the poles of the cell.

Telophase I—two new cells are formed, chromosome number is still diploid

Prophase II—chromosomes condense.

Metaphase II—spindle fibers form again, sister chromatids line up in the center of the cell, centromeres divide and sister chromatids separate.

Anaphase II—separated chromosomes move to opposite ends of cell.

Telophase II—four haploid cells form for each original sperm germ cell. One viable egg cell gets all the genetic information and three polar bodies form with no DNA. The nuclear membrane reforms and cytokinesis occurs.

Meiosis

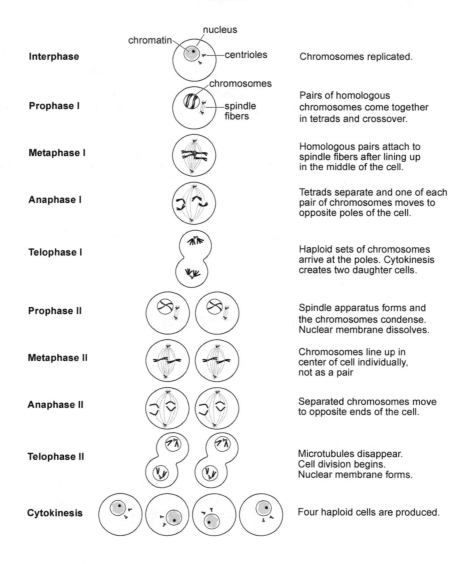

Interphase	Chromosomes replicated.
Prophase I	Pairs of homologous chromosomes come together in tetrads and crossover.
Metaphase I	Homologous pairs attach to spindle fibers after lining up in the middle of the cell.
Anaphase I	Tetrads separate and one of each pair of chromosomes moves to opposite poles of the cell.
Telophase I	Haploid sets of chromosomes arrive at the poles. Cytokinesis creates two daughter cells.
Prophase II	Spindle apparatus forms and the chromosomes condense. Nuclear membrane dissolves.
Metaphase II	Chromosomes line up in center of cell individually, not as a pair
Anaphase II	Separated chromosomes move to opposite ends of the cell.
Telophase II	Microtubules disappear. Cell division begins. Nuclear membrane forms.
Cytokinesis	Four haploid cells are produced.

Since it's not a perfect world, mistakes happen. Inheritable changes in DNA are called **mutations**. Mutations may be errors in replication or a spontaneous rearrangement of one or more segments by factors like radioactivity, drugs, or chemicals. The amount of the change is not as critical as where the change is. Mutations may occur on somatic or sex cells. Usually the ones on sex cells are more dangerous since they contain the basis of all information for the developing offspring. Mutations are not always bad. They are the basis of evolution, and if they make a more favorable variation that enhances the organism's survival, then they are beneficial. But, mutations may also lead to abnormalities, birth defects, and even death. There are several types of mutations; let's suppose a normal DNA sequence is A B C D E F. The mutation types are

Duplication—one base is repeated (A B C C D E F).

Inversion—a segment of the sequence is flipped around (A E D C B F).

Deletion—a base is left out (A B C E F).

Insertion or **translocation**—a segment from another place on the DNA is inserted in the wrong place (A B C R S D E F).

Breakage—a piece is lost (A B C).

Nondisjunction—This occurs during meiosis when chromosomes fail to separate properly. One sex cell may get both genes and another may get none. Depending on the chromosomes involved this may or may not be serious. Offspring end up with either an extra chromosome or are missing one. An example of nondisjunction is the Down syndrome, where three of chromosome #21 are present.

SKILL 6.5 Apply principles of Mendelian genetics in working monohybrid and dihybrid crosses and crosses involving linked genes.

Gregor Mendel is recognized as the father of genetics. His work in the late 1800's is the basis of our knowledge of genetics. Although unaware of the presence of DNA or genes, Mendel realized there were factors (now known as genes) that were transferred from parents to their offspring. Mendel worked with pea plants and fertilized the plants himself, keeping track of subsequent generations which led to the Mendelian laws of genetics. Mendel found that two factors governed each trait, one from each parent. Traits or characteristics came in several forms, known as alleles. For example, the trait of flower color had white alleles and purple alleles. Mendel formed three laws:

- **Law of dominance**—in a pair of alleles, one trait may cover up the allele of the other trait. Example: brown eyes are dominant to blue eyes.
- **Law of segregation**—only one of the two possible alleles from each parent is passed on to the offspring from each parent. (During meiosis, the haploid number insures that half the sex cells get one allele, half get the other).
- **Law of independent assortment**—alleles sort independently of each other. (Many combinations are possible depending on which sperm ends up with which egg. Compare this to the many combinations of hands possible when dealing a deck of cards).

A m**onohybrid cross** is a cross using only one trait. A **dihybrid cross** is a cross using two traits. More combinations are possible.

Punnet squares are used to show the possible ways that genes combine and indicate probability of the occurrence of a certain genotype or phenotype. One parent's genes are put at the top of the box and the other parent at the side of the box. Genes combine on the square just like numbers that are added in addition tables we learned in elementary school. In a monohybrid cross, there are four possible gene combinations. In a dihybrid cross, there are sixteen possible gene combinations

		pollen ♂			
		YR	Yr	yR	yr
pistil ♀	YR	◯ YYRR	◯ YYRr	◯ YyRR	◯ YyRr
	Yr	◯ YYRr	◖ YYrr	◯ YyRr	◖ Yyrr
	yR	◯ YyRR	◯ YyRr	◓ yyRR	◓ yyRr
	yr	◯ YyRr	◖ Yyrr	◓ yyRr	◓ yyrr

P   YYRR × yyrr
            ↓
F1   YyRr
            ↓
F2   1 - YYRR ⎤
       2 - YYRr ⎥
       2 - YyRR ⎬ ◯ 9 yellow round
       4 - YyRr ⎦

       1 - yyRR ⎤
       2 - yyRr ⎬ ◓ 3 green round

       1 - YYrr ⎤
       2 - Yyrr ⎬ ◯ 3 yellow wrinkled

       1 - yyrr ⎤◖ 1 green wrinkled

SKILL 6.6   **Apply principles of human genetics, including relationships between genotypes and phenotypes and causes and effects of disorders.**

A **dominant** trait is the stronger of the two traits. If a dominant gene is present, it will be expressed. Dominant traits are shown by a capital letter. **Recessive** traits the weaker of the two traits. In order for the recessive gene to be expressed, there must be two recessive genes present. Recessive traits are shown by a lower case letter.

Incomplete dominance means neither gene masks the other; a new phenotype is formed. For example, red flowers and white flowers may have equal strength. A heterozygote (Rr) would have pink flowers. If a problem occurs with a third phenotype, incomplete dominance is occurring. In **codominance,** genes may form new phenotypes. The ABO blood grouping is an example of codominance. A and B are of equal strength and O is recessive. Therefore, type A blood may have the genotypes of AA or AO, type B blood may have the genotypes of BB or BO, type AB blood has the genotype A and B, and type O blood has two recessive O genes.

Homozygous (purebred) means having two of the same genes present; an organism may be homozygous dominant with two dominant genes or homozygous recessive with two recessive genes. **Heterozygous** (hybrid) means having one dominant gene and one recessive gene. The dominant gene will be expressed due to the law of dominance.

Genotype refers to all the genes the organism has. Genes are represented with letters. AA, Bb, and tt are examples of genotypes. **Phenotype** is how the trait is expressed in an organism. Blue eyes, brown hair, and red flowers are examples of phenotypes.

Linkage occurs when genes are on the same chromosome and usually appear together unless crossing over has occurred in meiosis. (For example, blue eyes and blonde hair are linked genes.)

Lethal alleles are usually recessive due to the early death of the offspring. If a 2:1 ratio of alleles is found in offspring, a lethal gene combination is usually the reason. Some examples of lethal alleles include sickle cell anemia, Tay-Sachs disease, and cystic fibrosis. Usually the coding for an important protein is affected.

Inborn errors of metabolism occur when the protein affected is an enzyme. Examples include PKU (phenylketonuria) and albanism.

Polygenic characters occurs when many alleles code for a phenotype. There may be as many as twenty genes that code for skin color. This is why there is such a variety of skin tones. Another example is height. A couple of medium height may have very tall offspring.

There are **sex-influenced traits** because some traits are influenced by the sex hormones. Male pattern baldness is an example of a sex-influenced trait. Testosterone influences the expression of the gene. Mostly men lose their hair due to this trait.

SKILL 6.7 Analyze the genetic code and the roles of DNA and RNA in replication and protein synthesis.

The modern definition of a gene is a unit of genetic information. DNA makes up genes which, in turn, make up the chromosomes. DNA is wound tightly around proteins in order to conserve space. The DNA/protein combination makes up the chromosome. DNA controls the synthesis of proteins, thereby controlling the total cell activity. DNA is capable of making copies of itself.
Review of DNA structure:

1.   Made of nucleotides; a five carbon sugar, phosphate group and nitrogen base (either adenine, guanine, cytosine, or thymine).
2.   Consists of a sugar/phosphate backbone which is covalently bonded. The bases are joined down the center of the molecule and are attached by hydrogen bonds which are easily broken during replication.
3.   The amount of adenine equals the amount of thymine and the amount of

cytosine equals the amount of guanine.

4.   The shape is that of a twisted ladder called a double helix. The sugar/phosphates make up the sides of the ladder and the base pairs make up the rungs of the ladder.

DNA Replication

Enzymes control each step of the replication of DNA. The molecule untwists. The hydrogen bonds between the bases break and serve as a pattern for replication. Free nucleotides found inside the nucleus join on to form a new strand. Two new pieces of DNA are formed which are identical. This is a very accurate process. There is only one mistake for every billion nucleotides added. This is because there are enzymes (polymerases) present that proofread the molecule. In eukaryotes, replication occurs in many places along the DNA at once. The molecule may open up at many places like a broken zipper. In prokaryotic circular plasmids, replication begins at a point on the plasmid and goes in both directions until it meets itself.

Base pairing rules are important in determining a new strand of DNA sequence. The DNA nucleotides are A, G, C, and T. The rules are A bonds with T and C bonds with G. When the ladder separates, the new A, G, C, and T attach to the old DNA, and the DNA doubles.

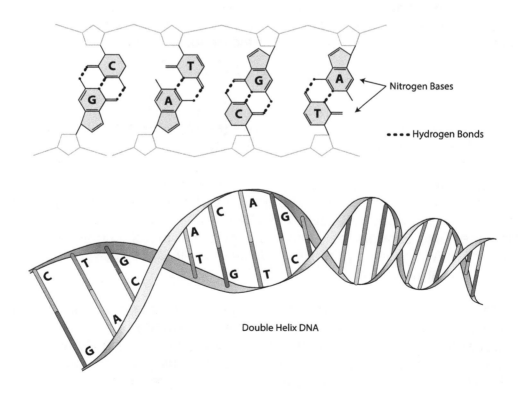

Double Helix DNA

Protein Synthesis

It is necessary for cells to manufacture new proteins for growth and repair of the organism. Protein synthesis is the process that allows the DNA code to be read and carried out of the nucleus into the cytoplasm in the form of RNA. This is where the ribosomes are found, which are the sites of protein synthesis. The protein is then assembled according to the instructions on the DNA. There are several types of RNA. Familiarize yourself with where they are found and their function.

- Messenger RNA (mRNA) copies the code from DNA in the nucleus and takes it to the ribosomes in the cytoplasm.
- Transfer RNA (tRNA) is free floating in the cytoplasm. Its job is to carry and position amino acids for assembly on the ribosome.
- Ribosomal RNA (rRNA) is found in the ribosomes. They make a place for the proteins to be made. rRNA is believed to have many important functions, so much research is currently being done currently in this area.

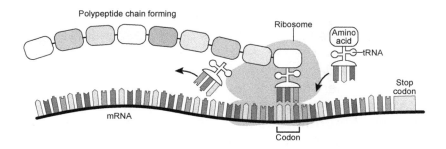

Along with enzymes and amino acids, the RNA's function is to assist in the building of proteins. There are two stages of protein synthesis:

The **transcription** phase allows for the assembly of mRNA and occurs in the nucleus where the DNA is found. The DNA splits open and an enzyme reads the code and "transcribes" the sequence onto a single strand of mRNA. For example, if the code on the DNA is T A C C T C G T A C G A , mRNA will be made reading: A U G G A G C A U G C U (Remember that uracil replaces thymine in RNA.) Each group of three bases is called a **codon**. The codon will eventually code for a specific amino acid to be carried to the ribosome. Start codons begin the building of the protein and stop codons end transcription. When the stop codon is reached, the mRNA separates from the DNA and leaves the nucleus for the cytoplasm.

The **translation** phase is the assembly of the amino acids to build the protein and occurs in the cytoplasm. The nucleotide sequence is translated to choose the correct amino acid sequence. As the rRNA translates the code at the ribosome, tRNA's that contain an **anticodon** seek out the correct amino acid and bring it back to the ribosome. For example, using the codon sequence from the example above, the mRNA reads A U G / G A G / C A U / G C U, the anticodons are U A C / C U C / G U A / C G A. The amino acid sequence would be Met (start) - Glu - His - Ala.

This whole process is accomplished through the assistance of **activating enzymes**. Each of the twenty amino acids has their own enzyme. The enzyme binds the amino acid to the tRNA. When the amino acids get close to each other on the ribosome, they bond together using peptide bonds. The start and stop codons are called nonsense codons. There is one start codon (AUG) and three stop codons. (UAA, UGA, and UAG). Addition mutations will cause the whole code to shift, thereby producing the wrong protein or, at times, no protein at all.

SKILL 6.8 Classify organisms based on the levels of biological taxonomy.

Carolus Linnaeus is termed the father of taxonomy. **Taxonomy** is the science of classification. Linnaeus based his system on morphology (study of structure). Later, evolutionary relationships (phylogeny) were also used to sort and group species. The modern classification system uses binomial nomenclature. This consists of a two word name for every species. The genus is the first part of the name and the species is the second part. Notice, in the levels explained below, that Homo sapiens is the scientific name for humans. Starting with the kingdom, the groups get smaller and more alike as one moves down the levels in the classification of humans: **kingdom**: Animalia, **phylum**: Chordata, **subphylum**: Vertebrata, **class**: Mammalia, **order**: Primate, **family**: Hominidae, **genus**: Homo, **species**: sapiens. Species are defined by the ability to successfully reproduce with members of their own kind. In the Plant kingdom, phyla are called divisions.

Kingdom Monera includes bacteria and blue-green algae, which are prokaryotic unicellular organisms and have no true nucleus. This group now includes Archeabacteria and Eubacteria.

Bacteria are classified according to their morphology (shape). **Bacilli** are rod shaped, **cocci** are round, and **spirilla** are spiral shaped. The **Gram stain** is a staining procedure used to identify bacteria. Gram-positive bacteria pick up the stain and turn purple. Gram-negative bacteria do not pick up the stain and are pink in color.

Kingdom Protista are eukaryotic, unicellular, some are photosynthetic, some are consumers. Microbiologists use methods of locomotion, reproduction, and how the organism obtains its food to classify protista.

Flagellates have a flagellum, ciliates have cilia, and ameboids move through use of pseudopodia. Protista reproduce by binary fission, which is simply dividing in half and is asexual. All new organisms are exact clones of the parent. Sexual modes provide more diversity for offspring. Bacteria can reproduce sexually through conjugation, where genetic material is exchanged. Some protista are photosynthetic organisms or producers, and convert sunlight to chemical energy. Others are consumers or heterotrophs and eat other living things. Saprophytes are consumers that live off dead or decaying material.

Kingdom Fungi includes eukaryotic, multicellular, and absorptive consumers, which contain a chitin cell wall.

Kingdom Plantae

Nonvascular plants are small in size, do not require vascular tissue (xylem and phloem) because individual cells are close to their environment. The nonvascular plants have no true leaves, stems or roots. **Division Bryophyta** (mosses and liverworts) have a dominant gametophyte generation. They possess rhizoids, which are root-like structures. Moisture in their environment is required for reproduction and absorption.

Vascular plants developed of vascular tissue which enabled these plants to grow in size. Xylem and phloem allowed for the transport of water and minerals up to the top of the plant, as well as transport food manufactured in the leaves to the bottom of the plant. All vascular plants have a dominant sporophyte generation. **Division Lycophyta** (club mosses) reproduce with spores and require water for reproduction. **Division Sphenophyta** (horsetails) also reproduce with spores. These plants have small, needle-like leaves and rhizoids and require moisture for reproduction. **Division Pterophyta** (ferns) reproduce with spores and flagellated sperm. These plants have a true stem and need moisture for reproduction.

Gymnosperms were the first plants to evolve with seeds which made them less dependent on water to assist in reproduction. Their seeds could travel by wind. Pollen from the male was also easily carried by the wind. Gymnosperms have cones which protect the seeds. **Division Cycadophyta** (cycads) look like palms with cones. **Divison Ghetophyta** are plants living in the desert. **Division Coniferophyta** (pines) have needles and cones. **Divison Ginkgophyta** have the ginkgo as its only member.

Angiosperms **(Division Anthophyta)** are the largest group in the plant kingdom. They are the flowering plants and produce true seeds for reproduction.

Kingdom Animalia

Annelida—the segmented worms. The annelids have specialized tissue. The circulatory system is more advanced in these worms and is a closed system with blood vessels. The nephridia are their excretory organs. They are hermaphrodidic and each worm fertilizes the other upon mating. They support themselves with a hydrostatic skeleton and have circular and longitudinal muscles for movement.

Mollusca—clams, octopus, soft bodied animals. These animals have a muscular foot for movement. They breathe through gills and most are able to make a shell for protection from predators. They have an open circulatory system, with sinuses bathing the body regions.

Arthropoda—insects, crustaceans and spiders. This is the largest group of the animal kingdom. Phylum arthropoda accounts for about 85% of all the animal species. Animals in the phylum arthropoda possess an exoskeleton made of chitin. They must molt to grow. Insects, for example, go through four stages of development. They begin as an egg, hatch into a larva, form a pupa, and then emerge as an adult. Arthropods breathe through gills, tracheae, or book lungs. Movement varies, with members being able to swim, fly, and crawl. There is a division of labor among the appendages (legs, antennae, etc.). This is an extremely successful phylum, with members occupying diverse habitats.

Echinodermata — sea urchins and starfish. These animals have spiny skin. Their habitat is marine. They have tube feet for locomotion and feeding.

Chordata — all animals with a notocord or a backbone. The classes in this phylum include Agnatha (jawless fish), Chondrichthyes (cartilage fish), Osteichthyes (bony fish), Amphibia (frogs and toads; gills which are replaced by lungs during development), Reptilia (snakes, lizards; the first to lay eggs with a protective covering), Aves (birds; warm-blooded with wings consisting of a particular shape and composition designed for flight), and Mammalia (warm blooded animals with body hair that bear their young alive, and possess mammary glands for milk production).

SKILL 6.9   Identify characteristics of viruses, bacteria, protists, and fungi.

Single-celled microorganisms were probably the first life forms inhabiting Earth. Scientists estimate that they developed approximately three billion years ago. Although they may seem simplistic, single celled organisms thrive and are abundant. A single celled eukaryotic organism is called a **protist.** When you look under a microscope the protists appearing animal-like are called **protozoans.** They do not have chloroplasts. They are usually classified by the way they move for food. Amoebas engulf other protists by flowing around and over them. The paramecium has a hair like structure that allows it to move back and forth like tiny oars searching for food. The euglena is an example of a protozoan that moves with a tail-like structure called a flagella. Plant-like protists have cell walls and float in the ocean.

Bacteria are the simplest microorganisms. A bacterial cell is surrounded by a cell wall, but there is no nucleus inside the cell. Most bacteria do not contain chlorophyll so they do not make their own food. The classification of bacteria is by shape. Cocci are round, bacilli are rod-shaped, and spirilla are spiral shaped.

Viruses cause the common cold by replicating once they get inside a host cell. However, they are not cells and cannot perform the processes of life, such as making new cellular material. Most scientists don't classify them as living organisms. They are much smaller than the smallest bacteria. A very simple bacterium might have thousands of genes. The HIV virus, which causes AIDS, has only nine genes.

Protists also gave rise to fungi, which are different from plants and animals. Yeasts are unicellular fungi. Mushrooms and lichen are multicellular organisms that are like plants because they are fixed in the ground. However, fungi do not manufacture their own food like plants. Their method of obtaining food is closer to that of animals.

SKILL 6.10   Differentiate between structures and functions of plant and animal cells and their organelles.

The structure of the cell is often related to the cell's function. Root hair cells differ from flower stamens or leaf epidermal cells. They all have different functions.

Animal cells are eukaryotic cells that contain the standard set of organelles, with the exception of plastids, and a cell wall. Some of the vacuoles contain food for the cell, while other vacuoles contain waste materials. Animal cells differ from plant cells because they have centrioles.

Plant cells are eukaryotic cells that contain the standard set of organelles. Some of the vacuoles contain food for the cell, while other vacuoles contain waste materials. In addition the large central vacuole is the cell fills with water and controls the cells turgor pressure. Plant cells differ from animal cells because they have both a cell wall and plastids (including chloroplasts).

SKILL 6.11   Identify plant structures and their functions.

The specialization of plant tissues enables plants to grow larger. Be familiar with the following tissues and their functions:

- **Xylem**—The tube-shaped part of plants that transports water and mineral from the roots to the rest of the plant.
- **Phloem**—Elongated tubes that transports food (glucose) and other nutrients throughout the plant.
- **Cortex**— Region of the root used for storage of food and water.
- **Epidermis**—Protective covering of plant.
- **Endodermis**—Controls movement between the cortex and the cell interior.
- **Pericycle**—Meristematic tissue which can divide when necessary.
- **Pith**—Tissue in stems used for storage.
- **Sclerenchyma cell**—A rigid supportive plant cell for stems.
- **Stomata**—Openings on the underside of leaves that let carbon dioxide in and water out (transpiration).
- **Guard cells**—Control the size of the stomata. If the plant has to conserve water, the stomata will close.
- **Palisade mesophyll**—Site of photosynthesis that contains the chloroplasts in leaves.
- **Spongy mesophyll**—Plant tissue with open spaces in the leaf that allows for gas circulation.
- **Seed coat**—Protective covering on a seed.
- **Cotyledon**—Small seed leaf that emerges when the seed germinates.
- **Endosperm**—A nutrient-rich tissue that supplies food in the seed.
- **Apical meristem**—Embryonic plant tissue in an area of cell division allowing for growth.

Flowers are the reproductive organs of the plant. Know the following functions and locations:

- **Pedicel**—Supports the weight of the flower.
- **Receptacle**—Holds the floral organs at the base of the flower.
- **Sepals**—Green leaf-like parts that cover the flower prior to blooming.
- **Petals**—Contain coloration by pigments, whose purpose is to attract insects to assist in pollination.
- **Anther**—Male part that produces pollen.
- **Filament**—Supports the anther; the filament and anther make up the **stamen**.
- **Stigma**—Female part that holds pollen grains that came from the male part.
- **Style**—Tube that leads to the ovary (female).
- **Ovary**—Contains the ovules; the stigma, style and ovary make up the **carpel**.

SKILL 6.12 Identify the major steps of plant processes (e.g., photosynthesis, respiration, transpiration, reproduction).

Photosynthesis is the process by which plants make carbohydrates from the energy of the sun, carbon dioxide, and water. Oxygen is a waste product. Photosynthesis occurs in the chloroplast where the pigment chlorophyll traps sun energy. It is divided into two major steps:

- Light reactions—Sunlight is trapped, water is split, and oxygen is given off. ATP is made and hydrogen atoms reduce NADP to NADPH2. The light reactions occur in light. The products of the light reactions enter into the dark reactions (Calvin cycle).

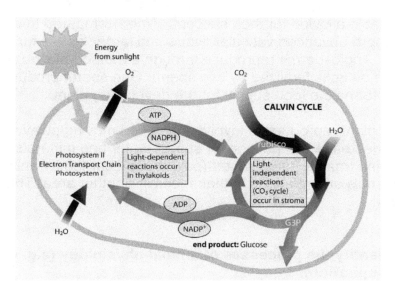

- Dark Reactions—Carbon dioxide enters during the dark reactions, which can occur with or without the presence of light. The energy transferred from NADPH2 and ATP allow for the fixation of carbon into glucose.

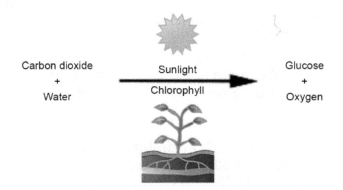

Plants break down the products of photosynthesis through **cellular respiration**. Glucose, with the help of oxygen, breaks down and produces carbon dioxide and water as waste. Approximately fifty percent of the products of photosynthesis are used by the plant for energy.

Water travels up the xylem of the plant through the process of **transpiration**. Water sticks to itself (cohesion) and to the walls of the xylem (adhesion). As it evaporates through the stomata of the leaves, the water is pulled up the column from the roots. Environmental factors such as heat and wind increase the rate of transpiration. High humidity will decrease the rate of transpiration.

Angiosperms are the largest group in the plant kingdom. They are the flowering plants and produce true seeds for **reproduction**. They arose about seventy million years ago when the dinosaurs were disappearing. The land was drying up and their ability to produce seeds that could remain dormant until conditions became acceptable allowed for their success. When compared to other plants, they also had more advanced vascular tissue and larger leaves for increased photosynthesis. Angiosperms reproduce through a method of **double fertilization**. An ovum is fertilized by two sperm. One sperm produces the new plant, the other forms the food supply for the developing plant.

The success of plant reproduction involves the seed moving away from the parent plant to decrease competition for space, water and minerals. Seeds may be carried by wind (maple trees), water (palm trees), carried by animals (burrs) or ingested by animals and released in their feces in another area. This is called **seed dispersal**.

SKILL 6.13   Identify the processes of animal physiology (e.g. digestion, respiration).

Animal respiration takes in oxygen and gives off waste gases. For instance a fish uses its gills to extract oxygen from the water. Bubbles are evidence that waste gases are expelled. Respiration without oxygen is called anaerobic respiration. Anaerobic respiration in animal cells is also called lactic acid fermentation. The end products are lactic acid and carbon dioxide.

Animal reproduction can be asexual or sexual. Geese lay eggs. Animals such as bear cubs, deer, and rabbits are born alive. Some animals reproduce frequently while others do not. Some animals only produce one baby yet others produce many (clutch size).

Animal digestion breaks down carbohydrates, fats, and proteins. Some animals only eat meat (carnivores) while others only eat plants (herbivores). Many animals do both (omnivores). Nature has created animals with structural adaptations so they may obtain food through sharp teeth or long facial structures. Many organs are needed to digest food. The process begins with the mouth. Certain animals, such as birds, have beaks to puncture wood or allow for large fish to be consumed. The tooth structure of a beaver is designed to cut down trees. Tigers are known for their sharp teeth used to rip hides from their prey. Enzymes are catalysts that help speed up chemical reactions by lowering effective activation energy. Enzyme rate is affected by temperature, pH, and the amount of substrate. Saliva contains the enzyme amylase that changes starches into sugars.

Animal circulation refers to the flow of blood. The blood temperature of all mammals stays constant regardless of the outside temperature. This is called warm-blooded, while cold-blooded animals' circulation will vary with the temperature. Amphibians and fish are cold-blooded.

SKILL 6.14   Identify the structures of the organs and organ systems of various kinds of animals, including humans.

The function of the **skeletal system** is support. Vertebrates have an endoskeleton, with muscles attached to bones. Skeletal proportions are controlled by area to volume relationships. Body size and shape is limited due to the forces of gravity. Surface area is increased to improve efficiency in all organ systems.

The function of the **muscular system** is movement. There are three types of muscle tissue. Skeletal muscle is voluntary. These muscles are attached to bones. Smooth muscle is involuntary. It is found in organs and enable functions such as digestion and respiration. Cardiac muscle is a specialized type of smooth muscle.

The neuron is the basic unit of the **nervous system**. It consists of an axon, which carries impulses away from the cell body, the dendrite, which carries impulses toward the cell body, and the cell body, which contains the nucleus. Synapses are spaces between neurons. Chemicals called neurotransmitters are found close to the synapse. The myelin sheath, composed of Schwann cells, covers the neurons and provides insulation.

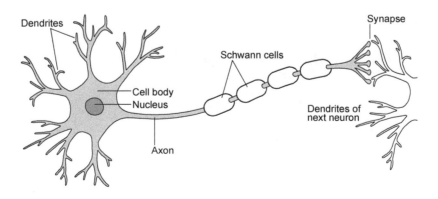

The function of the **digestive system** is to break down food and absorb it into the blood stream where it can be delivered to all cells of the body for use in cellular respiration. As animals evolved, digestive systems changed from simple absorption to a system with a separate mouth and anus, capable of allowing the animal to become independent of a host.

The **respiratory system** functions in the gas exchange of oxygen (needed) and carbon dioxide (waste). It delivers oxygen to the bloodstream and picks up carbon dioxide for release out of the body. Simple animals diffuse gases from and to their environment. Gills allow aquatic animals to exchange gases in a fluid medium by removing dissolved oxygen from the water. Lungs maintain a fluid environment for gas exchange in terrestrial animals.

The function of the **circulatory system** is to carry oxygenated blood and nutrients to all cells of the body and return carbon dioxide waste to be expelled from the lungs. Animals evolved from an open system to a closed system with vessels leading to and from the heart.

The Human Body

The **axial skeleton** consists of the bones of the skull and vertebrae. The **appendicular skeleton** consists of the bones of the legs, arms, tail, and shoulder girdle. Bone is a connective tissue. Parts of the bone include compact bone which gives strength, spongy bone which contains red marrow to make blood cells, yellow marrow in the center of long bones to store fat cells, and the periosteum which is the protective covering on the outside of the bone. A **joint** is defined as a place where two bones meet. Joints enable movement. **Ligaments** attach bone to bone. **Tendons** attach bones to muscles.

Muscles can only contract; therefore they work in antagonistic pairs to allow back and forward movement. Muscle fibers are made of groups of myofibrils which are made of groups of sarcomeres. Actin and myosin are proteins which make up the sarcomere.

Concerning the physiology of muscle contraction, a nerve impulse strikes a muscle fiber. This causes calcium ions to flood the sarcomere. Calcium ions allow ATP to expend energy. The myosin fibers creep along the actin, causing the muscle to contract. Once the nerve impulse has passed, calcium is pumped out and the contraction ends.

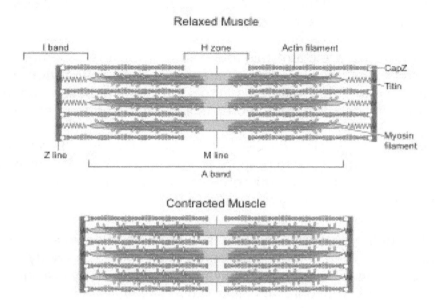

Relaxed Muscle

Contracted Muscle

Nerve action depends on depolarization and an imbalance of electrical charges across the neuron. A polarized nerve has a positive charge outside the neuron. A depolarized nerve has a negative charge outside the neuron. Neurotransmitters turn off the sodium pump which results in depolarization of the membrane. This wave of depolarization (as it moves from neuron to neuron) carries an electrical impulse. This is actually a wave of opening and closing gates that allows for the flow of ions across the synapse. Nerves have an action potential. There is a threshold of the level of chemicals that must be met or exceeded in order for muscles to respond. This is called the *all or none* response.

The **reflex arc** is the simplest nerve response. The brain is bypassed. When a stimulus (like touching a hot stove) occurs, sensors in the hand send the message directly to the spinal cord. This stimulates motor neurons that contract the muscles to move the hand.

Voluntary nerve responses involve the brain. Receptor cells send the message to sensory neurons that lead to association neurons. The message is taken to the brain. Motor neurons are stimulated and the message is transmitted to effector cells that cause the end effect.

Concerning the organization of the nervous system, the somatic nervous system is controlled consciously. It consists of the central nervous system (brain and spinal cord) and the peripheral nervous system (nerves that extend from the spinal cord to the muscles). The autonomic nervous system is unconsciously controlled by the hypothalamus of the brain. Smooth muscles, the heart and digestion are some processes controlled by the autonomic nervous system. The sympathetic nervous system works opposite from the parasympathetic nervous system. For example, if the sympathetic nervous system stimulates an action, the parasympathetic nervous system would end that action.

Neurotransmitters are chemicals released by exocytosis. Some neurotransmitters stimulate, while others inhibit, action. **Acetylcholine** is the most common neurotransmitter; it controls muscle contraction and heartbeat. The enzyme acetylcholinesterase breaks it down to end the transmission.

Epinephrine is responsible for the "fight or flight" reaction. It causes an increase in heart rate and blood flow to prepare the body for action. It is also called adrenaline. **Endorphins** and **enkephalins** are natural pain killers and are released during serious injury and childbirth.

The function of the **digestive system** is to break food down and absorb it into the blood stream where it can be delivered to all cells of the body for use in cellular respiration. The teeth and saliva begin digestion by breaking food down into smaller pieces and lubricating it so it can be swallowed. The lips, cheeks, and tongue form a bolus (ball) of food. It is carried down the pharynx by the process of peristalsis (wave like contractions) and enters the stomach through the cardiac sphincter which closes to keep food from going back up. In the stomach, pepsinogen and hydrochloric acid form pepsin, the enzyme that breaks down proteins. The food is broken down further by this chemical action and is turned into chyme. The pyloric sphincter muscle opens to allow the food to enter the small intestine. Most nutrient absorption occurs in the small intestine. Its large surface area, accomplished by its length and protrusions called villi and microvilli allow for a great absorptive surface. Upon arrival into the small intestine, chyme is neutralized to allow the enzymes found there to function. Any food left after the trip through the small intestine enters the large intestine. The large intestine functions to reabsorb water and produce vitamin K. The feces, or remaining waste, are passed out through the anus.

Although not part of the digestive tract, the **accessory organs** function in the production of necessary enzymes and bile. The pancreas makes many enzymes to break down food in the small intestine. The liver makes bile, which breaks down and emulsifies fatty acids.

In the respiratory system, air enters the mouth and nose, where it is warmed, moistened and filtered of dust and particles. Cilia in the trachea trap unwanted material in mucus, which can be expelled. The trachea splits into two bronchial tubes and the bronchial tubes divide into smaller and smaller bronchioles in the lungs. The internal surface of the lung is composed of **alveoli**, which are thin walled air sacs. These allow for a large surface area for gas exchange. The alveoli are lined with capillaries. Oxygen diffuses into the bloodstream and carbon dioxide diffuses out to be exhaled. The oxygenated blood is carried to the heart and delivered to all parts of the body.

The **thoracic cavity** holds the lungs. A muscle, the diaphragm, below the lungs, is an adaptation that makes inhalation possible. As the volume of the thoracic cavity increases, the diaphragm muscle flattens out and inhalation occurs. When the diaphragm relaxes, exhalation occurs.

Be familiar with the parts of the heart and the path blood takes from the heart to the lungs, through the body and back to the heart. Unoxygenated blood enters the heart through the inferior and superior **vena cava**. The first chamber it encounters is the right **atrium**. It goes through the tricuspid valve to the right **ventricle**, on to the pulmonary arteries, and then to the lungs where it is oxygenated. It returns to the heart through the pulmonary vein into the left atrium. It travels through the bicuspid valve to the left ventricle where it is pumped to all parts of the body through the aorta.

The **sinoatrial node** (SA node) is the pacemaker of the heart. Located on the right atrium, it is responsible for contraction of the right and left atrium. The **atrioventricular node** (AV node) is located on the left ventricle, and is responsible for contraction of the ventricles.

Blood vessels include:

- **Arteries**—Lead away from the heart. All arteries carry oxygenated blood except the pulmonary artery going to the lungs. Arteries are under high pressure.
- **Arterioles**—Arteries branch off to form these smaller passages.
- **Capillaries**—Arterioles branch off to form tiny capillaries that reach every cell. Blood moves slowest here due to the small size; only one red blood cell may pass at a time to allow for diffusion of gases into and out of cells. Nutrients are also absorbed by the cells from the capillaries.
- **Venules**—Capillaries combine to form larger venules. These vessels are now carry waste products from the cells.
- **Veins**—Venules combine to form larger veins, leading back to the heart. Veins and venules have thinner walls than arteries because they are not under as much pressure. Veins contain valves to prevent the backward flow of blood due to gravity.

Components of the blood include:

- **Plasma**—60% of the blood is plasma. It contains salts called electrolytes, nutrients, and waste. It is the liquid part of blood.
- **Erythrocytes**—Also called red blood cells; they contain hemoglobin which carries oxygen molecules.
- **Leukocytes**—Also called white blood cells. White blood cells are larger than red cells. They are phagocytic and can engulf invaders. White blood cells are not confined to the blood vessels and can enter the interstitial fluid between cells.

- **Platelets**—Assist in blood clotting. Platelets are made in the bone marrow.

In **blood clotting**, the neurotransmitter that initiates blood vessel constriction following an injury is called serotonin. A material called prothrombin is converted to thrombin with the help of thromboplastin. The thrombin is then used to convert fibrinogen to fibrin which traps red blood cells to form a scab and stop blood flow.

The **immune system** protects against disease by identifying and killing pathogens. **Nonspecific defense mechanisms** do not target specific pathogens, but are a whole body response. Nonspecific mechanisms are seen as symptoms of an infection. These mechanisms include the skin, mucous membranes, and cells of the blood (white blood cells) and lymph (macrophages). Fever is a result of an increase in white blood cells. Pyrogens are released by white blood cells, which set the body's thermostat to a higher temperature. This inhibits the growth of microorganisms. It also increases metabolism to increase phagocytosis and body repair.

Specific defense mechanisms recognize foreign material and respond by destroying the invader. These mechanisms are specific in purpose and diverse in type. They are able to recognize individual pathogens. They are able to differentiate between foreign material and body cells. Memory of the invaders provides immunity upon further exposure.

Antigens are any foreign particle that invades the body. **Antibodies** are manufactured by the body, they recognize and latch onto antigens, hopefully destroying them. **Immunity** is the body's ability to recognize and destroy an antigen before it causes harm. Active immunity develops after recovery from an infectious disease (chicken pox) or after a vaccination (mumps, measles, rubella). Passive immunity may be passed from one individual to another. It is not permanent. A good example is the immunities passed from mother to a nursing child.

The function of the **excretory system** is to rid the body of nitrogenous wastes in the form of urea. The functional unit of excretion are the nephrons, which make up the kidneys. Antidiuretic hormone (ADH), which is made in the hypothalamus and stored in the pituitary, is released when differences in osmotic balance occur. This will cause more water to be reabsorbed. As the blood becomes more dilute, ADH release ceases.

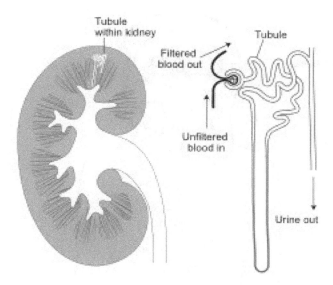

The Bowman's capsule contains the glomerulus, a tightly packed group of capillaries. The glomerulus is under high pressure. Waste and fluids leak out due to pressure. Filtration is not selective in this area. Selective secretion by active and passive transport occurs in the proximal convoluted tubule. Unwanted molecules are secreted into the filtrate. Selective secretion also occurs in the loop of Henle. Salt is actively pumped out of the tube and much water is lost due to the hyperosmosity of the inner part (medulla) of the kidney. As the fluid enters the distal convoluted tubule, more water is reabsorbed. Urine forms in the collecting duct which leads to the ureter then to the bladder where it is stored. Urine is passed from the bladder through the urethra. The amount of water reabsorbed back into the body is dependent upon how much water or fluids an individual has consumed. Urine can be very dilute or very concentrated if dehydration is present.

The function of the **endocrine system** is to manufacture proteins called hormones. Hormones are released into the bloodstream and are carried to a target tissue where they stimulate an action. Hormones may build up over time to cause their effect, as in puberty or the menstrual cycle. Hormones are specific and fit receptors on the target tissue cell surface. The receptor activates an enzyme which converts ATP to cyclic AMP. Cyclic AMP (cAMP) is a second messenger from the cell membrane to the nucleus. The genes found in the nucleus turn on or off to cause a specific response.

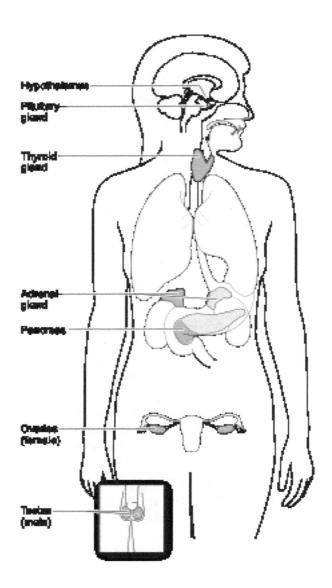

There are two classes of hormones. **Steroid hormones** come from cholesterol and cause sexual characteristics and mating behavior. These hormones include estrogen and progesterone in females and testosterone in males. **Peptide hormones** are made in the pituitary, adrenal glands (kidneys), and the pancreas. They include the following:

- **Follicle stimulating hormone (FSH)**—production of sperm or egg cells.
- **Luteinizing hormone (LH)**—functions in ovulation.
- **Luteotropic hormone (LTH)**—assists in production of progesterone.
- **Growth hormone (GH)**—stimulates growth.
- **Antidiuretic hormone (ADH)**—assists in retention of water.
- **Oxytocin**—stimulates labor contractions at birth and let—down of milk.
- **Melatonin**—regulates circadian rhythms and seasonal changes.

- **Epinephrine (adrenaline)**—causes fight or flight reaction of the nervous system.
- **Thyroxin**—increases metabolic rate.
- **Calcitonin**—removes calcium from the blood.
- **Insulin**—decreases glucose level in blood.
- **Glucagon**—increases glucose level in blood.

Hormones work on a feedback system. The increase or decrease in one hormone may cause the increase or decrease in another. The release of hormones causes a specific response.

Sexual reproduction greatly increases diversity due to the many combinations possible through meiosis and fertilization. Gametogenesis is the production of the sperm and egg cells. Spermatogenesis begins at puberty in the male. One spermatozoa produces four sperm. The sperm mature in the seminiferous tubules located in the testes. Oogenesis, the production of egg cells is usually complete by the birth of a female. Egg cells are not released until menstruation begins at puberty. Meiosis forms one ovum with all the cytoplasm and three polar bodies which are reabsorbed by the body. The ovum are stored in the ovaries and released each month from puberty to menopause.

Path of the sperm: Sperm are stored in the seminiferous tubules in the testes where they mature. Mature sperm are found in the epididymis located on top of the testes. After ejaculation, the sperm travels up the vas deferens where they mix with semen made in the prostate and seminal vesicles and travel out the urethra.

Path of the egg: Eggs are stored in the ovaries. Ovulation releases the egg into the fallopian tubes which are ciliated to move the egg along. Fertilization normally occurs in the fallopian tube. If pregnancy does not occur, the egg passes through the uterus and is expelled through the vagina during menstruation. Levels of progesterone and estrogen stimulate menstruation. In the event of pregnancy, hormonal levels are affected by the implantation of a fertilized egg, so menstruation does not occur.

If fertilization occurs, the zygote implants in about two to three days in the uterus. Implantation promotes secretion of human chorionic gonadotropin (HCG). This is what is detected in pregnancy tests. The HCG keeps the level of progesterone elevated to maintain the uterine lining in order to feed the developing embryo until the umbilical cord forms. Labor is initiated by oxytocin which causes labor contractions and dilation of the cervix. Prolactin and oxytocin cause the production of milk.

SKILL 6.15 Analyze behaviors or adaptations of animals and plants that enable them to survive.

Animal communication is any behavior by one animal that affects the behavior of another animal. Animals use body language, sound, and smell to communicate. Perhaps the most common type of animal communication is the presentation or movement of distinctive body parts. Many species of animals reveal or conceal body parts to communicate with potential mates, predators, and prey. In addition, many species of animals communicate with sound. Examples of vocal communication include the mating songs of birds and frogs and warning cries of monkeys. Finally, many animals release scented chemicals called pheromones and secrete distinctive odors from specialized glands to communicate with other animals. Pheromones are important in reproduction and mating and glandular secretions of long lasting smells alert animals to the presence of others.

Ecological and behavioral factors affect the interrelationships among organisms in many ways. Two important ecological factors are environmental conditions and resource availability. Important types of organismal behaviors include competitive, instinctive, territorial, and mating.

Environmental conditions, such as climate, influence organismal interrelationships by changing the dynamics of the ecosystem. Changes in climate such as moisture levels and temperature can alter the environment, changing the characteristics that are advantageous. For example, an increase in temperature will favor those organisms that can tolerate the temperature change. Thus, those organisms gain a competitive advantage. In addition, the availability of necessary resources influences interrelationships. For example, when necessary resources are scarce, interrelationships are more competitive than when resources are abundant.

As previously mentioned, organisms **compete** for scarce resources. In addition, organisms compete with members of their own species for mates and territory. Many competitive behaviors involve rituals and dominance hierarchies. Rituals are symbolic activities that often settle disputes without undue harm. For example, dogs bare their teeth, erect their ears, and growl to intimidate competitors. A dominance hierarchy, or pecking order, organizes groups of animals, simplifying interrelationships, conserving energy, and minimizing the potential for harm in a community.

Instinctive, or innate, behavior is common to all members of a given species and is genetically preprogrammed. Environmental differences do not affect instinctive behaviors. For example, baby birds of many types and species beg for food by raising their heads and opening their beaks.

Many animals act aggressively to protect their territory from other animals. Animals **protect territories** for use in feeding, mating, and rearing of young.

Mating behaviors are very important interspecies interactions. The search for a mate with which to reproduce is an instinctive behavior. Mating interrelationships often involve ritualistic and territorial behaviors that are often competitive.

Behavior may be innate or learned. **Innate behaviors** are behaviors that are inborn or instinctual. An environmental stimulus such as the length of day or temperature results in a behavior. Hibernation among some animals is an innate behavior. A behavior that is modified due to past experience is called **learned behavior**.

SKILL 6.16   Interpret cell theory and how its discovery relates to the process of science.

The cell theory states in its most elementary form that all living things are composed of one or more cells. Robert Hooke discovered the cell walls of cork in 1665. The first man to witness a live cell under a microscope was Antonie van Leeuwenhoek. The cell theory was completed in 1858 when Rudolf Virchow concluded that all cells come from pre-existing cells.

The modern theory adds to this that energy flow (metabolism and biochemistry) occurs within cells. Also, cells contain hereditary information (DNA) that is passed from cell to cell during cell division.

There are some exceptions to cell theory. The first cell did not originate from a pre-existing cell. Also, viruses reproduce in a host as if they were living organisms, but are not cells. The other exception is that there are certain organelles (mitochondria and chloroplasts) that reproduce independently of the cell.

SKILL 6.17   Identify how evolution is supported by the fossil record, comparative anatomy, embryology, biogeography, molecular biology, genetics, and observed change.

Biologists have identified two million different species of organisms. The least complex organisms are bacteria and the most complex are present-day humans. Fossils show that bacteria-like organisms appeared on Earth 3.5 billion years ago and evolved into modern humans, whose fossils appeared 150,000 years ago. Fossils of chimpanzees appeared 8 million years ago and that of dinosaurs 200 million years ago. The dates of these fossils are determined by the half-lives of radioactive substances. In short, the fossil record supports what is called common descent with modifications.

While a turtle appears to be very different from a chimpanzee, the embryos of a turtle and a chimpanzee are much more similar. This is supportive of the idea chimpanzees and turtles descended from the same organism. Furthermore, the anatomies of adult species are not as great as it seems. The forelimbs of whales, cats, and bats are very similar even though their forelimbs are used in different ways.

The geographic distribution of species is called biogeography. The tropical animals of South America are more closely related to species of South American deserts than to species in the African tropics. The reason is that species migrate from one environment to another and adapt to the different conditions in the new environment.

The molecular machinery of all organisms are very similar. They use, for example, the same amino acids to build proteins. The DNA of living organisms, which control heredity, is also very similar.

Evolutionary change has been directly observed in the protozoa that causes malaria, the HIV virus, and E. coli bacteria.

SKILL 6.18 Evaluate the roles of adaptation, genetic variation, mutation, and extinction in natural selection.

The adaptation of species to their habitat is one the basic phenomena of biology. Polar bears, for example, are white to make them less visible to their prey. According to Jean-Baptiste Lamark (1744–1829), giraffes have long necks because of stretching to get leaves high on trees. In other words, species adapt because they acquire characteristics in coping with the environment and pass those characteristics to offspring. According to the mechanism proposed by Charles Darwin:

1) The birth of more individuals than the environment can support leads to a struggle for survival.
2) Individuals whose inherited characteristics fit them best to the environment are likely to leave more offspring than less fit individuals.
3) This unequal ability of individuals to survive and reproduce will lead to a gradual change in a population, with favorable characteristics accumulating over the generations.

The continuity of traits from one generation to the next is called heredity, but there is also variation, called genetic variation. Natural selection is the differential success rate in reproduction, and its result is adaptation. Artificial selection occurs in the breeding of domesticated plants and animals.

The two processes that generate genetic variation are mutation of genes and sexual recombination. Must mutations occur in body cells and die with the individual. Mutations that change gametes (male or female germ cells) can be passed on to offspring. In humans, there is about one mutation for every 100,000 to 200,000 replications of genes.

SKILL 6.19 Interpret the impact of biotechnology on the individual, society, and the environment, including medical and ethical issues.

Biotechnology has applications in four major areas: health care, agriculture, industrial uses of crops and other products, and environmental uses.

The field of modern biotechnology is thought to have largely begun on June 16, 1980, when the United States Supreme Court ruled that a genetically-modified microorganism could be patented. The case involved the development of a bacterium that was capable of breaking down crude oil spilled by oil tankers.

Genetic engineering, recombinant DNA technology, and gene splicing are terms that apply to the direct manipulation of an organism's genes. Genetic engineering uses the techniques of molecular cloning and transformation to alter the structure and characteristics of genes directly. Genetic engineering has improved agricultural production. Bacteria, modified by these techniques, have been used to manufacture synthetic human insulin. Biotechnology is also commonly associated with landmark breakthroughs in new medical therapies to treat hepatitis B, hepatitis C, cancers, arthritis, hemophilia, bone fractures, multiple sclerosis, and cardiovascular disorders.

Genetic testing involves the direct examination of the DNA molecule itself. A scientist scans a patient's DNA sample for mutated sequences. Genetic testing is used for the identification of unaffected individuals who carry one copy of a gene for a disease that requires two copies for the disease to manifest, determining sex, forensic/identity testing, and estimating the risk of developing adult-onset cancers.

Gene therapy may be used for treating, or even curing, genetic and acquired diseases like cancer and AIDS by using normal genes to supplement or replace defective genes or to bolster a normal function such as immunity.

COMPETENCY 7.0   KNOWLEDGE OF THE EFFECTS OF PHYSICAL
                   AND BIOLOGICAL FACTORS ON THE
                   ENVIRONMENT

SKILL 7.1   Identify components and sequences of biogeochemical cycles
            (e.g., carbon, oxygen, hydrogen, nitrogen).

Essential elements are recycled through an ecosystem. At times, the element
needs to be fixed into a useable form. Cycles are dependent on plants, algae,
and bacteria to fix nutrients for use by animals.

Water cycle—Two percent of all the available water is fixed and held in ice or
the bodies of organisms. Available water includes surface water (lakes, ocean,
and rivers) and ground water (aquifers, wells). Ninety-six percent of all available
water is from ground water. Water is recycled through the processes of
evaporation and precipitation. The water present now is the water that has been
here since our atmosphere formed.

Carbon cycle—Ten percent of all available carbon in the air (from carbon
dioxide gas) is fixed by photosynthesis. Plants fix carbon in the form of glucose,
animals eat the plants and are able to obtain their source of carbon. When
animals release carbon dioxide through respiration, the plants again have a
source of carbon to fix.

Nitrogen cycle—Eighty percent of the atmosphere is in the form of nitrogen gas.
Nitrogen must be fixed and taken out of the gaseous form to be incorporated into
an organism. Only a few genera of bacteria have the correct enzymes to break
the triple bond between nitrogen atoms. These bacteria live within the roots of
legumes (peas, beans, alfalfa) and add bacteria to the soil so it may be taken up
by the plant. Nitrogen is necessary to make amino acids and the nitrogenous
bases of DNA.

Phosphorus cycle—Phosphorus exists as a mineral and is not found in the
atmosphere. Fungi and plant roots have structures called mycorrhizae that are
able to fix insoluble phosphates into useable phosphorus. Urine and decayed
matter returns phosphorus to the Earth where it can be fixed in the plant.
Phosphorus is needed for the backbone of DNA and for the manufacture of ATP.

The Carbon Cycle

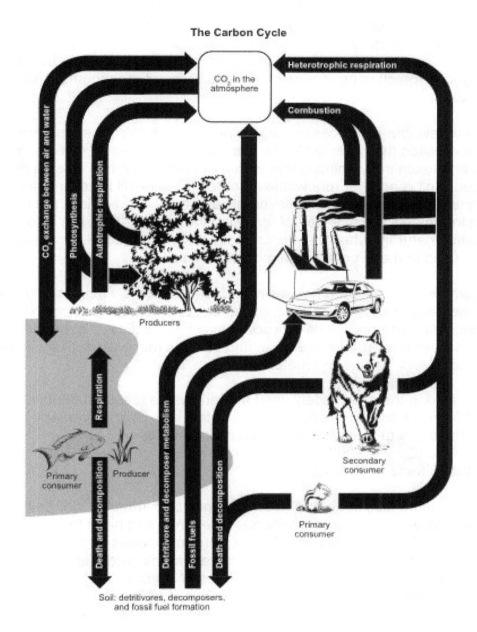

SKILL 7.2 **Identify issues related to the development, use, and conservation of natural resources.**

A **renewable resource** is one that is replaced naturally. Living renewable resources are plants and animals. Plants are renewable because they grow and reproduce. Sometimes renewal of the resource doesn't keep up with the demand. Such is the case with trees. Since the housing industry uses lumber for frames and homebuilding they are often cut down faster than new trees can grow. Now there are specific tree farms. Special methods allow trees to grow faster.

A second renewable resource is animals. They renew by the process of reproduction. Some wild animals need protection on refuges. As the population of humans increases resources are used faster. Cattle are used for their hides and for food. Some animals like deer are killed for sport. Each state has an environmental protection agency with divisions of forest management and wildlife management.

Non-living renewable resources are water, air, and soil. Water is renewed in a natural cycle called the water cycle. Air is a mixture of gases. Oxygen is given off by plants and taken in by animals that, in turn, expel the carbon dioxide that the plants need. Soil is another renewable resource. Fertile soil is rich in minerals. When plants grow they remove the minerals and make the soil less fertile. Chemical treatments are one way of renewing the composition. It is also accomplished naturally when the plants decay back into the soil. The plant material is used to make compost to mix with the soil.

Nonrenewable resources are not easily replaced in a timely fashion. Minerals are nonrenewable resources. Quartz, mica, salt, and sulfur are some examples. Mining depletes these resources so society may benefit. Glass is made from quartz, electronic equipment from mica, and salt has many uses. Sulfur is used in medicine, fertilizers, paper, and matches.

Metals are among the most widely used nonrenewable resource. Metals must be separated from the ore. Iron is our most important ore. Gold, silver, and copper are often found in a more pure form called native metals.

Causes and Effects of Pollutants

Pollutants are impurities in air and water that may be harmful to life. Spills from barges carrying large quantities of oil pollute beaches and harm fish. All acids contain hydrogen. Acidic substances from factories and car exhausts dissolve in rain water forming **acid rain.** Acid rain forms predominantly from pollutant oxides in the air (usually nitrogen-based NO_x or sulfur-based SO_x), which become hydrated into their acids (nitric or sulfuric acid). When the rain falls onto stone, the acids can react with metallic compounds and gradually wear the stone away.

Radioactivity is the breaking down of atomic nuclei by releasing particles or electromagnetic radiation. Radioactive nuclei give off radiation in the form of streams of particles or energy. Alpha particles are positively charged particles consisting of two protons and two neutrons. It is the slowest form of radiation. It can be stopped by paper! Beta particles are electrons. They are produced when a neutron in the nucleus breaks up into a proton and an electron. The proton remains inside the nucleus, increasing its atomic number by one. But the electron is given off. They can be stopped by aluminum. Gamma rays are electromagnetic waves with extremely short wavelengths. They have no mass. They have no charge so they are not deflected by an electric field.

Gamma rays travel at the speed of light. It takes a thick block of lead to stop them. Uranium is the source of radiation and therefore is radioactive. Marie Curie discovered new elements called radium and polonium that actually give off more radiation than uranium.

The major concern with radioactivity is in the case of a nuclear disaster. Medical misuse is also a threat. Radioactivity ionizes the air it travels through. It is strong enough to kill cancer cells or dangerous enough to cause illness or even death. Gamma rays can penetrate the body and damage cells. Protective clothing is needed when working with gamma rays. Electricity from nuclear energy uses uranium-235. The devastation of the Russian nuclear power plant disaster has evacuated entire regions as the damage to the land and food source will last for hundreds of years.

SKILL 7.3 Relate environmental factors to the adaptation and survival rates of organisms.

Charles Darwin defined the theory of natural selection in the mid-1800's. Through the study of finches on the Galapagos Islands, Darwin theorized that nature selects the traits that are advantageous to the organism. Those that do not possess the desirable trait die and do not pass on their genes. Those more fit to survive reproduce, thus increasing that gene in the population. Darwin listed four principles to define natural selection:

1.   The individuals in a certain species vary from generation to generation.
2.   Some of the variations are determined by the genetic makeup of the species.
3.   More individuals are produced than will survive.
4.   Some traits allow for better survival of an animal.

Certain factors increase the chances of variability in a population, thus leading to evolution. Items that increase variability include mutations, sexual reproduction, immigration, and large population. Items that decrease variation would be natural selection, emigration, small population, and random mating.

Genes that happen to come together determine the makeup of the gene pool. Animals that use mating behaviors may be successful or unsuccessful. An animal that lacks attractive plumage or has a weak mating call will not attract the female, thereby eventually limiting that gene in the gene pool. Mechanical isolation, where sex organs do not fit the female, has an obvious disadvantage. This is called **sexual selection.**

SKILL 7.4   Identify the major characteristics of world biomes and communities, including succession and interrelationships of organisms.

Ecology is the study of organisms, where they live and their interactions with the environment. A **population** is a group of the same species in a specific area. A **community** is a group of populations residing in the same area. Communities that are ecologically similar in regards to temperature, rainfall and the species that live there are called **biomes**. Specific biomes include:

- **Marine** biome covers 75% of the Earth. This biome is organized by the depth of the water. The intertidal zone is from the tide line to the edge of the water. The littoral zone is from the water's edge to the open sea. It includes coral reef habitats and is the most densely populated area of the marine biome. The open sea zone is divided into the epipelagic zone and the pelagic zone. The epipelagic zone receives more sunlight and has a larger number of species. The ocean floor is called the benthic zone and is populated with bottom feeders.
- **Tropical rain forest** temperature is constant (25 C°), and rainfall exceeds 200 cm per year. Located around the area of the equator, the rain forest has abundant, diverse species of plants and animals.
- **Savanna** temperatures range from 0–25 C° depending on the location. Rainfall is from 90 to 150 cm per year. Plants include shrubs and grasses. The savanna is a transitional biome between the rain forest and the desert.
- **Desert** temperatures range from 10–38 C°. Rainfall is under 25 cm per year. Plant species include xerophytes and succulents. Lizards, snakes, and small mammals are common animals.
- **Temperate deciduous forest** temperature ranges from –24 to 38 C°. Rainfall is between 65 to 150 cm per year. Deciduous trees are common, as well as deer, bear and squirrels.
- **Taiga** temperatures range from –24 to 22 C°. Rainfall is between 35 to 40 cm per year. Taiga is located very north and very south of the equator, getting close to the poles. Plant life includes conifers and plants that can withstand harsh winters. Animals include weasels, mink, and moose.
- **Tundra** temperatures range from –28 to 15 C°. Rainfall is limited, ranging from 10 to 15 cm per year. The tundra is located even further north and south than the taiga. Common plants include lichens and mosses. Animals include polar bears and musk ox.
- **Polar or permafrost** temperature ranges from –40 to 0 C°. It rarely gets above freezing. Rainfall is below 10 cm per year. Most water is bound up as ice. Life is limited.

Succession is an orderly process of replacing a community that has been damaged or beginning one where no life previously existed. Primary succession occurs after a community has been totally wiped out by a natural disaster or where life never existed before, as in a flooded area. Secondary succession takes place in communities that were once flourishing but were disturbed by some source, either man or nature, but were not totally stripped. A climax community is a community that is established and flourishing.

There are a number of feeding relationships between species in an ecosystem:

- **Parasitism**—Two species that occupy a similar place; the parasite benefits from the relationship, the host is harmed.
- **Commensalism**—Two species that occupy a similar place; neither species is harmed or benefits from the relationship.
- **Mutualism (symbiosis)**—Two species that occupy a similar place; both species benefit from the relationship.
- **Competition**—Two species that occupy the same habitat or eat the same food are said to be in competition with each other.
- **Predation**—Animals that eat other animals are called predators. The animals they feed on are called the prey. Population growth depends upon competition for food, water, shelter, and space. The amount of predators determines the amount of prey, which in turn affects the number of predators.

Carrying capacity is the total amount of life a habitat can support. Once the habitat runs out of food, water, shelter, or space, the carrying capacity decreases, and then stabilizes.

Ecological problems exist because nonrenewable resources are fragile and must be conserved for use in the future. Man's impact and knowledge of conservation will control our future.

Biological magnification arises because chemicals and pesticides accumulate along the food chain. Tertiary consumers have more accumulated toxins than animals at the bottom of the food chain.

Fuel sources have been depleted because of strip mining and the overuse of oil reserves. At the current rate of consumption, conservation or alternate fuel sources will guarantee our future fuel sources.

Although technology gives us many advances, **pollution** is a side effect of production. Waste disposal and the burning of fossil fuels have polluted our land, water and air. Global warming and acid rain are two results of the burning of hydrocarbons and sulfur.

Global warming is the increase in the average temperature of Earth's near-surface air and oceans. Rainforest depletion and the use of fossil fuels and aerosols have caused an increase in carbon dioxide production. This leads to a decrease in the amount of oxygen which is directly proportional to the amount of ozone. As the ozone layer depletes, more heat enters our atmosphere and is trapped. This causes an overall warming effect which may eventually melt polar ice caps, causing a rise in water levels and changes in climate which will affect weather systems world-wide.

An **endangered species** is a population of an organism that is at risk of becoming extinct because it is either few in numbers, or threatened by changing environmental or predation parameters. The construction of homes to house people in our world has caused the destruction of habitat for other animals leading to their extinction. Three major crops feed the world (rice, corn, wheat). The planting of these foods harm habitats and push animals residing there into other habitats causing overpopulation or extinction.

SKILL 7.5   Identify how biotic and abiotic factors influence ecosystems.

Biotic factors refer to living things in an ecosystem; plants, animals, bacteria, fungi, etc. If one population in a community increases, it affects the ability of another population to succeed by limiting the available amount of food, water, shelter and space.

Abiotic factors are the non-living aspects of an ecosystem; soil quality, rainfall, and temperature. Changes in climate and soil can cause effects at the beginning of the food chain, thus limiting or accelerating the growth of populations.

Abiotic factors vary in the environment. It is also difficult to determine the types and numbers of organisms that exist in that environment. Factors which determine the types and numbers of organisms of a species in an ecosystem are called limiting factors. Many limiting factors restrict the growth of populations in nature.

Carrying capacity is the maximum number of organisms the resources of an ecosystem can support. The carrying capacity of the environment is limited by the available abiotic and biotic resources (limiting factors), as well as the ability of ecosystems to recycle the residue of dead organisms through the activities of bacteria and fungi.

The arrival of the human species has greatly altered the biotic and abiotic factors for much of life on Earth. An example of this would include how annual average temperature common to the Arctic restricts the growth of trees, as the subsoil is permanently frozen. Another example is the effect that climate change has on migratory birds. The anticipated increase in cloudiness over the arctic could itself become a factor in ozone depletion. The clouds, formed from condensed nitric acid and water, tend to increase snowfall, which accelerates depletion of stratospheric nitrogen. There is a circular relationship between how biotic and abiotic factors influence environment conditions and then how environmental conditions in turn effect biotic and abiotic factors.

SKILL 7.6 **Analyze interactions between microorganisms and the environment.**

Although bacteria and fungi may cause disease, they are also beneficial for use as medicines and food. Penicillin is derived from a fungus that is capable of destroying the cell wall of bacteria. Most antibiotics work in this way. Viral diseases have been fought through the use of vaccination, where a small amount of the virus is introduced so the immune system is able to recognize it upon later infection. Antibodies are more quickly manufactured when the host has had prior exposure. Viruses are difficult to treat because antibiotics are ineffective against them. That is why doctors do not usually prescribe antibiotics for those who have a cold or the flu—common viral infections. While some yeasts can cause illness, Brewer's yeast is a fungus that humans use to make bread and to ferment wine. In addition, many microbes are decomposers, helping to clear away dead organisms and clean the forest floor of debris.

SKILL 7.7 **Identify the effects of homeostasis on the survivability of an organism.**

All living organisms respond and adapt to their environments. Homeostasis is the result of regulatory mechanisms that help maintain an organism's internal environment within tolerable limits.

The molecular composition of the immediate environment outside of the organism is not the same as it is inside and the temperature outside may not be optimal for metabolic activity within the organism. Homeostasis is the control of these differences between internal and external environments. There are three homeostatic systems to regulate these differences.

Osmoregulation deals with maintenance of the appropriate level of water and salts in body fluids for optimum cellular functions.

Excretion is the elimination of metabolic waste products from the body including excess water.

Thermoregulation maintains the internal, or core body temperature of the organism within a tolerable range for metabolic and cellular processes. For example, in humans and mammals, constriction and dilation of blood vessels near the skin help maintain body temperature.

SKILL 7.8   Relate the interactions of biotic and abiotic factors to the flow of energy and biomass within a system.

Biogeochemical cycling is the movement of chemicals between the biotic (living) and abiotic (non-living) parts of an ecosystem. Respiration and photosynthesis play an important role in the cycling of oxygen and carbon. Respiration is the process in which an individual organism uses oxygen and releases carbon dioxide to the atmosphere during energy producing reactions. Photosynthesis, the reverse of respiration, is the process in which an individual plant or microorganism uses the carbon from carbon dioxide to produce carbohydrates with oxygen as a by-product.

Two major forms of carbon in the environment are carbon dioxide gas in the atmosphere and organic macromolecules in living things. Photosynthesis by plants and microorganisms converts carbon dioxide to carbohydrates, removing carbon from the atmosphere and storing it as biomass. Conversely, aerobic and anaerobic respiration by plants, animals, and microorganisms returns carbon to the environment in the form of carbon dioxide or methane gas, respectively.

The main driving force in the oxygen cycle is photosynthesis. Plants and microorganisms perform photosynthesis to produce glucose, releasing oxygen gas to the environment as a by-product. Animals, plants, and microorganisms remove oxygen from the environment, using it to break down glucose in an energy yielding reaction that produces carbon dioxide and water.

SKILL 7.9   Analyze the relationship between natural factors and human activities as they affect Florida's ecosystems.

An ecosystem is a community of plants and animals that live together. Ecosystems found in South Florida include flatwoods, coral reefs, dunes, marshes, swamps, hammocks, and mangroves. Florida is also the home of the well-known Everglades National Park.

The most extensive terrestrial ecosystem in Florida is the pine **flatwoods**. This evolved under frequent fire, seasonal drought, and flooded soil conditions. The pine flatwoods can be divided into two groups: the North Florida flatwoods which are typically open woodlands dominated by pine trees and the South Florida flatwoods which are typically savannas. The flatwoods consist primarily of various pine trees and an understory of shrubs such as the saw palmetto, wax myrtle, wildflowers, ferns, and blueberries. Of the underbrush, the Chapman's rhododendron is currently listed as threatened/endangered. Plants that grow in the pinelands must be resistant to fire because pinelands are maintained by fire.

Fires are beneficial to the pines because young pine seedlings require lots of sunlight to survive, and the fires destroy hardwood competitors. When fires occur, hardwood seedlings and other understory plants are affected, but the thick bark of the pine resists fire damage. Wildlife found here include deer, squirrels, bobcats, skunks, opossums, raccoons, birds, snakes, and tortoises.

Southern Florida's ecosystem contains the only living continuous **coral reef** system adjacent to the continental U.S. Over 30 different kinds of corals, including the star and staghorn corals are found in Florida waters. Florida waters are the principal nursery for the commercial and sport fisheries in Florida.

Dunes are created by wind, but are held in place by grasses that trap sand grains as they are being moved across the beach. Dunes stabilized by grasses protect the coast against winds and pounding waves. Florida beaches are important nesting sites for sea turtles and shorebirds. A loss of beach habitat to real estate development, erosion, and rising sea level has caused a decline in the nesting shorebird and sea turtle populations.

Freshwater marshes are generally wetlands with an open expanse of grasses and other grass-like plants. They have standing water for much of the year and act as natural filters, slowing down the water's movement and allowing the settling of particles. Animals found in the marsh can include fish, mollusks, shrimp, frogs, snakes, alligators, and the threatened Florida panther.

Freshwater swamps are wet, wooded areas where standing water occurs for at least part of the year. The freshwater swamps may have cypress trees, bay trees or hardwoods. Other plants found in swamps include epiphytes (air plants) growing on trees, vines, and ferns. Wood storks, herons, otters, black bear, and the Florida panther are only a few of the animals that find food, homes, and nesting sites in Florida's swamps.

Hardwood hammocks are small areas of hardwood trees that can grow on natural rises of land. In Florida, hammocks occur in marshes, pinelands, and mangrove swamps. Hammocks may contain many different species of trees such as the sabal palm, live oak, red maple, mahogany, gumbo limbo, and cocoplum. Wildlife in hammocks can include tree snails, raccoons, opossums, birds, snakes, lizards, tree frogs, as well as large mammals.

Three species of **mangroves** are found in Florida: the red mangrove, black mangrove, and white mangrove. Red mangroves grow along the water's edge, followed by black, with white mangroves growing mostly inland. Mangroves grow in saltwater and in areas frequently flooded by saltwater. Mangroves provide protected habitat, breeding grounds, and nursery areas to many land and marine animals. Mangroves also provide shoreline protection from wind, waves, and erosion. Of special note is the presence of the beloved manatee, who can be found here, especially where its preferred food source, seagrass, resides.

**COMPETENCY 8.0   KNOWLEDGE OF CLASSROOM AND
                      LABORATORY MANAGEMENT**

**SKILL 8.1   Identify legal and ethical requirements for proper use, care,
              handling, and disposal of organisms.**

Animals which are not obtained from recognized sources should not be used for
dissections. Decaying animals or those of unknown origin may harbor
pathogens and/or parasites. Specimens should be rinsed before handling. Latex
gloves are desirable. If gloves are not available, students with sores or scratches
should be excused from the activity. Formaldehyde is a carcinogen and should
be avoided or disposed of according to district regulations. Students objecting to
dissections for moral reasons should be given an alternative assignment.

No dissections may be performed on living mammalian vertebrates or birds.
Lower order life and invertebrates may be used. Biological experiments may be
done with all animals except mammalian vertebrates or birds. No physiological
harm may result to the animal. All animals housed and cared for in the school
must be handled in a safe and humane manner. Animals are not to remain on
school premises during extended vacations unless adequate care is provided.

Pathogenic organisms must never be used for experimentation. Students should
adhere to the following rules at all times when working with **microorganisms** to
avoid accidental contamination:

1.   Treat all microorganisms as if they were pathogenic.
2.   Maintain sterile conditions at all times

**SKILL 8.2   Identify the safe and appropriate techniques used in
              preparation, storage, dispensing, and supervision of materials
              used in science instruction.**

Hot plates should be used whenever possible to avoid the risk of burns or fire. If
Bunsen burners are used, the following precautions should be followed:

1.   Know the location of fire extinguishers and safety blankets and train
      students in their use. Long hair and long sleeves should be secured and
      out of the way.
2.   Turn the gas all the way on and make a spark with the striker. The
      preferred method to light burners is to use strikers rather than matches.
3.   Adjust the air valve at the bottom of the Bunsen burner until the flame
      shows an inner cone.
4.   Adjust the flow of gas to the desired flame height by using the adjustment
      valve.
5.   Do not touch the barrel of the burner (it is hot).

Graduated cylinders are used for precise measurements. They should always be placed on a flat surface. The surface of the liquid will form a meniscus (lens-shaped curve). The measurement is read at the *bottom* of this curve.

Electronic balances are easier to use, but more expensive. An electronic balance should always be tared (returned to zero) before measuring and using it on a flat surface. Substances should always be placed on a piece of paper to avoid spills and/or damage to the instrument. **Triple beam balances** must be used on a level surface. There are screws located at the bottom of the balance to make any adjustments. Start with the largest counterweight first and proceed toward the last notch that does not tip the balance. Do the same with the next largest, etc., until the pointer remains at zero. The total mass is the total of all the readings on the beams. Again, use paper under the substance to protect the equipment.

A **buret** is used to dispense precisely measured volumes of liquid. A stopcock is used to control the volume of liquid being dispensed.

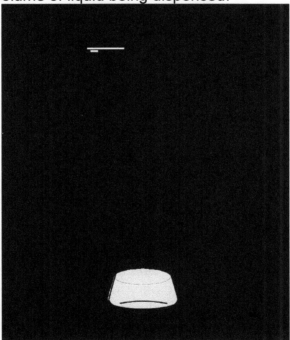

Light microscopes are commonly used in laboratory experiments. Several procedures should be followed to properly care for this equipment:

- Clean all lenses with lens paper only.
- Carry microscopes with two hands; one on the arm and one on the base.
- Always begin focusing on low power, then switch to high power.
- Store microscopes with the low power objective down.
- Always use a coverslip when viewing wet mount slides.
- Bring the objective down to its lowest position then focus by moving up to
- avoid breaking the slide or scratching the lens.

Wet-mount slides should be made by placing a drop of water on the specimen and then putting a glass coverslip on top of the drop of water. Dropping the coverslip at a forty-five degree angle will help in avoiding air bubbles. Total magnification is determined by multiplying the ocular (usually 10X) and the objective (usually 10X on low, 40X on high).

SKILL 8.3   Identify appropriate substitutions for materials and activities necessary for effective science instruction.

Lab materials are readily available from the many school suppliers that routinely send their catalogues to schools. Many times, common materials are available at the local grocery store. The use of locally available flora and fauna both reduces the cost and familiarizes students with the organisms where they live. Innovation and networking with other science teachers will assist in keeping costs of lab materials to a minimum.

SKILL 8.4   Identify the federal and state legal requirements for safe preparation, use, storage and disposal of chemicals and other materials.

All science labs should contain the following items of safety equipment. The following are requirements by law.

- Fire blanket which is visible and accessible
- Ground-fault circuit Interrupters (GFCI) within two feet of water supplies
- Emergency shower capable of providing a continuous flow of water
- Signs designating room exits
- Emergency eye wash station which can be activated by the foot or forearm
- Eye protection for every student and a means of sanitizing equipment
- Emergency exhaust fans providing ventilation to the outside of the building
- Master cut-off switches for gas, electric, and compressed air. Switches must have permanently attached handles. Cut-off switches must be clearly labeled.
- An ABC fire extinguisher
- Storage cabinets for flammable materials

Also recommended, but not required by law:

- Chemical spill control kit
- Fume hood with a motor which is spark proof
- Protective laboratory aprons made of flame retardant material
- Signs which will alert people to potential hazardous conditions
- Containers for broken glassware, flammables, corrosives, and waste.

- Containers should be labeled.

It is the responsibility of teachers to provide a safe environment for their students. Proper supervision greatly reduces the risk of injury and a teacher should never leave a class for any reason without providing alternate supervision. After an accident, two factors are considered; foreseeability and negligence.

Foreseeability is the anticipation that an event may occur under certain circumstances. **Negligence** is the failure to exercise ordinary or reasonable care. Safety procedures should be a part of the science curriculum and a well-managed classroom is important to avoid potential lawsuits

The **right-to-know statutes** cover science teachers who work with potentially hazardous chemicals. Briefly, the law states that employees must be informed of potentially toxic chemicals. An inventory must be made available if requested. The inventory must contain information about the hazards and properties of the chemicals. Training must be provided in the safe handling and interpretation of the material safety data sheet (MSDA).

The following chemicals are potential carcinogens and are not allowed in school facilities:
acrylonitrile, arsenic compounds, asbestos, benzidine, benzene, cadmium compounds, chloroform, chromium compounds, ethylene oxide, ortho-toluidine, Nickel powder, Mercury.

All laboratory solutions should be prepared as directed in the lab manual. Care should be taken to avoid contamination. All glassware should be rinsed thoroughly with distilled water before using, and cleaned well after use. Safety goggles should be worn while working with glassware in case of an accident. All solutions should be made with distilled water as tap water contains dissolved particles which may affect the results of an experiment. Chemical storage should be located in a secured, dry area. Chemicals should be stored in accordance with reactability. Acids are to be locked in a separate area. Used solutions should be disposed of according to local disposal procedures. Any questions regarding safe disposal or chemical safety may be directed to the local fire department.

SKILL 8.5   Use multiple assessment tools and strategies to identify and address student misconceptions.

Helping students to understand the scientific concepts that are being taught and overcoming misconceptions is accomplished by providing students with an excellent learning experience. Classroom demonstrations and providing students with the equipment and time to perform their own experiments and make their own observations are more effective than classroom lectures and verbal explanations.

Students should be given the time and opportunity to work with the concepts themselves so they can construct their own knowledge and understandings. Working in groups to solve problems or answer questions is one way to achieve this. A simple tool is to have students partner with one other student and explain the concept to each other. Asking students open-ended questions will indicate how much students understand.

The least effective assessment tool for eliminating misconceptions is multiple-choice or true and false questions. An effective technique is to ask students to predict what will happen before doing the demonstration. Also, you can ask students for their theories before giving them the scientifically correct theory. There are many common misconceptions about science. The following are a few scientific misconceptions that are or have been common in the past:

- The Earth is the center of the solar system.
- The Earth is the largest object in the solar system.
- Rain comes from the holes in the clouds.
- Acquired characteristics can be inherited.
- The eye receives upright images.
- Energy is a thing.
- Heat is not energy.

SKILL 8.6 Select appropriate strategies for teaching scientific inquiry.

Scientific inquiry can be taught be giving students activities than enable them to learn each science process skill one at a time or in one large project. Students could be asked to design an investigation to test an hypotheses that is given to them. For example, *The higher the height a ball drops, the higher it will bounce.* Or they can be given a problem and asked to construct an hypotheses. For example, *What determines a person's pulse rate?*

Similar activities can be designed for the science skills of observing, classifying, predicting, making inferences, and identifying variables. Observations can be taught by having students write down their observations and identify the sense used in making it. Classification can be taught by giving students a group of objects or diagrams to classify.

The scientific method is the basic process behind science. It involves several steps beginning with hypothesis formulation and working through to the conclusion:

Posing a question. Although many discoveries happen by chance, the standard thought process of a scientist begins with forming a question to research. The more limited the question, the easier it is to set up an experiment to answer it.

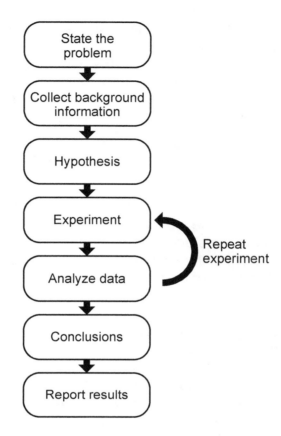

Form a hypothesis. Once the question is formulated take an educated guess about the answer to the problem or question. This "best guess" is your hypothesis.

Doing the test. To make a test fair, data from an experiment must have a variable or any condition that can be changed such as temperature or mass. A good test will try to manipulate as few variables as possible so as to see which variable is responsible for the result. A control is an extra setup in which all the conditions are the same except for the variable being tested.

Observe and record the data. Reporting of the data should state specifics of how the measurements were calculated. A graduated cylinder needs to be read with proper procedures. As beginning students, technique must be part of the instructional process so as to give validity to the data.
Drawing a conclusion. After recording data, you compare your data with that of other groups. A conclusion is the judgment derived from the data results.

Graphing data. Graphing utilizes numbers to demonstrate patterns. The patterns offer a visual representation, making it easier to draw conclusions.

Write report. A report has many sections. It should include a specific title and tell exactly what is being studied. The abstract is a summary of the report written at the beginning of the paper. The purpose should always be defined and will state the problem. The purpose should include the hypothesis (educated guess) of what is expected from the outcome of the experiment. It is important to describe exactly what was done to prove or disprove a hypothesis. Drawings, graphs and illustrations should be included to support information. Observations are objective, whereas analyses and interpretations are subjective. A conclusion should explain why the results of the experiment either proved or disproved the hypothesis.

Learning can be broadly divided into two kinds—active and passive. Active learning involves, as the name indicates, a learning atmosphere full of action whereas in passive learning students are taught in an un stimulating and inactive atmosphere. Active learning involves and draws students into it, thereby interesting them to the point of participating and purposely engaging in learning.

SKILL 8.7   Identify appropriate technological tools that facilitate the learning of science.

There are many technological tools available to teachers to help them design and prepare effective lessons. Computer skills are invaluable for creating hand-outs, slide presentations, images, and videos. The internet provides ready-to-use Web lessons, quizzes, grading rubrics, and classroom calendars.

These technological resources are also available to students for various kinds homework assignments and classroom activities. Students can be given research projects that involve using the internet and/or the library. Distinguishing between the two is really no longer valid because library databases and catalogs can be accessed from home and school computers.

There are also computer programs that simulate experiments in physics and chemistry. These are called *virtual laboratories* and give students the same hands-on experience of an actual laboratory experiment.

COMPETENCY 9.0   KNOWLEDGE OF PROCESS SKILLS AND APPLICATION OF SCIENTIFIC INQUIRY

SKILL 9.1   Apply appropriate scientific process skills to observe and analyze natural phenomena and communicate findings.

Science may be defined as a body of knowledge that is systematically derived from study, observations, and experimentation. Its goal is to identify and establish principles and theories that may be applied to solve problems.

Pseudoscience, on the other hand, is a belief that is not warranted. There is no scientific methodology or application. Some of the more classic examples of pseudoscience include witchcraft, alien encounters, or any topics that are explained by hearsay.

Science requires that hypotheses and theories be testable, that is, verifiable or falsifiable by experimentation or observations. Science also is limited to the study of observable phenomena or knowledge gained by the senses. The concepts used in science generally have what are called *operational definitions.* A kilogram, for example, is the mass of a platinum-iridium bar maintained by the International Bureau of Weights and Measures

SKILL 9.2   Apply scientific inquiry, including scientific methods to investigations.

Scientific inquiry starts with observation. Observation is a very important skill by itself, since it leads to experimentation and finally communicating the experimental findings to the society/public. After observing, a question is formed, which starts with *why* or *how*. To answer these questions, experimentation is necessary. Between observation and experimentation, there are three more important steps. These are: gathering information (or researching about the problem), hypothesis, and designing the experiment.

Designing an experiment is very important since it involves identifying the control, constants, independent variables and dependent variables. A control/standard is something we compare our results with at the end of the experiment. It is like a reference. Constants are the factors we have to keep constant in an experiment to get reliable results. Independent variables are factors we change in an experiment. It is very important to bear in mind that there should be more constants than variables to obtain reproducible results in an experiment.

Classifying is grouping items according to their similarities. It is important for students to realize relationships and similarity as well as differences to reach a reasonable conclusion in a lab experience.

After the experiment is done, it is repeated and results are graphically presented. The results are then analyzed and conclusions drawn.

It is the responsibility of the scientists to share the knowledge they obtain through their research.

After the conclusion is drawn, the final step is communication. In this age, a lot of emphasis is put on the way and the method of communication. The conclusions must be communicated by clearly describing the information using accurate data, visual presentation like graphs (bar/line/pie), tables/charts, diagrams, artwork, and other appropriate media like PowerPoint presentations. Modern technology must be used whenever it is necessary. The method of communication must be suitable to the audience.

Written communication is as important as oral communication. This is essential for submitting research papers to scientific journals, newspapers and other magazines.

SKILL 9.3 Apply knowledge of mathematics and technology to scientific investigation.

Science uses the metric system as it is accepted worldwide and allows easier comparison among experiments done by scientists around the world. Learn the following basic units and prefixes:

meter — measure of length
liter — measure of volume
gram — measure of mass

deca-(meter, liter, gram)= 10X the base unit   **deci** = 1/10 the base unit
hecto-(meter, liter, gram)= 100X the base unit   **centi** = 1/100 the base unit
kilo-(meter, liter, gram) = 1000X the base unit   **milli** = 1/1000 the base unit

Graphing is an important skill to visually display collected data for analysis. The two types of graphs most commonly used are the **line graph** and the **bar graph** (histogram). Line graphs are set up to show two variables represented by one point on the graph. The X axis is the horizontal axis and represents the independent variable. Independent variables are those that would be changed by the experimenter. A common example of an independent variable is time. Time proceeds regardless of anything else occurring. The Y axis is the vertical axis and represents the dependent variable. Dependent variables are observed to see how they are affected by the change to the independent variable. An example of a dependent variable would be the increase in the height of a plant. Graphs should be calibrated at equal intervals. If one space represents one day, the next space may not represent ten days. A best-fit line is drawn to join the points and may not include all the points in the data. Axes must always be labeled for the graph to be meaningful. A good title will describe both the dependent and the independent variables. Bar graphs are set up similarly in regards to axes, but points are not plotted. Instead, the dependent variable is set up as a bar where the X-axis intersects with the Y-axis. Each bar is a separate item of data and is not joined by a continuous line.

The following are examples of technology used to further scientific knowledge:

Chromatography uses the principles of capillary action to separate substances such as plant pigments. Molecules of a larger size will move slower up the paper, whereas smaller molecules will move more quickly, producing lines of pigments.

Spectrophotometry uses percent light absorbance to measure a color change, thus giving qualitative data a quantitative value.

Centrifugation involves spinning substances at a high speed. The more dense part of a solution will settle to the bottom of the test tube, while the lighter material will stay on top. Centrifugation is used to separate blood into blood cells and plasma, with the heavier blood cells settling to the bottom.

Electrophoresis uses electrical charges of molecules to separate them according to their size. The molecules, such as DNA or proteins, are pulled through a gel toward either the positive end of the gel box (if the material has a negative charge) or the negative end of the gel box (if the material has a positive charge).

Satellites have improved our ability to communicate and transmit radio and television signals. Navigational abilities have been greatly improved through the use of satellite signals. Sonar uses sound waves to locate objects and is especially useful under water. The sound waves bounce off the object and are used to assist in location. Seismographs record vibrations in the Earth and allow us to measure Earthquake activity.

SKILL 9.4 Compare the methods used in the pursuit of scientific explanation as applied in different fields of science such ad geology, astronomy, physics, and biology.

Physics is characterized by the use of mathematical equations to understand phenomena in a fundamental and ultimate manner. Chemists, for example, know the significance of 2, 8, 18, and 32 electrons in an atom and know how to derive these numbers from the equations of quantum mechanics. But the discovery of the equations was a discovery in physics, not chemistry. Astronomy is a branch of physics, because astronomers use the equations of general relativity and elementary particles.

Chemistry studies the composition, structure, and properties of matter and condensed matter physics studies the macroscopic and microscopic physical properties of matter. This means that it is difficult to define the boundary between physics and chemistry.

Biology on the other hand is the study of living organisms, entities that reproduce and metabolize. It is generally considered that the question of what caused life is not a question in biology, even though there is some scientific speculation and conjecture on this question. There is very little mathematics in biology except in the area of the biology of cells and the chemical processes of life. At this level, biology can be considered the application of chemistry to living things.

Another major branch of the natural sciences, as opposed to the social sciences, is Earth science. Earth science includes the history of Earth's materials and the processes that formed them. The study of weather is part of Earth science.

SKILL 9. 5   Identify the traits of scientists and how they affect the development of scientific knowledge.

Most scientists spend their working hour applying science to help satisfy human needs. Putting science to this use is called *technology*. Technology requires research using the same techniques pure scientists use to discover truths about the natural world. It also requires the same education and work habits. However, pure science is concerned with knowledge for its own sake. Individuals who devote their lives to this are motivated by a love of science. Discovering new scientific truths is very difficult and can take many years.

Albert Einstein published four papers in 1905 any one of which would have made him a prominent scientist. However, he also spent twenty years trying to develop a unified field theory without success. Scientists are driven by the conviction that the universe is intelligible and the confidence that effort and hard work can result in success.

SKILL 9.6   Identify the assumptions of scientific knowledge (e.g., durable, open to change).

Physicists in the 19th century thought light traveled in a substance that was both rigid and highly rarefied. It had to be rigid because light traveled very fast and it has to be very rarefied because it could not be detected in a vacuum. In 1887, scientist measured the speed of light accurately enough to see if there was a luminous ether, as they called the substance. There was no ether and it became clear that certain assumptions about electric and magnetic fields were false and that light traveled in a vacuum. In short, the model of electromagnetic radiation was improved upon. Scientists always considered current theories to be tentative and subject to change.

Another example is the replacement of the Newtonian laws of motion with relativity. In this case, Newton's laws are approximations of the currently accepted laws of motion.

SKILL 9.7 Identify which questions can be answered through science and which questions are outside the boundaries of scientific investigation.

Science is concerned with knowledge gained from our senses: seeing, hearing, and touching. Such knowledge can be given operational definitions. It does not concern concepts, such as free will and supernatural beings, which do not have operational definitions. Nor it is concerned with moral questions of right and wrong and questions concerning the meaning of life. Such questions are the subject matter of other methods of inquiry.

Stephen Jay Gould, a famous evolutionary biologist, coined the phrase "nonoverlapping magisteria" to indicate that there were different methods of inquiry that addressed different issues.

SKILL 9.8 Evaluate the impact of the historical and cultural development of science on the advancement of scientific knowledge.

Science began with the agricultural revolution 10,000 years ago because there was apparently a body of knowledge than enabled humans to increase production. One might also put the beginning at the invention of fire one or two million years earlier. Pythagoras' theorem (circa 490 BC) was actually recorded on Mesopotamian cuneiform tablets in 1800 BC. Ancient Greeks discovered the principle behind buoyancy and the approximate radius of Earth. Indians made considerable discoveries in mathematics and astronomy from the 5th to 15th centuries AD. During this period, there were many pure and applied scientific discoveries in China: compasses, movable-type printing, atlases of stars, cast iron, the iron plough, the wheelbarrow, the suspension bridge, solid fuel rocket, and many more.

The scientific method began with Muslim scientists in the Middle Ages, not only because of their achievements in optics, mathematics, chemistry, and astronomy, but because philosophers of the Arab Empire explicitly advocated the need for experiments, observations, and measurements.

The rise of science in the West began with the rise of universities in the 12 century. Roger Bacon (1224–1294) is considered one of the early advocates of the scientific method. In 1277, the Bishop of Paris declared certain Aristotelian propositions, such as nature abhorring a vacuum, to be heretical. This is regarded by some historians of science as being the beginning of modern science because the bishop and his advisors at the University of Paris were using reason to arrive at a scientific truth. Aristotle's ideas about science were considered heretical because they implied God's power was not infinite.

In the 14th century, there was scientific progress in kinematics, but the Scientific Revolution began in the 16th century with the heliocentric theory of Nicolaus Copernicus. In 1605, Johannes Kepler discovered that planets orbit the sun in elliptical, not circular paths. In 1677, Isaac Newton derived Kepler's laws from the second law of motion.

In the 19th century, science became a profession and an institution in Western nation-states. The economic progress was due in part to the technological advances made possible by science and scientific progress was made possible by the economic progress.

SKILL 9.9 Compare the development, use, benefits, and limitations of theories, laws, hypotheses, and models.

Some things happen at too fast or too slow a rate, or are too small or too large for use to see. In these cases, we have to rely on indirect evidence to develop models of what is intangible. Once data has been collected and analyzed, it is useful to generalize the information by creating a model. A model is a conceptual representation of a phenomenon. Models are useful in that they clarify relationships, helping us to understand the phenomenon and make predictions about future outcomes. The natural sciences and social sciences employ modeling for this purpose.

A theory is a model that explains the phenomenon. In physics, there are some theories that are so well established that they are called laws. For example, Newton's laws of motion, the universal law of gravity, the law of definite proportions in chemistry, and the laws of thermodynamics.

Many scientific models are mathematical in nature and contain a set of variables linked by logical and quantitative relationships. These mathematical models may include functions, tables, formulas, and graphs. Typically, such mathematical models include assumptions that restrict them to very specific situations. Often this means they can only provide an approximate description of what occurs in the natural world. These assumptions, however, prevent the model from becoming overly complicated. For a mathematical model to fully explain a natural or social phenomenon, it would have to contain many variables and could become too cumbersome to use. Accordingly, it is critical that assumptions be carefully chosen and thoroughly defined.

Certain models are abstract and simply contain sets of logical principles rather than relying on mathematics. These types of models are generally more vague and are more useful for discovering and understanding new ideas. Abstract models can also include actual physical models built to make concepts more tangible. Abstract models, to an even greater extent than mathematical models, make assumptions and simplify actual phenomena.

Proper scientific models must be able to be tested and verified using experimental data. Often these experimental results are necessary to demonstrate the superiority of a model when two or more conflicting models seek to explain the same phenomenon. Computer simulations are increasingly used in both testing and developing mathematical and even abstract models. These types of simulations are especially useful in situations, such as ecology or manufacturing, where experiments are not feasible or variables are not fully under control.

SKILL 9.10 Analyze the interdependence between scientific knowledge and economic, political, social, and ethical concerns.

The stem cell controversy is the ethical debate centered on research involving the creation, use, and destruction of human embryonic stem cells. The usefulness of such research is a scientific question that is part of the ethical and political debate.

Another area where economic concerns are important is global warming. This refers to the increase in the average temperature of the Earth's near-surface air and the oceans since the mid-twentieth century and its projected continuation. It is believed by many scientific societies and academies of science that man-made greenhouse gases are responsible for most of the observed temperature increase. Natural phenomena such as solar variation and volcanoes probably had a small warming effect from pre-industrial times to 1950 and a small cooling effect afterward.

There are a number of negative consequences of this global warming. Rising sea levels and the expansion of subtropical deserts are a concern. Most national governments have signed and ratified the Kyoto Protocol aimed at reducing greenhouse gas emissions.

Environmentalism is a social movement that seeks to influence the political process by lobbying, activism, and education in order to protect natural resources and ecosystems. The first environmentalist was King Edward I of England who banned the burning of sea-coal by proclamation in London in 1272, after its smoke had become a problem.

Some claim that food additives, such as artificial sweeteners, colorants, preserving agents, and flavorings may cause health problems such as increasing the risk of cancer or ADHD. Several recent studies have also shown that artificial sweeteners, such as Aspartame, may increase risks of obesity.

Sample Test

DIRECTIONS: Read each item and select the best response.

1. **The measure of the pull of the Earth's gravity on an object is called _____ .**
   (Average Rigor) (Skill 1.1)

   A. mass number
   B. atomic number
   C. mass
   D. weight

2. **A seltzer tablet changing into bubbles is an example of:**
   (Rigorous) (Skill 1.1)

   A. A physical change.
   B. A chemical change.
   C. Conversion.
   D. Diffusion.

3. **When heat is added to most solids, they expand. Why is this the case?**
   (Average Rigor) (Skill 1.2)

   A. The molecules get bigger.
   B. The faster molecular motion leads to greater distance between the molecules.
   C. The molecules develop greater repelling electric forces.
   D. The molecules form a more rigid structure.

4. **If the volume of a confined gas is increased, what happens to the pressure of the gas? You may assume that the gas behaves ideally, and that temperature and number of gas molecules remain constant.**
   (Average Rigor) (Skill 1.3)

   A. The pressure increases.
   B. The pressure decreases.
   C. The pressure stays the same.
   D. There is not enough information given to answer this question.

5. **Based on the description of the model of atom below, give the name of the individual(s) that developed the model.**
   1. **Matter is made up of atoms.**
   2. **Atoms of an element are similar to each other.**
   3. **Atoms of different elements are different from each other.**
   4. **Atoms combine with each other to form new kinds of compounds.**
   (Rigorous) (Skill 1.4)

   A. Ernest Rutherford.
   B. Neils Bohr.
   C. John Dalton.
   D. Democritus Thompson.

6. **Vinegar is an example of a _____ .**
    (Easy) (Skill 1.5)

    A. strong acid
    B. strong base
    C. weak acid
    D. weak base

7. **Which of the following will not change in a chemical reaction?**
    (Average Rigor) (Skill 1.6)

    A. Number of moles of products.
    B. Atomic number of one of the reactants.
    C. Mass (in grams) of one of the reactants.
    D. Rate of reaction.

8. **Which parts of an atom are located inside the nucleus?**
    (Easy) (Skill 1.7)

    A. Electrons and neutrons.
    B. Protons and neutrons.
    C. Protons only.
    D. Neutrons only.

9. **What part of an atom has to change to create another isotope of an element?**
    (Rigorous) (Skill 1.7)

    A. The number of electrons.
    B. The number of neutrons.
    C. The arrangement of the electrons.
    D. The number of protons.

10. **The elements in the modern periodic table are arranged _____ .**
    (Easy) (Skill 1.8)

    A. in numerical order by atomic number
    B. randomly
    C. in alphabetical order by chemical symbol
    D. in numerical order by atomic mass

11. **Which of the following is not a property of metalloids?**
    (Rigorous) (Skill 1.8)

    A. Metalloids are solids at standard temperature and pressure.
    B. Metalloids can conduct electricity to a limited extent.
    C. Metalloids are found in groups 13 through 17.
    D. Metalloids all favor ionic bonding.

12. **The two strands of a DNA molecule are held together by what kind of bond?**
    (Average Rigor) (Skill 1.9)

    A. Polar-covalent.
    B. Ionic.
    C. Non-polar covalent
    D. Hydrogen.

13. **Carbon bonds with hydrogen by _____ .**
(Rigorous) (Skill 1.9)

A. ionic bonding
B. non-polar covalent bonding
C. polar covalent bonding
D. strong nuclear force

14. **Which reaction below is a decomposition reaction?**
(Rigorous) (Skill 1.10)

A. $HCl + NaOH \rightarrow NaCl + H_2O$.
B. $C + O_2 \rightarrow CO_2$.
C. $2H_2O \rightarrow 2H_2 + O_2$.
D. $CuSO_4 + Fe \rightarrow FeSO_4 + Cu$.

15. **Which of the following is a correct explanation for astronaut 'weightlessness'?**
(Easy) (Skill 2.1)

A. Astronauts continue to feel the pull of gravity in space, but they are so far from Earth that the force is small.
B. Astronauts continue to feel the pull of gravity in space, but spacecraft have such powerful engines that those forces dominate, reducing effective weight.
C. Astronauts do not feel the pull of gravity in space, because space is a vacuum.
D. Astronauts do not feel the pull of gravity in space, because black hole forces dominate the force field, reducing their masses.

16. **The force of gravity on Earth causes all bodies in free fall to _____ .**
(Average Rigor) (Skill 2.1)

A. fall at the same speed
B. accelerate at the same rate
C. reach the same terminal velocity
D. move in the same direction

17. **All of the following are considered Newton's laws except for:**
(Easy) (Skill 2.2)

A. An object in motion will continue in motion unless acted upon by an outside force.
B. For every action force, there is an equal and opposite reaction force."
C. Nature abhors a vacuum.
D. Mass can be considered the ratio of force to acceleration.

18. **Newton's Laws are taught in science classes because _____ .**
(Rigorous) (Skill 2.2)

A. they are an absolutely correct analysis of inertia, gravity, and forces.
B. they are a close approximation to correct physics, for usual Earth conditions.
C. they accurately incorporate relativity into studies of forces.
D. Newton was a well-respected scientist in his time.

19. The picture shows a view from slightly above of a teacher swinging a yoyo over their head. The teacher would be holding onto the string in the center of the circle, and the circle itself describes the path of the yoyo. Arrows 1,2 and 3 describe the forces on the yoyo. Which answer below names the forces correctly?

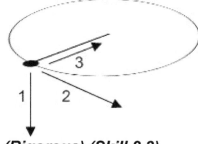

(Rigorous) (Skill 2.3)

A. 1 is inertia, 2 is centripetal force, 3 is gravity.
B. 1 is centripedal force, 2 is gravity, 3 is inertia.
C. 1 is gravity, 2 is inertia, 3 is centripetal.
D. 1 is gravity, 2 is inertia, 3 is centrifugal.

20. Sound can be transmitted in all of the following except _____.

(Easy) (Skill 2.4)

A. air
B. water
C. a diamond
D. a vacuum

21. Which of the following is not a factor in how different materials will conduct seismic waves?
(Average Rigor) (Skill 2.4)

A. Density.
B. Incompressibility.
C. Rigidity.
D. Tensile strength.

22. The speed of light is different in different materials. This is responsible for _____ .
(Average Rigor) (Skill 2.5)

A. interference
B. refraction
C. reflection
D. relativity

23. As a train approaches, the whistle sounds _____ .
(Rigorous) (Skill 2.5)

A. higher, because it has a higher apparent frequency
B. lower, because it has a lower apparent frequency
C. higher, because it has a lower apparent frequency
D. lower, because it has a higher apparent frequency

24. Resistance is measured in units called _____ .
   (Average Rigor) (Skill 2.6)

   A. watts
   B. volts
   C. ohms
   D. current

25. A light bulb is connected in series with a rotating coil within a magnetic field. The brightness of the light may be increased by any of the following except:
   (Rigorous) (Skill 2.7)

   A. Rotating the coil more rapidly.
   B. Using more loops in the coil.
   C. Using a different color wire for the coil.
   D. Using a stronger magnetic field.

26. Which component(s) of an atom is most responsible for the magnetic properties of a substance?
   (Average Rigor) (Skill 2.8)

   A. Electrons.
   B. Protons.
   C. Neutrons.
   D. Electrons and Protons.

27.	The Hoover Dam is perhaps the most famous hydroeletric dam in North America. Which on of the follwing best describes how Hydroelectric dams generate their power? *(Rigorous) (Skill 2.9)*

A.	Gravity imparts kinetic energy onto the falling water, which acts as a mechanical force turning the generator turbines. The turbines contain a coil of wire, and as the turbine spins it spins the coil of wire. This generates an electrical current in the wire that is then sent out to the power grid.

B.	Gravity imparts kinetic energy onto the falling water, which acts as a mechanical force turning the generator turbines. When the turbines spin they spin a series of electromagnets inside a coil of copper wire. This generates an electrical current in the wire that is then sent out to the power grid.

C.	Gravity imparts potential energy onto the falling water, which acts as a mechanical force turning the generator turbines. When the turbines spin they spin a series of electromagnets inside a coil of copper wire. This generates an electrical current in the wire that is then sent out to the power grid.

D.	Gravity imparts kinetic energy onto the falling water, which acts as a mechanical force turning the generator turbines. When the turbines spin they spin a series of permanent magnets inside a coil of copper wire. This generates an electrical current in the wire that is then sent out to the power grid.

28. **A newton is fundamentally a measure of _____ .**
(Average Rigor) (Skill 2.10)

    A. force
    B. momentum
    C. energy
    D. gravity

29. **A cup of hot liquid and a cup of cold liquid are both sitting in a room at comfortable room temperature and humidity. Both cups are thin plastic. Which of the following is a true statement?**
(Average Rigor) (Skill 3.1)

    A. There will be condensation on the outside of the hot liquid cup, and also condensation on the outside of the cold liquid cup.
    B. There will be condensation on the outside of the hot liquid cup, but not on the cold liquid cup.
    C. There will be condensation on the outside of the cold liquid cup, but not on the hot liquid cup.
    D. There will not be condensation on the outside of either cup.

30. **Which of the following is not true about phase change in matter?**
(Rigorous) (Skill 3.1)

    A. Solid water and liquid ice can coexist at water's freezing point.
    B. At 7 degrees Celsius, water is always in liquid phase.
    C. Matter changes phase when enough energy is gained or lost.
    D. Different phases of matter are characterized by differences in molecular motion.

31. **All of the following measure energy except for _____.**
(Average Rigor) (Skill 3.2)

    A. joules
    B. calories
    C. watts
    D. ergs

32. **The transfer of heat by electromagnetic waves is called _____ .**
(Easy) (Skill 3.3)

    A. conduction
    B. convection
    C. phase change
    D. radiation

33. A long silver bar has a temperature of 50 degrees Celsius at one end and 0 degrees Celsius at the other end. The bar will reach thermal equilibrium (barring outside influence) by the process of heat

_____.
(Average Rigor) (Skill 3.3)

A. conduction
B. convection
C. radiation
D. phase change

34. When you step out of the shower, the floor feels colder on your feet than the bathmat. Which of the following is the correct explanation for this phenomenon?
(Average Rigor) (Skill 3.4)

A. The floor is colder than the bathmat.
B. Your feet have a chemical reaction with the floor, but not the bathmat.
C. Heat is conducted more easily into the floor.
D. Water is absorbed from your feet into the bathmat.

35. A boulder sitting on the edge of a cliff has which type of energy?
(Easy) (Skill 3.5)

A. Kinetic energy.
B. Latent energy.
C. No energy.
D. Potential energy.

36. A ball rolls down a smooth hill. You may ignore air resistance. Which of the following is a true statement?
(Average Rigor) (Skill 3.5)

A. The ball has more energy at the start of its descent than just before it hits the bottom of the hill, because it is higher up at the beginning.
B. The ball has less energy at the start of its descent than just before it hits the bottom of the hill, because it is moving more quickly at the end.
C. The ball has the same energy throughout its descent, because positional energy is converted to energy of motion.
D. The ball has the same energy throughout its descent, because a single object (such as a ball) cannot gain or lose energy.

37. **What is the main obstacle to using nuclear fusion for obtaining electricity?** *(Average Rigor) (Skill 3.6)*

    A. Nuclear fusion produces much more pollution than nuclear fission.
    B. There is no obstacle; most power plants us nuclear fusion today.
    C. Nuclear fusion requires very high temperature and activation energy.
    D. The fuel for nuclear fusion is extremely expensive.

38. **In a fission reactor, "heavy water" is used to** _____ . *(Rigorous) (Skill 3.6)*

    A. terminate fission reactions.
    B. slow down neutrons.
    C. rehydrate the chemicals.
    D. initiate a chain reaction.

39. **The electromagnetic radiation with the longest wave length is/are** _____ . *(Easy) (Skill 3.7)*

    A. radio waves
    B. red light
    C. X-rays
    D. ultraviolet light

40. **A converging lens produces a real image** _____ . *(Rigorous) (Skill 3.8)*

    A. always
    B. never
    C. when the object is within one focal length of the lens.
    D. when the object is further than one focal length from the lens.

41. **You have four pulley set-ups (in order to solve the problem you don't need the number and size of the pulleys), each with a weight of 1 Newton attched at one end. Based on the energy used to lift the mass and how far the mass was lifted, which of the systems was the most efficient?** *(Rigorous) (Skill 3.9)*

    A. 3 Joules lifted the mass 2 meters.
    B. 10 Joules lifted the mass 8 meters.
    C. 4 Joules lifted the mass 3.6 meters.
    D. 7.5 Joules lifted the mass 6 meters.

42. As in all processess, plant growth must deal with the law of conservation of mass and energy. Most people recongize the Sun as the source of a plant's energy however what is the primary source of the mass of plants?
(Rigorous) (Skill 3.10)

A. Water absorbed through the roots.
B. Nutrient's and minerals absorbed through the roots.
C. Carbon absorbed through the roots.
D. Carbon absorbed through the stomata.

43. Identify which of the answers has correctly paired the terms with their definitions?

I. Amperes 1. Electrical potential
II. Volts   2. Electrical resistance
III. Ohms   3. Energy flow
IV. Watts   4. Electric current

(Rigorous) (Skill 3.11)

A. I:1, II:3, III:4, IV:2
B. I:3, II:1, III:2, IV:4
C. I:4, II:1, III:2, IV:3
D. I:3, II:4, III:2, IV:3

44. A 10 ohm resistor and a 50 ohm resistor are connected in parallel. If the current in the 10 ohm resistor is 5 amperes, the current (in amperes) running through the 50 ohm resistor is
(Rigorous) (Skill 3.12)

A. 1
B. 50
C. 25
D. 60

45. _____ are cracks in the plates of the Earth's crust, along which the plates move.
(Easy) (Skill 4.1)

A. Faults
B. Ridges
C. Earthquakes
D. Volcanoes

46. Which of the following is not a type of volcano?
(Average Rigor) (Skill 4.2)

A. Shield volcanoes.
B. Composite volcanoes.
C. Stratus volcanoes.
D. Cinder cone volcanoes.

47. Although Yellowstone has many unique geological features, Its entirety is encompassed by one type of geological feature. What is that feature?
(Rigorous) (Skill 4.2)

A. Caldera.
B. Glacial trough.
C. Shield volcano.
D. Laccolith.

48. The end of a geologic era is most often characterized by?
(Average Rigor) (Skill 4.3)

   A. A general uplifting of the crust.
   B. The extinction of the dominant plants and animals
   C. The appearance of new life forms.
   D. All of the above.

49. The result of radioactive decay is?
(Average Rigor) (Skill 4.4)

   A. Parent element.
   B. Daughter element.
   C. Half-life.
   D. An unstable atom.

50. A contour line that has tiny comb-like lines along the inner edge indicates a?
(Average Rigor) (Skill 4.5)

   A. Depression
   B. Mountain
   C. Valley
   D. River

51. Surface ocean currents are caused by which of the following?
(Rigorous) (Skill 4.6)

   A. Temperature.
   B. Density changes in water.
   C. Wind.
   D. Tidal forces.

52. Which of these best decribes the seafloor along the majority of Florida's Atlantic shoreline?
(Average Rigor) (Skill 4.7)

   A. Continental slope.
   B. Continental rise.
   C. Continental shelf.
   D. Seamount.

53. Mount Kīlauea on the island of Hawaii, is a very active volcano that has continuous lava flow into the ocean near it. What is the name of the type of shoreline created at the point where the lava flows meet the water?
(Rigorous) (Skill 4.7)

   A. Stacking.
   B. Submerged.
   C. Developing.
   D. Emergent.

54. The salinity of ocean water is closest to _____ .
(Average Rigor) (Skill 4.8)

   A. 0.035 %
   B. 0.35 %
   C. 3.5 %
   D. 35 %

55. Fossils are usually found in _____ rock.
(Easy) (Skill 4.9)

   A. igneous
   B. sedimentary
   C. metamorphic
   D. cumulus

56. Which of the following is a type of igneous rock?
(Rigorous) (Skill 4.9)

A. Quartz.
B. Granite.
C. Obsidian.
D. All of the above.

57. Igneous rocks can be classified according to which of the following?
(Easy) (Skill 4.10)

A. Texture.
B. Composition.
C. Formation process.
D. All of the above.

58. Which of these is a true statement about loamy soil?
(Average Rigor) (Skill 4.10)

A. Loamy soil is gritty and porous.
B. Loamy soil is smooth and a good barrier to water.
C. Loamy soil is hostile to microorganisms.
D. Loamy soil is velvety and clumpy.

59. Recently, New Hampshire's famous Old Man in the Mountain collapsed. What type of erosion was the principal cause of this?
(Rigorous) (Skill 4.11)

A. Physical weathering.
B. Chemical weathering.
C. Exfoliation.
D. Frost wedging.

60. Which layer of the atmosphere would you expect most weather to occur?
(Average Rigor) (Skill 4.12)

A. Troposphere.
B. Thermosphere.
C. Mesosphere.
D. Stratosphere.

61. Which of the following instruments measures wind speed?
(Easy) (Skill 4.13)

A. A barometer.
B. An anemometer.
C. A thermometer.
D. A weather vane.

62. The theory of 'continental drift' is supported by which of the following?
(Average Rigor) (Skill 4.14)

A. The way the shapes of South America and Europe fit together.
B. The way the shapes of Europe and Asia fit together.
C. The way the shapes of South America and Africa fit together.
D. The way the shapes of North America and Antarctica fit together.

63. A fossils of a dinosaur genus known as Saurolophus have been found in both Western North America, and in Mongolia. What is the most likely explanation for these findings?
    (Rigorous) (Skill 4.14)

    A. Convergent evolution
    B. This genus of dinosaurs were powerful swimmers that swam across the Bering Strait.
    C. At one time all land masses were connected in a land form known as Pangaea, and so the dinosaurs could have easily walked from what is now Mongolia to what is now Western North America.
    D. Although Asia and North American were separate continents at the time, low sea levels made it possible for the dinosaurs to walk from one continent to the other.

64. What is the most accurate description of the water cycle?
    (Rigorous) (Skill 4.15)

    A. Rain comes from clouds, filling the ocean. The water then evaporates and becomes clouds again.
    B. Water circulates from rivers into groundwater and back, while water vapor circulates in the atmosphere.
    C. Water is conserved except for chemical or nuclear reactions, and any drop of water could circulate through clouds, rain, ground-water, and surface-water.
    D. Water flows toward the oceans, where it evaporates and forms clouds, which causes rain, which in turn flow back to the oceans after it falls.

65. When water falls to a cave floor and evaporates, it may deposit calcium carbonate. This process leads to the formation of which of the following?
    (Easy) (Skill 4.16)

    A. Stalactites.
    B. Stalagmites.
    C. Fault lines.
    D. Sedimentary rocks.

66. **Quicksand is created by the Interaction of very fine sand and water. The process that creates quicksand is callled _____ .**
    (Rigorous) (Skill 4.16)

    A. Absorption
    B. Percolation
    C. Leaching
    D. Runoff

67. **What is the source for most of the United States' drinking water?**
    (Rigorous) (Skill 4.17)

    A. Desalinated ocean water.
    B. Surface water (lakes, streams, mountain runoff).
    C. Rainfall into municipal reservoirs.
    D. Groundwater.

68. **Which of the following is the best explanation of the fundamental concept of uniformitarianism?**
    (Rigorous) (Skill 4.18)

    A. The types and varieties of life between will see a uniform progression over time.
    B. The physical, chemical and biological laws that operate in the geologic past operate in the same way today.
    C. Debris from catastrophic events (i.e. volcanoes, and meteorites) will be evenly distributed over the affected area.
    D. The frequency and intensity of major geologic events will remain consistent over long periods of time.

69. **The phases of the moon are the result of its _____ in relation to the sun.**
    (Average Rigor) (Skill 5.1)

    A. revolution
    B. rotation
    C. position
    D. inclination

70. Neap tides are especially weak tides that occur when the Sun and Moon are in a perpindicular arrangment to the Earth, and "Spring Tides" are espically strong tides that occur when the Sun and Moon are in line. At which combination of lunar phases do these tides occur (respectively)?
(Rigorous) (Skill 5.1)

A. Half-moon, and full moon.
B. Quarter moon, and new moon.
C. Gibbous moon, and quarter moon.
D. Full moon and new moon.

71. A star's brightness is referred to as:
(Average Rigor) (Skill 5.2)

A. Magnitude.
B. Mass.
C. Apparent magnitude.
D. Intensity.

72. A telescope that collects light by using a concave mirror and can produce small images is called a

_____.
(Average Rigor) (Skill 5.3)

A. radioactive telescope
B. reflecting telescope
C. refracting telescope
D. optical telescope

73. Which of the following units is not a measure of distance?
(Easy) (Skill 5.4)

A. AU (astronomical unit).
B. Light year.
C. Parsec.
D. Lunar year.

74. Which of the following is the best definition for meteorite?
(Easy) (Skill 5.5)

A. A meteorite is a mineral composed of mica and feldspar.
B. A meteorite is material from outer space, that has struck the Earth's surface.
C. A meteorite is an element that has properties of both metals and nonmetals.
D. A meteorite is a very small unit of length measurement.

75. The planet with true retrograde rotation is:
(Rigorous) (Skill 5.5)

A. Pluto.
B. Uranus.
C. Venus.
D. Saturn.

76. **What is the main difference between the condensation hypothesis and the tidal hypothesis for the origin of the solar system?**
(Rigorous) (Skill 5.6)

A. The tidal hypothesis can be tested, but the condensation hypothesis cannot.
B. The tidal hypothesis proposes a near collision of two stars pulling on each other, but the condensation hypothesis proposes condensation of rotating clouds of dust and gas.
C. The tidal hypothesis explains how tides began on planets such as Earth, but the condensation hypothesis explains how water vapor became liquid on Earth.
D. The tidal hypothesis is based on Aristotelian physics, but the condensation hypothesis is based on Newtonian mechanics.

77. **Identify the correct sequence of organization of living things from lower to higher order:**
(Easy) (Skill 6.1)

A. Cell, organelle, organ, tissue, system, organism.
B. Cell, tissue, organ, organelle, system, organism.
C. Organelle, cell, tissue, organ, system, organism.
D. Organelle, tissue, cell, organ, system, organism.

78. **Which of the following is not a necessary characteristic of living things?**
(Average Rigor) (Skill 6.1)

A. Movement.
B. Reduction of local entropy.
C. Ability to cause change in local energy form.
D. Reproduction.

79. **Which of the following features is/are found in eukaryotic cells but not in prokaryotic cells?**

1. **Nucleus**
2. **Mitochondria**
3. **Cytoskeleton**
4. **Vacules**

(Easy) (Skill 6.2)

A. 4 Only.
B. 1 and 2.
C. 1, 2 and 4.
D. 1, 2 and 3.

80. What cell organelle contains the cell's stored food?
(Rigorous) (Skill 6.3)

A. Vacuoles.
B. Golgi Apparatus.
C. Ribosomes.
D. Lysosomes.

81. The first stage of mitosis is called _____ .
(Average Rigor) (Skill 6.4)

A. telophase
B. anaphase
C. prophase
D. mitophase

82. Klinefelter syndrome is a condition in which a person is born with two X chromosomes and one Y chromosome. What process during meiosis would cause this to happen?
(Rigorous) (Skill 6.4)

A. Inversion.
B. Translocation.
C. Non-disjunction.
D. Arrangement failure.

83. A white flower is crossed with a red flower. Which of the following is a sign of incomplete dominance?
(Average Rigor) (Skill 6.5)

A. Pink flowers.
B. Red flowers.
C. White flowers.
D. No flowers.

84. A carrier of a genetic disorder is heterozygous for a disorder that is recessive in nature. Hemophilia is a sex-linked disorder. This means that:
(Easy) (Skill 6.6)

A. Only females can be carriers.
B. Only males can be carriers.
C. Both males and females can be carriers.
D. Neither females nor males can be carriers.

85. A child has type O blood. Her father has type A blood, and her mother has type B blood. What are the genotypes of the father and mother, respectively?
(Average Rigor) (Skill 6.6)

A. AO and BO.
B. AA and AB.
C. OO and BO.
D. AO and BB.

86. Amino acids are carried to the ribosome in protein synthesis by _____ .
(Average Rigor) (Skill 6.7)

A. transfer RNA (tRNA)
B. messenger RNA (mRNA)
C. ribosomal RNA (rRNA)
D. transformation RNA (trRNA)

87. Which is the correct sequence of insect development?
(Easy) (Skill 6.8)

A. Egg, pupa, larva, adult.
B. Egg, larva, pupa, adult.
C. Egg, adult, larva, pupa.
D. Pupa, egg, larva, adult.

88. Echinodermata are best known for what characteristic?
(Average Rigor) (Skill 6.8)

A. Their slimy skin.
B. Their Dry Habitat.
C. Their tube feet.
D. Their tentacles.

89. Laboratory researchers have classified fungi as distinct from plants because the cell walls of fungi _____ .
(Rigorous) (Skill 6.8)

A. contain chitin
B. contain yeast
C. are more solid
D. are less solid

90. Diatoms are one of the primary contributors to photosynethis in the oceans. They also have a unique cell wall made up of silicate, which often makes them sink in the water. Although some diatoms might form colonies most are single celled. Diatoms are usually nonmotile, although in many species the gametes have flagella. Based on this information which answer is the best identification of Diatoms.
(Rigorous) (Skill 6.9)

A. Protozoans.
B. Euglenas.
C. Protists.
D. Blue-Green Algae.

91. Which plant tissues contain chloroplasts?
(Average Rigor) (Skill 6.11)

A. Stomata.
B. Palisade mesophyll.
C. Spongy Mesophyll.
D. Endosperm.

92. The process of Transpiration requires which of the following?

1 Xylem
2 Stomata
3 Roots
4 Capillary action

(Rigorous) (Skill 6.12)

A. 1 and 2.
B. 2 and 3.
C. 1, 2, 3, and 4.
D. 1 and 3.

93. Enzymes speed up reactions by _____ .
(Average Rigor) (Skill 6.13)

A. utilizing ATP
B. lowering pH, allowing reaction speed to increase
C. increasing volume of substrate
D. lowering energy of activation

94. A product of anaerobic respiration in animals is _____ .
(Rigorous) (Skill 6.13)

A. carbon dioxide
B. lactic acid
C. oxygen
D. sodium chloride

95. Multiple sclerosis is an autoimmune disease that prevents nerves that are being attacked from being properly insulated, thus preventing normal propagation of the nerve signal. Which part of the nervous system is the most likely target of the body's immune system in this diease?
(Rigorous) (Skill 6.14)

A. Axon.
B. Synapse.
C. Dendrite.
D. Myelin.

96. Many male birds sing long complicated songs that describe thier identity and the area of land that they claim. Which of the answers below is the best decription of this behavior?
(Rigorous) (Skill 6.15)

A. Innate territorial behavior.
B. Learned competitive behavior.
C. Innate mating behavior.
D. Learned territorial behavior.

97. **What are the most significant and prevalent elements in the biosphere?**
(Easy) (Skill 7.1)

   A. Carbon, hydrogen, oxygen, nitrogen, phosphorus.
   B. Carbon, hydrogen, sodium, iron, calcium.
   C. Carbon, oxygen, sulfur, manganese, iron.
   D. Carbon, hydrogen, oxygen, nickel, sodium, nitrogen.

98. **Which of the following is found in the least abundance in organic molecules?**
(Rigorous) (Skill 7.1)

   A. Phosphorus.
   B. Potassium.
   C. Carbon.
   D. Oxygen.

99. **Which of the following is the most accurate definition of a non-renewable resource?**
(Average Rigor) (Skill 7.2)

   A. A nonrenewable resource is never replaced once used.
   B. A nonrenewable resource is replaced on a timescale that is very long relative to human life spans.
   C. A nonrenewable resource is a resource that can only be manufactured by humans.
   D. A nonrenewable resource is a species that has already become extinct.

100. **Which of the following is the best example of an explanation of the theory of evolution?**
(Rigorous) (Skill 7.3)

A. Giraffes need to reach higher for leaves to eat, so their necks stretch. The giraffe babies are then born with longer necks. Eventually, there are more long-necked giraffes in the population.

B. Giraffes with longer necks are able to reach more leaves, so they eat more and have more babies than other giraffes. Eventually, there are more long-necked giraffes in the population.

C. Giraffes want to reach higher for leaves to eat, so they release enzymes into their bloodstream, which in turn causes fetal development of longer-necked giraffes. Eventually, there are more long-necked giraffes in the population.

D. Giraffes with long necks are more attractive to other giraffes, so they get the best mating partners and have more babies. Eventually, there are more long-necked giraffes in the population.

101. **A wrasse (fish) cleans the teeth of other fish by eating away plaque. This is an example of _____ between the fish.**
(Average Rigor) (Skill 7.4)

A. parasitism
B. symbiosis (mutualism)
C. competition
D. predation

102. **Which one of the following biomes makes up the greatest percentage of the biosphere?**
(Rigorous) (Skill 7.4)

A. Desert.
B. Tropical rain forest.
C. Marine.
D. Temperate deciduous forest.

103. **Which of the following is not a common type of acid in 'acid rain' or acidified surface water?**
(Average Rigor) (Skill 7.5)

A. Nitric acid.
B. Sulfuric acid.
C. Carbonic acid.
D. Hydrofluoric acid.

104. **Viruses are responsible for many human diseases including all of the following except _____?**
(Easy) (Skill 7.6)

A. influenza
B. AIDS
C. the common cold
D. strep throat

105. Extensive use of antibacterial soap has been found to increase the virulence of certain infections in hospitals. Which of the following might be an explanation for this phenomenon?
(Average Rigor) (Skill 7.6)

A. Antibacterial soaps do not kill viruses.
B. Antibacterial soaps do not incorporate the same antibiotics used as medicine.
C. Antibacterial soaps kill a lot of bacteria, and only the hardiest ones survive to reproduce.
D. Antibacterial soaps can be very drying to the skin.

106. Which of the following hormones is least involved in the process of osmoregulation?
(Rigorous) (Skill 7.7)

A. Antidiuretic hormone.
B. Melatonin.
C. Calcitonin.
D. Gulcagon.

107. What makes up the largest abiotic portion of the nitrogen cycle?
(Average Rigor) (Skill 7.8)

A. Nitrogen fixing bacteria.
B. Nitrates.
C. Decomposers.
D. Atmosphere.

108. Which of the following abiotic factors maintains Florida's most extensive terrestrial ecosystem?
(Rigorous) (Skill 7.9)

A. Rain.
B. Flooding.
C. Fire.
D. Wind.

109. Formaldehyde should not be used in school laboratories for the following reason:
(Average Rigor) (Skill 8.1)

A. It smells unpleasant.
B. It is a known carcinogen.
C. It is expensive to obtain.
D. It is explosive.

110. Experiments may be done with any of the following animals except _____ .
(Rigorous) (Skill 8.1)

A. birds
B. invertebrates
C. lower order life
D. frogs

111. **When measuring the volume of water in a graduated cylinder, where does one read the measurement?**
(Average Rigor) (Skill 8.2)

A. At the highest point of the liquid.
B. At the bottom of the meniscus curve.
C. At the closest mark to the top of the liquid
D. At the top of the plastic safety ring.

112. **In a science experiment, a student needs to repeatedly dispense very small measured amounts of liquid into a well-mixed solution. Which of the following is the best choice for his/her equipment to use?**
(Rigorous) (Skill 8.2)

A. Pipette, stirring rod, beaker.
B. Burette with burette stand, stir-plate, beaker.
C. Volumetric flask, dropper, stirring rod.
D. Beaker, graduated cylinder, stir-plate.

113. **Many times science teachers are faced with the dilemna of not having enough funds to perform all the wonderful science laboratory exercises that they find. Which of these items might help with this problem?**
(Easy) (Skill 8.3)

A. Getting supplies at hardware and grocery stores.
B. Applying for Grant Money.
C. Use of School Gardens or natural areas.
D. All of the above.

114. **Who should be notified in the case of a serious chemical spill?**
(Average Rigor) (Skill 8.4)

A. The custodian.
B. The fire department or their municipal authority.
C. The science department chair.
D. The school board.

115. **What is the scientific method?**
(Average Rigor) (Skill 9.1)

   A. It is the process of doing an experiment and writing a laboratory report.
   B. It is the process of using open inquiry and repeatable results to establish theories.
   C. It is the process of reinforcing scientific principles by confirming results.
   D. It is the process of recording data and observations.

116. **Which of the following is not an acceptable way for a student to acknowledge sources in a laboratory report?**
(Rigorous) (Skill 9.1)

   A. The student tells his/her teacher what sources s/he used to write the report.
   B. The student uses footnotes in the text, with sources cited, but not in correct MLA format.
   C. The student uses endnotes in the text, with sources cited, in correct MLA format.
   D. The student attaches a separate bibliography, noting each use of sources.

117. **Which of the following data sets is properly represented by a bar graph?**
(Average Rigor) (Skill 9.2)

   A. Number of people choosing to buy cars, vs. Color of car bought.
   B. Number of people choosing to buy cars, vs. Age of car customer.
   C. Number of people choosing to buy cars, vs. Distance from car lot to customer home.
   D. Number of people choosing to buy cars, vs. Time since last car purchase.

118. **Which is the correct order of methodology?**

   1. **collecting data**
   2. **planning a controlled experiment**
   3. **drawing a conclusion**
   4. **hypothesizing a result**
   5. **re-visiting a hypothesis to answer a question**

(Easy) (Skill 9.3)

   A. 1,2,3,4,5.
   B. 4,2,1,3,5.
   C. 4,5,1,3,2.
   D. 1,3,4,5,2.

119. When designing a scientific experiment, a student considers all the factors that may influence the results. The process goal is to _____.
    (Average Rigor) (Skill 9.3)

    A. recognize and manipulate independent variables
    B. recognize and record independent variables
    C. recognize and manipulate dependent variables
    D. recognize and record dependent variables

120. In an experiment measuring the inhibition effect of different antibiotic discs on bacteria grown in Petri dishes, what are the independent and dependent variables respectively?
    (Rigorous) (Skill 9.4)

    A. Number of bacterial colonies and the antibiotic type.
    B. Antibiotic type and the distance between antibiotic and the closest colony.
    C. Antibiotic type and the number of bacterial colonies.
    D. Presence of bacterial colonies and the antibiotic type.

121. Koch's postulates on microbiology include all of the following except:
    (Rigorous) (Skill 9.5)

    A. The same pathogen must be found in every diseased person.
    B. The pathogen must be isolated and grown in culture.
    C. The same pathogen must be isolated from the experimental animal.
    D. Antibodies that react to the pathogen must be found in every diseased person.

122. If one inch equals 2.54 cm how many mm in 1.5 feet? (APPROXIMATELY)
    (Easy) (Skill 9.6)

    A. 18 mm.
    B. 1800 mm.
    C. 460 mm.
    D. 4,600 mm.

123. Separating blood into blood cells and plasma involves the process of _____ .
    (Average Rigor) (Skill 9.6)

    A. electrophoresis
    B. centrifugation
    C. spectrophotometry
    D. chromatography

124. **Which type of student activity is most likely to expose a student's misconceptions about science?**
(Average Rigor) (Skill 9.7)

A. Multiple-choice and fill-in-the-blank worksheets.
B. Laboratory activities, where the lab is laid out step by step with no active thought on the part of the student.
C. Teacher-led demonstrations.
D. Laboratories in which the student are forced to critically consider the steps taken and the results.

125. **Which of the following is not an appropriate aspect of scientific attitude?**
(Rigorous) (Skill 9.8)

A. Scientific curiosity.
B. Scientific open-mindedness.
C. Scientific conformity.
D. Scientific skepticism.

Answer Key

1.	D	26.	A	51.	C	76.	B	101.	B
2.	B	27.	B	52.	C	77.	C	102.	C
3.	B	28.	A	53.	D	78.	A	103.	D
4.	B	29.	C	54.	C	79.	D	104.	D
5.	C	30.	B	55.	B	80.	A	105.	C
6.	C	31.	C	56.	D	81.	C	106.	B
7.	B	32.	D	57.	D	82.	C	107.	D
8.	B	33.	A	58.	D	83.	A	108.	C
9.	B	34.	C	59.	D	84.	A	109.	B
10.	A	35.	D	60.	A	85.	A	110.	A
11.	D	36.	C	61.	B	86.	A	111.	B
12.	D	37.	C	62.	C	87.	B	112.	B
13.	C	38.	B	63.	D	88.	C	113.	D
14.	C	39.	A	64.	C	89.	A	114.	B
15.	A	40.	D	65.	B	90.	C	115.	B
16.	B	41.	C	66.	B	91.	B	116.	A
17.	C	42.	D	67.	D	92.	C	117.	A
18.	B	43.	C	68.	B	93.	D	118.	B
19.	C	44.	A	69.	C	94.	B	119.	A
20.	D	45.	A	70.	B	95.	D	120.	B
21.	D	46.	C	71.	A	96.	D	121.	D
22.	B	47.	A	72.	B	97.	A	122.	C
23.	A	48.	D	73.	D	98.	B	123.	C
24.	C	49.	B	74.	B	99.	B	124.	D
25.	C	50.	A	75.	C	100.	B	125.	C

Rigor Table

	Easy %20	Average Rigor %40	Rigorous %40
Question #	17, 20, 32, 35, 39, 45, 55, 57, 61, 65, 73, 74, 77, 79, 84, 87, 97, 104, 113, 118, 122	12, 16, 21, 22, 24, 26, 28, 29, 31, 33, 34, 36, 37, 46, 48, 49, 50, 52, 54, 58, 60, 62, 69, 71, 72, 78, 81, 83, 85, 86, 88, 91, 93, 99, 101, 103, 105, 107, 109, 111, 114, 115, 117, 119, 123, 124	2, 5, 9, 11, 13, 14, 18, 19, 23, 25, 27, 30, 38, 40, 41, 42, 43, 44, 47, 51, 53, 56, 59, 63, 64, 66, 67, 68, 70, 75, 76, 80, 82, 89, 90, 92, 94, 95, 96, 98, 100, 102, 106, 108, 110, 112, 116, 120, 121, 125

Rationales with Sample Questions

1.   The measure of the pull of the Earth's gravity on an object is called
         _____. *(Average Rigor) (Skill 1.1)*

         A. mass number
         B. atomic number
         C. mass
         D. weight

Answer: D. weight.
To answer this question, recall that mass number is the total number of protons and neutrons in an atom, atomic number is the number of protons in an atom, and mass is the amount of matter in an object. The only remaining choice is (D), weight, which is correct because weight is the force of gravity on an object.

2.   A seltzer tablet changing into bubbles is an example of: *(Rigorous) (Skill 1.1)*

         A. A physical change.
         B. A chemical change.
         C. Conversion.
         D. Diffusion.

Answer: B. A chemical change.
A physical change is a change that does not produce a new substance. Conversion is usually used when discussing phase changes of matter, diffusion occurs in aspects of a mixture when the concentration is equalized. A seltzer tablet changing into bubbles produces a new substance—gas—which is a characteristic of chemical changes.

3.   **When heat is added to most solids, they expand. Why is this the case?** *(Average Rigor) (Skill 1.2)*

   A. The molecules get bigger.
   B. The faster molecular motion leads to greater distance between the molecules.
   C. The molecules develop greater repelling electric forces.
   D. The molecules form a more rigid structure.

Answer: B. The faster molecular motion leads to greater distance between the molecules.

The atomic theory of matter states that matter is made up of tiny, rapidly moving particles. These particles move more quickly when warmer, because temperature is a measure of average kinetic energy of the particles. Warmer molecules therefore move further away from each other, with enough energy to separate from each other more often and for greater distances. The individual molecules do not get bigger, by conservation of mass, eliminating answer (A). The molecules do not develop greater repelling electric forces, eliminating answer (C). Occasionally, molecules form a more rigid structure when becoming colder and freezing (such as water)—but this gives rise to the exceptions to heat expansion, so it is not relevant here, eliminating answer (D). Therefore, the answer is (B).

4.   **If the volume of a confined gas is increased, what happens to the pressure of the gas? You may assume that the gas behaves ideally, and that temperature and number of gas molecules remain constant.** *(Average Rigor) (Skill 1.3)*

   A. The pressure increases.
   B. The pressure decreases.
   C. The pressure stays the same.
   D. There is not enough information given to answer this question.

Answer: B. The pressure decreases.

Because we are told that the gas behaves ideally, you may assume that it follows the ideal gas law, i.e. $PV = nRT$. This means that an increase in volume must be associated with a decrease in pressure (i.e. higher T means lower P), because we are also given that all the components of the right side of the equation remain constant. Therefore, the answer must be (B).

5.   Based on the description of the model of atom below, give the name of the individual(s) that developed the model.

   1. Matter is made up of atoms.
   2. Atoms of an element are similar to each other.
   3. Atoms of different elements are different from each other.
   4. Atoms combine with each other to form new kinds of compounds.

   (Rigorous) (Skill 1.4)

   A. Ernest Rutherford.
   B. Neils Bohr.
   C. John Dalton.
   D. Democritus Thompson.

Answer: C. John Dalton.
Democritus was the name of a greek philosopher that developed the first atomic theory of matter. It was until the 1780's that a school teacher expanded on this to create the model with the rules above. Thompson was the last name of a British scientist that (in the late 1800's) first looked in the electrical charge in an atom, and developed a model were negitive particles were equally mixed in a cloud of positive material. Later experiments by Ernest Rutherford brought about the idea of an atom with a nucleus and orbiting electrons. Neil Bohr refined Rutherfords model into the one that we use today, by stating that electrons have limited stable orbits that they can be in.

6.   Vinegar is an example of a _____ . *(Easy) (Skill 1.5)*

   A. strong acid
   B. strong base
   C. weak acid
   D. weak base

Answer: C. weak acid
The main ingredient in vinegar is acetic acid, a weak acid. Vinegar is a useful acid in science classes, because it makes a frothy reaction with bases such as baking soda (e.g. in the quintessential volcano model). Vinegar is not a strong acid, such as hydrochloric acid, because it does not dissociate as fully or cause as much corrosion. It is not a base. Therefore, the answer is (C).

7.   **Which of the following will not change in a chemical reaction?** *(Average Rigor) (Skill 1.6)*

   A. Number of moles of products.
   B. Atomic number of one of the reactants.
   C. Mass (in grams) of one of the reactants.
   D. Rate of reaction.

Answer: B. Atomic number of one of the reactants.
Atomic number, i.e. the number of protons in a given element, is constant unless involved in a nuclear reaction. Meanwhile, the amounts (measured in moles (A) or in grams(C)) of reactants and products change over the course of a chemical reaction, and the rate of a chemical reaction (D) may change due to internal or external processes. Therefore, the answer is (B).

8.   **Which parts of an atom are located inside the nucleus?** *(Easy) (Skill 1.7)*

   A. Electrons and neutrons.
   B. Protons and neutrons.
   C. Protons only.
   D. Neutrons only.

Answer: B. Protons and neutrons.
Protons and neutrons are located in the nucleus, while electrons move around outside the nucleus. This is consistent only with answer (B).

9.   **What part of an atom has to change to create another isotope of an element?** *(Rigorous) (Skill 1.7)*

   A. The number of electrons.
   B. The number of neutrons.
   C. The arrangement of the electrons.
   D. The number of protons.

Answer: B. The number of neutrons.
A change in the number of electrons (answer (A)) creates an ion. The change in the arrangement of the electrons (answer (C)), could change the reactivity of an atom temporarily. A change of the number of Protons (answer D)), will change the atom into an ion and/or isotope of another element (this usually only happens in nuclear reactions). Answer (B) is the only one that does not change the relative charge of an atom, while changing the weight of and atom, which in essence is what an isotope is.

10.   The elements in the modern periodic table are arranged _____ .
       (Easy) (Skill 1.8)

       A. in numerical order by atomic number
       B. randomly
       C. in alphabetical order by chemical symbol
       D. in numerical order by atomic mass

Answer: A. In numerical order by atomic number.
Although the first periodic tables were arranged by atomic mass, the modern table is arranged by atomic number, i.e. the number of protons in each element. (This allows the element list to be complete and unique.) The elements are not arranged either randomly or in alphabetical order. The answer to this question is therefore (A).

11.   Which of the following is not a property of metalloids? *(Rigorous)*
       (Skill 1.8)

       A. Metalloids are solids at standard temperature and pressure.
       B. Metalloids can conduct electricity to a limited extent.
       C. Metalloids are found in groups 13 through 17.
       D. Metalloids all favor ionic bonding.

Answer: D. Metalloids all favor ionic bonding.
Metalloids are substances that have characteristics of both metals and nonmetals, including limited conduction of electricity and solid phase at standard temperature and pressure. Metalloids are found in a 'stair-step' pattern from Boron in group 13 through astatine in group 17. Some metalloids, e.g. silicon, favor covalent bonding. Others, e.g. astatine, can bond ionically. Therefore, the answer is (D). Recall that metals/nonmetals/metalloids are not strictly defined by periodic table group, so their bonding is unlikely to be consistent with one another.

12.   **The two strands of a DNA molecule are held together by what kind of bond?** *(Average Rigor) (Skill 1.9)*

   A. Polar-covalent.
   B. Ionic.
   C. Non-polar covalent
   D. Hydrogen.

Answer: D. Hydrogen.
If covalent bonding (polar or non-polar) was used to join the strands of DNA together the bonds would require a great deal of energy to seperate, making transcription and copying difficult. Ionic bonds are not stable enough in solution to maintain the double helix. Hydrogen bonds form between the complementary base pair in the DNA, 2 bonds for adenine and thymine, and 3 bonds between cytosine and guanine.

13.   **Carbon bonds with hydrogen by _____ .** *(Rigorous) (Skill 1.9)*

   A. ionic bonding
   B. non-polar covalent bonding
   C. polar covalent bonding
   D. strong nuclear force

Answer: C. polar covalent bonding
Each carbon atom contains four valence electrons, while each hydrogen atom contains one valence electron. A carbon atom can bond with one or more hydrogen atoms, such that two electrons are shared in each bond. This is covalent bonding, because the electrons are shared (In ionic bonding, atoms must gain or lose electrons to form ions. The ions are then electrically attracted in oppositely-charged pairs.). Covalent bonds are always polar when between two non-identical atoms, so this bond must be polar (*Polar* means that the electrons are shared unequally, forming a pair of partial charges, i.e. poles.). In any case, the strong nuclear force is not relevant to this problem. The answer to this question is therefore (C).

14. **Which reaction below is a decomposition reaction?** *(Rigorous) (Skill 1.10)*

   A. $HCl + NaOH \rightarrow NaCl + H_2O$.
   B. $C + O_2 \rightarrow CO_2$.
   C. $2H_2O \rightarrow 2H_2 + O_2$.
   D. $CuSO_4 + Fe \rightarrow FeSO_4 + Cu$.

Answer: C. $2H_2O \rightarrow 2H_2 + O_2$.
To answer this question, recall that a decomposition reaction is one in which there are fewer reactants (on the left) than products (on the right). This is consistent only with answer (C). Meanwhile, note that answer (A) shows a double-replacement reaction (in which two sets of ions switch bonds), answer (B) shows a synthesis reaction (in which there are fewer products than reactants), and answer (D) shows a single-replacement reaction (in which one substance replaces another in its bond, but the other does not get a new bond).

15. **Which of the following is a correct explanation for astronaut 'weightlessness'?** *(Easy) (Skill 2.1)*

   A. Astronauts continue to feel the pull of gravity in space, but they are so far from Earth that the force is small.
   B. Astronauts continue to feel the pull of gravity in space, but spacecraft have such powerful engines that those forces dominate, reducing effective weight.
   C. Astronauts do not feel the pull of gravity in space, because space is a vacuum.
   D. Astronauts do not feel the pull of gravity in space, because black hole forces dominate the force field, reducing their masses.

Answer: A. Astronauts continue to feel the pull of gravity in space, but they are so far from planets that the force is small.
Gravity acts over tremendous distances in space (theoretically, infinite distance, though certainly at least as far as any astronaut has traveled). However, gravitational force is inversely proportional to distance squared from a massive body. This means that when an astronaut is in space, s/he is far enough from the center of mass of any planet that the gravitational force is small, and s/he feels 'weightless.' Space is mostly empty (i.e. vacuum), and there are some black holes, and spacecraft do have powerful engines. However, none of these has the effect attributed to it in the incorrect answer choices (B), (C), or (D). The answer to this question must therefore be (A).

16. **The force of gravity on Earth causes all bodies in free fall to _____ .** *(Average Rigor) (Skill 2.1)*

   A. fall at the same speed
   B. accelerate at the same rate
   C. reach the same terminal velocity
   D. move in the same direction

Answer: B. accelerate at the same rate
Gravity causes approximately the same acceleration on all falling bodies close to Earth's surface. (It is only approximately" because there are very small variations in the strength of Earth's gravitational field.) More massive bodies continue to accelerate at this rate for longer, before their air resistance is great enough to cause terminal velocity, so answers (A) and (C) are eliminated. Bodies on different parts of the planet move in different directions (always toward the center of mass of Earth), so answer (D) is eliminated. Thus, the answer is (B).

17. **All of the following are considered Newton's laws except for:** *(Easy)* *(Skill 2.2)*

   A. An object in motion will continue in motion unless acted upon by an outside force.
   B. For every action force, there is an equal and opposite reaction force."
   C. Nature abhors a vacuum.
   D. Mass can be considered the ratio of force to acceleration.

Answer: C. Nature abhors a vacuum.
Newton's laws include his law of inertia [an object in motion (or at rest) will stay in motion (or at rest) until acted upon by an outside force] (A), his law that Force = Mass × Acceleration (D), and his equal-and-opposite force law (B). Therefore, the answer to this question is (C), because "Nature abhors a vacuum" is not one of these.

18. **Newton's Laws are taught in science classes because _____.** *(Rigorous) (Skill 2.2)*

   A. they are an absolutely correct analysis of inertia, gravity, and forces.
   B. they are a close approximation to correct physics, for usual Earth conditions.
   C. they accurately incorporate relativity into studies of forces.
   D. Newton was a well-respected scientist in his time.

Answer: B. they are a close approximation to correct physics, for usual Earth conditions.

Although Newton's laws are often taught as fully correct for inertia, gravity, and forces, it is important to realize that Einstein's work (and that of others) has indicated that Newton's laws are reliable only at speeds much lower than that of light. This is reasonable, though, for most middle- and high-school applications. At speeds close to the speed of light, relativity considerations must be used. Therefore, the only correct answer is (B).

19. **The picture shows a view from slightly above of a teacher swinging a yoyo over their head. The teacher would be holding onto the string in the center of the circle, and the circle itself describes the path of the yoyo. Arrows 1,2 and 3 describe the forces on the yoyo. Which answer below names the forces correctly?** *(Rigorous) (Skill 2.3)*

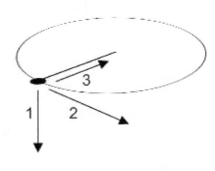

   A. 1 is inertia, 2 is centripetal force, 3 is gravity.
   B. 1 is centripedal force, 2 is gravity, 3 is inertia.
   C. 1 is gravity, 2 is inertia, 3 is centripetal.
   D. 1 is gravity, 2 is inertia, 3 is centrifugal.

Answer: C. 1 is gravity, 2 is inertia, 3 is centripetal.

Althrough the yoyo is not falling gravity is still pulling the yoyo towards the Earth (making it arrow 1). Other forces are acting to offset this force. Arrow 2 indicates a force that would take the yoyo in a straight path, this force is inertia. All objects in motion will travel in a straight line unless an outside force acts upon it. If you have trouble visualizing this, just imagine what will happen to the yoyo if the string breaks. Arrow 3 is the centripetal force being provided by the string, this is the force that creates the circular motion. The centrifugal force is in the opposite direction of the centripetal force.

20.   **Sound can be transmitted in all of the following except _____ .**
       (Easy) (Skill 2.4)

       A. air
       B. water
       C. a diamond
       D. a vacuum

Answer: D. a vacuum
Sound, a longitudinal wave, is transmitted by vibrations of molecules. Therefore, it can be transmitted through any gas, liquid, or solid. However, it cannot be transmitted through a vacuum, because there are no particles present to vibrate and bump into their adjacent particles to transmit the waves. This is consistent only with answer (D). (It is interesting also to note that sound is actually faster in solids and liquids than in air.)

21.   **Which of the following is not a factor in how different materials will conduct seismic waves?** *(Average Rigor) (Skill 2.4)*

       A. Density.
       B. Incompressibility.
       C. Rigidity.
       D. Tensile strength.

Answer: D. Tensile strength.
Density affects the speed at which seismic waves travel through the material. Incompressibility has to do with how quickly a material compresses and rebounds as the waves hit it. The more compressable a material (and thus the slower the rebound) the slower the wave travels trhough the material. Seismic waves create a shearing force as they travel through a material, rigidity is the measure of the material's resistance to that shearing force. Tensile strength measures how far something can be stretched before breaking. Since seismic waves compress materials and are not stretching them that makes answer (D) the correct answer.

22. **The speed of light is different in different materials. This is responsible for _____ .** *(Average Rigor) (Skill 2.5)*

   A. interference
   B. refraction
   C. reflection
   D. relativity

Answer: B. refraction
Refraction (B) is the bending of light because it hits a material at an angle wherein it has a different speed. (This is analogous to a cart rolling on a smooth road. If it hits a rough patch at an angle, the wheel on the rough patch slows down first, leading to a change in direction.) Interference (A) is when light waves interfere with each other to form brighter or dimmer patterns; reflection (C) is when light bounces off a surface; relativity (D) is a general topic related to light speed and its implications, but not specifically indicated here. Therefore, the answer is (B).

23. **As a train approaches, the whistle sounds _____ .** *(Rigorous) (Skill 2.5)*

   A. higher, because it has a higher apparent frequency
   B. lower, because it has a lower apparent frequency
   C. higher, because it has a lower apparent frequency
   D. lower, because it has a higher apparent frequency

Answer: A. higher, because it has a higher apparent frequency
By the Doppler effect, when a source of sound is moving toward an observer, the wave fronts are released closer together, i.e. with a greater apparent frequency. Higher frequency sounds are higher in pitch. This is consistent only with answer (A).

24. **Resistance is measured in units called _____ .** *(Average Rigor) (Skill 2.6)*

   A. watts
   B. volts
   C. ohms
   D. current

Answer: C. ohms
A watt is a unit of energy. Potential difference is measured in a unit called the volt. Current is the number of electrons per second that flow past a point in a circuit. An ohm is the unit for resistance. The correct answer is (C).

25. **A light bulb is connected in series with a rotating coil within a magnetic field. The brightness of the light may be increased by any of the following except:** *(Rigorous) (Skill 2.7)*

   A. Rotating the coil more rapidly.
   B. Using more loops in the coil.
   C. Using a different color wire for the coil.
   D. Using a stronger magnetic field.

Answer: C. Using a different color wire for the coil.
To answer this question, recall that the rotating coil in a magnetic field generates electric current, by Faraday's law. Faraday's law states that the amount of emf generated is proportional to the rate of change of magnetic flux through the loop. This increases if the coil is rotated more rapidly (A), if there are more loops (B), or if the magnetic field is stronger (D). Thus, the only answer to this question is (C).

26. **Which component(s) of an atom is most responsible for the magnetic properties of a substance?** *(Average Rigor) (Skill 2.8)*

   A. Electrons.
   B. Protons.
   C. Neutrons.
   D. Electrons and Protons.

Answer: A. Electrons.
Electrons are most responsible for the magnetic properties of a substance because they are rotating about their own axis and creating a tiny magnet. They also rotate around the nucleus of the atom, producing a current loop and magnetic field. Protons have a spin magnetic moment also, but their magnetic fields tend to cancel out. There is an exception with ferromagnetism which is caused by the magnetic properties of the nuclei of the substances.

27. The Hoover Dam is perhaps the most famous hydroeletric dam in North America. Which on of the follwing best describes how Hydroelectric dams generate their power? *(Rigorous) (Skill 2.9)*

    A. Gravity imparts kinetic energy onto the falling water, which acts as a mechanical force turning the generator turbines. The turbines contain a coil of wire, and as the turbine spins it spins the coil of wire. This generates an electrical current in the wire that is then sent out to the power grid.

    B. Gravity imparts kinetic energy onto the falling water, which acts as a mechanical force turning the generator turbines. When the turbines spin they spin a series of electromagnets inside a coil of copper wire. This generates an electrical current in the wire that is then sent out to the power grid.

    C. Gravity imparts potential energy onto the falling water, which acts as a mechanical force turning the generator turbines. When the turbines spin they spin a series of electromagnets inside a coil of copper wire. This generates an electrical current in the wire that is then sent out to the power grid.

    D. Gravity imparts kinetic energy onto the falling water, which acts as a mechanical force turning the generator turbines. When the turbines spin they spin a series of permanent magnets inside a coil of copper wire. This generates an electrical current in the wire that is then sent out to the power grid.

Answer: B. Gravity imparts kinetic energy onto the falling water, which acts as a mechanical force turning the generator turbines. When the turbines spin they spin a series of electromagnets inside a coil of copper wire. This generates an electrical current in the wire that is then sent out to the power grid.

Most electric generators work in a process that reverses the process that is used in electric motors. In a motor an electomagnetic spins in response to the electric current traveling through the coils around it thus creating the mechnical force that drives the motor. A generator just needs a source of mechanical energy to reverse the process and create an electric current.

28.   **A newton is fundamentally a measure of _____ .**
       (Average Rigor) (Skill 2.10)

   A. force
   B. momentum
   C. energy
   D. gravity

Answer: A. force
In SI units, force is measured in newtons. Momentum and energy each have different units, without equivalent dimensions. A newton is a (kilogram × meter)/(second)^2, while momentum is measured in (kilogram × meter)/(second) and energy, in Joules, is kilogram ×(meter/second)^2. Although "gravity" can be interpreted as the force of gravity, i.e. measured in Newtons, fundamentally it is not required. Therefore, the answer is (A).

29.   **A cup of hot liquid and a cup of cold liquid are both sitting in a room at comfortable room temperature and humidity. Both cups are thin plastic. Which of the following is a true statement?**
       (Average Rigor) (Skill 3.1)

   A. There will be condensation on the outside of the hot liquid cup, and also condensation on the outside of the cold liquid cup.
   B. There will be condensation on the outside of the hot liquid cup, but not on the cold liquid cup.
   C. There will be condensation on the outside of the cold liquid cup, but not on the hot liquid cup.
   D. There will not be condensation on the outside of either cup.

Answer: C. There will be condensation on the outside of the cold liquid cup, but not on the hot liquid cup.
Condensation forms on the outside of a cup when the contents of the cup are colder than the surrounding air, and the cup material is not a perfect insulator. This happens because the air surrounding the cup is cooled to a lower temperature than the ambient room, so it has a lower saturation point for water vapor. Although the humidity had been reasonable in the warmer air, when that air circulates near the colder region and cools, water condenses onto the cup's outside surface. This phenomenon is also visible when someone takes a hot shower, and the mirror gets foggy. The mirror surface is cooler than the ambient air, and provides a surface for water condensation. Furthermore, the same phenomenon is why defrosters on car windows send heat to the windows—the warmer window does not permit as much condensation. Therefore, the correct answer is (C).

30. **Which of the following is not true about phase change in matter?** *(Rigorous) (Skill 3.1)*

   A. Solid water and liquid ice can coexist at water's freezing point.
   B. At 7 degrees Celsius, water is always in liquid phase.
   C. Matter changes phase when enough energy is gained or lost.
   D. Different phases of matter are characterized by differences in molecular motion.

Answer: B. At 7 degrees Celsius, water is always in liquid phase.
According to the molecular theory of matter, molecular motion determines the 'phase' of the matter and the energy in the matter determines the speed of molecular motion. Solids have vibrating molecules that are in fixed relative positions; liquids have faster molecular motion than their solid forms, and the molecules may move more freely but must still be in contact with one another; gases have even more energy and more molecular motion. (Other phases, such as plasma, are yet more energetic.) At the freezing point or boiling point of a substance, both relevant phases may be present. For instance, water at zero degrees Celsius may be composed of some liquid and some solid, or all liquid, or all solid. Pressure changes, in addition to temperature changes, can cause phase changes. For example, nitrogen can be liquefied under high pressure, even though its boiling temperature is very low. Therefore, the correct answer must be (B). Water may be a liquid at that temperature, but it may also be a solid, depending on ambient pressure.

31. **All of the following measure energy except for _____** *(Average Rigor) (Skill 3.2)*

   A. joules
   B. calories
   C. watts
   D. ergs

Answer: C. watts
Energy units must be dimensionally equivalent to force × length, which equals (mass)x(length squared)/(time squared). Joules, calories, and ergs are all metric measures of energy. Joules are the SI units of energy, while calories are used to allow water to have a specific heat of one unit. Ergs are used in the cgs (centimeter-gram-second) system, for smaller quantities. Watts, however, are units of power, i.e. joules per second. Therefore, the answer is (C).

32.   **The transfer of heat by electromagnetic waves is called _____ .**
        (Easy) (Skill 3.3)

        A. conduction
        B. convection
        C. phase change
        D. radiation

Answer: D. radiation.
Heat transfer via electromagnetic waves (which can occur even in a vacuum) is called radiation. Heat can also be transferred by direct contact (conduction), by fluid current (convection), and by matter changing phase, but these are not relevant here. The answer to this question is therefore (D).

33.   **A long silver bar has a temperature of 50 degrees Celsius at one end and 0 degrees Celsius at the other end. The bar will reach thermal equilibrium (barring outside influence) by the process of heat**

        _____.
        (Average Rigor) (Skill 3.3)

        A. conduction
        B. convection
        C. radiation
        D. phase change

Answer: A. conduction
Heat conduction is the process of heat transfer via solid contact. The molecules in a warmer region vibrate more rapidly, jostling neighboring molecules and accelerating them. This is the dominant heat transfer process in a solid with no outside influences. Recall, also, that convection is heat transfer by way of fluid currents; radiation is heat transfer via electromagnetic waves; phase change can account for heat transfer in the form of shifts in matter phase. The answer to this question must therefore be (A).

34.   When you step out of the shower, the floor feels colder on your feet than the bathmat. Which of the following is the correct explanation for this phenomenon?
        (Average Rigor) (Skill 3.4)

        A. The floor is colder than the bathmat.
        B. Your feet have a chemical reaction with the floor, but not the bathmat.
        C. Heat is conducted more easily into the floor.
        D. Water is absorbed from your feet into the bathmat.

Answer: C. Heat is conducted more easily into the floor.
When you step out of the shower and onto a surface, the surface is most likely at room temperature, regardless of its composition, eliminating answer (A). Your feet feel cold when heat is transferred from them to the surface, which happens more easily on a hard floor than a soft bathmat. This is because of differences in specific heat (the energy required to change temperature, which varies by material). Therefore, the answer must be (C), i.e. heat is conducted more easily into the floor from your feet.

35.   A boulder sitting on the edge of a cliff has which type of energy?
        (Easy) (Skill 3.5)

        A. Kinetic energy.
        B. Latent energy.
        C. No energy.
        D. Potential energy.

Answer: D. Potential energy.
Answer (A) would be true if the boulder fell off the cliff and started falling. Answer (C) would be a difficult condition to find since it would mean that no outside forces where operating on an object, and gravity is difficult to avoid. Answer (B) might be a good description of answer (D) which is the correct energy. The boulder has potential energy is imparted from the force of gravity.

36.   **A ball rolls down a smooth hill. You may ignore air resistance. Which of the following is a true statement?**
       (Average Rigor) (Skill 3.5)

       A. The ball has more energy at the start of its descent than just before it hits the bottom of the hill, because it is higher up at the beginning.
       B. The ball has less energy at the start of its descent than just before it hits the bottom of the hill, because it is moving more quickly at the end.
       C. The ball has the same energy throughout its descent, because positional energy is converted to energy of motion.
       D. The ball has the same energy throughout its descent, because a single object (such as a ball) cannot gain or lose energy.

Answer: C. The ball has the same energy throughout its descent, because positional energy is converted to energy of motion.

The principle of conservation of energy states that (except in cases of nuclear reaction, when energy may be created or destroyed by conversion to mass), "Energy is neither created nor destroyed, but may be transformed." Answers (A) and (B) give you a hint in this question—it is true that the ball has more potential energy when it is higher, and that it has more kinetic energy when it is moving quickly at the bottom of its descent. However, the total sum of all kinds of energy in the ball remains constant, if we neglect 'losses' to heat/friction. Note that a single object can and does gain or lose energy when the energy is transferred to or from a different object. Conservation of energy applies to systems, not to individual objects unless they are isolated. Therefore, the answer must be (C).

37.   **What is the main obstacle to using nuclear fusion for obtaining electricity?** *(Average Rigor) (Skill 3.6)*

       A. Nuclear fusion produces much more pollution than nuclear fission.
       B. There is no obstacle; most power plants us nuclear fusion today.
       C. Nuclear fusion requires very high temperature and activation energy.
       D. The fuel for nuclear fusion is extremely expensive.

Answer: C. Nuclear fusion requires very high temperature and activation energy.

Nuclear fission is the usual process for power generation in nuclear power plants. This is carried out by splitting nuclei to release energy. The sun's energy is generated by nuclear fusion, i.e. combination of smaller nuclei into a larger nucleus. Fusion creates much less radioactive waste, but it requires extremely high temperature and activation energy, so it is not yet feasible for electricity generation. Therefore, the answer is (C).

38.   In a fission reactor, heavy water is used to _____ .
       (Rigorous) (Skill 3.6)

       A. terminate fission reactions
       B. slow down neutrons
       C. rehydrate the chemicals
       D. initiate a chain reaction

Answer: B. slow down neutrons
Heavy water is used in a nuclear [fission] reactor to slow down neutrons to control the nuclear reactions. It does not terminate the reaction, and it does not initiate the reaction. Also, although the reactor takes advantage of water's other properties (e.g. high specific heat for cooling), the water does not "rehydrate" the chemicals. Therefore, the answer is (B).

39.   The electromagnetic radiation with the longest wave length is/are
       _____. *(Easy) (Skill 3.7)*

       A. radio waves
       B. red light
       C. X-rays
       D. ultraviolet light

Answer: A. radio waves
As one can see on a diagram of the electromagnetic spectrum, radio waves have longer wave lengths (and smaller frequencies) than visible light, which in turn has longer wave lengths than ultraviolet or X-ray radiation. If you did not remember this sequence, you might recall that wave length is inversely proportional to frequency, and that radio waves are considered much less harmful (less energetic, i.e. lower frequency) than ultraviolet or X-ray radiation. The correct answer is therefore (A).

40.   **A converging lens produces a real image _____.**
        (Rigorous) (Skill 3.8)

        A. always
        B. never
        C. when the object is within one focal length of the lens
        D. when the object is further than one focal length from the lens

Answer: D. When the object is further than one focal length from the lens
A converging lens produces a real image whenever the object is far enough from the lens (outside one focal length) so that the rays of light from the object can hit the lens and be focused into a real image on the other side of the lens. When the object is closer than one focal length from the lens, rays of light do not converge on the other side; they diverge. This means that only a virtual image can be formed, i.e. the theoretical place where those diverging rays would have converged if they had originated behind the object. Thus, the correct answer is (D).

41.   **You have four pulley set-ups (in order to solve the problem you don't need the number and size of the pulleys), each with a weight of 1 Newton attched at one end. Based on the energy used to lift the mass and how far the mass was lifted, which of the systems was the most efficient?**
        (Rigorous) (Skill 3.9)

        A. 3 Joules lifted the mass 2 meters.
        B. 10 Joules lifted the mass 8 meters.
        C. 4 Joules lifted the mass 3.6 meters.
        D. 7.5 Joules lifted the mass 6 meters.

Answer: C. 4 Joules lifted the mass 3.6 meters.
Percent efficiency is useful energy produced divided by energy used times 100%. A joule is equal to the amount of energy required to move an object with a force of 1 newton a distance of 1 meter. So the useful energy produced is calculated from multipling the height lifted by the 1 Newton to get how many useful joules were produced, after that the rest is straight arithmetic.

Answer A: (2 m × 1 N / 3 J) × 100 % = 66.67%
Answer B: (8 m × 1 N / 10 J) × 100 % = 80%
Answer C: (3.6 m ×1 N / 4 J) × 100 % = 90%
Answer D: (6 m × 1 N / 7.5 J) × 100 % = 80%

42. As in all processess, plant growth must deal with the law of conservation of mass and energy. Most people recongize the Sun as the source of a plant's energy however what is the primary source of mass in plants? *(Rigorous) (Skill 3.10)*

    A. Water absorbed through the roots.
    B. Nutrient's and minerals absorbed through the roots.
    C. Carbon absorbed through the roots.
    D. Carbon absorbed through the stomata.

Answer: D. Carbon absorbed through the stomata.
Although water, nutrients, and minerals are absorbed through the roots by a plant, they do not make up the bulk of the added mass when a plant grows. Most of the added mass during plant growth is in the form of organic compounds, meaning the plant needs a large source of carbon to grow. Carbon dioxide taken in by the plant when it opens it's stomata is usually turned into glucose by photosynthesis. This glucose can then be either metabolized for energy or altered to form the other organic compounds the plant requires.

43. Identify which of the answers has correctly paired the terms with their definitions?

    I. Amperes   1. Electrical potential
    II. Volts   2. Electrical resistance
    III. Ohms   3. Energy flow
    IV. Watts   4. Electric current

(Rigorous) (Skill 3.11)

    A. I:1, II:3, III:4, IV:2
    B. I:3, II:1, III:2, IV:4
    C. I:4, II:1, III:2, IV:3
    D. I:3, II:4, III:2, IV:3

Answer: C. I:4, II:1, III:2, IV:3
Electrical quantities are most often measured as amperes (electric current), watts (energy flow), volts (electrical potential), and ohms (resistance). The term electrical quantity has fallen out of favor among scientists and is now more often referred to as *charge*.

44.   A 10 ohm resistor and a 50 ohm resistor are connected in parallel. If
        the current in the 10 ohm resistor is 5 amperes, the current (in
        amperes) running through the 50 ohm resistor is
        (Rigorous) (Skill 3.12)

        A. 1
        B. 50
        C. 25
        D. 60

Answer: A. 1
To answer this question, use Ohm's law, which relates voltage to current and
resistance: $V = IR$ where V is voltage; I is current; R is resistance. We also use
the fact that in a parallel circuit, the voltage is the same across the branches.
Because we are given that in one branch, the current is 5 amperes and the
resistance is 10 ohms, we deduce that the voltage in this circuit is their product,
50 volts (from $V = IR$). We then use $V = IR$ again, this time to find I in the second
branch. Because V is 50 volts, and R is 50 ohm, we calculate that I has to be 1
ampere. This is consistent only with answer (A).

45.   _____ are cracks in the plates of the Earth's crust, along
        which the plates move. *(Easy) (Skill 4.1)*

        A. Faults
        B. Ridges
        C. Earthquakes
        D. Volcanoes

Answer: A. Faults
Faults are cracks in the Earth's crust, and when the Earth moves, an earthquake
results. Faults may lead to mismatched edges of ground, forming ridges, and
ground shape may also be determined by volcanoes. The answer to this question
must therefore be (A).

46.   Which of the following is not a type of volcano?
       (Average Rigor) (Skill 4.2)

       A. Shield volcanoes.
       B. Composite volcanoes.
       C. Stratus volcanoes.
       D. Cinder cone volcanoes.

Answer: C. Stratus volcanoes.
There are three types of volcanoes. Shield volcanoes (A) are associated with non-violent eruptions and repeated lava flow over time. Composite volcanoes (B) are built from both lava flow and layers of ash and cinders. Cinder cone volcanoes (D) are associated with violent eruptions, such that lava is thrown into the air and becomes ash or cinder before falling and accumulating. 'Stratus' (C) is a type of cloud, not volcano, so it is the correct answer to this question.

47.   Although Yellowstone has many unique geological features, Its entirety is encompassed by one type of geological feature. What is that feature? *(Rigorous) (Skill 4.2)*

       A. Caldera.
       B. Glacial trough.
       C. Shield volcano.
       D. Laccolith.

Answer: A. Caldera
Although several times in history glaciers have covered where Yellowstone is currently, they did not create the depression that the park sits in. The other three answers all have to do with magma near the surface at one time or another. A laccolith is created when magma forces its way between two rock layers and creates an obvious dome. Although it is likely that there are laccoliths inside Yellowstone, it is not the feature that contains the whole park. Yellowstone is a volcano, it is not however a shield volcano, it does not constantly have lava flowing out of it. Yellowstone is the site of one of the few known supervolcanoes. At least three times in its history it has exploded, blowing out millions of tons of rock and debris, and creating bowl like depressions known as caldera.

48.   **The end of a geologic era is most often characterized by?**
        (Average Rigor) (Skill 4.3)

        A. A general uplifting of the crust.
        B. The extinction of the dominant plants and animals
        C. The appearance of new life forms.
        D. All of the above.

Answer: D. All of the above.
Any of these things can be used to characterize the end of a geologic era, and often a combination of factors are applied to determining the end of an era.

49.   **The result of radioactive decay is?**
        (Average Rigor) (Skill 4.4)

        A. Parent element.
        B. Daughter element.
        C. Half-life.
        D. An unstable atom.

Answer: B. Daughter element
Radioactive decay causes the mother element (the unstable element) to change into a daughter element (stable element). The mother-daughter relationship of produced nuclides during the series of isotope decay is the basis for radiometric dating. Although many isotopes are used in radiometric dating, the most widely known method is referred to as carbon-14 dating. Knowing the half-life (how long it takes for half of the material to decay) is the key factor in the radiometric dating process.

50.   **A contour line that has tiny comb-like lines along the inner edge indicates a?** *(Average Rigor) (Skill 4.5)*

        A. Depression
        B. Mountain
        C. Valley
        D. River

Answer: A. Depression
Contour lines are shown as closed circles in elevated areas and as lines with miniature perpendicular lined edges where depressions exist. These little lines are called hachure marks.

51.   **Surface ocean currents are caused by which of the following?**
       (Rigorous) (Skill 4.6)

       A. Temperature.
       B. Density changes in water.
       C. Wind.
       D. Tidal forces.

Answer: C. Wind
A current is a large mass of continuously moving oceanic water. Surface ocean currents are mainly wind-driven and occur in all of the world's oceans (example: the Gulf Stream). This is in contrast to deep ocean currents which are driven by changes in density. Surface ocean currents are classified by temperature. Tidal forces cause changes in ocean level however they do not effect surface currents.

52.   **Which of these best decribes the seafloor along the majority of Florida's Atlantic shoreline?** ***(Average Rigor) (Skill 4.7)***

       A. Continental slope.
       B. Continental rise.
       C. Continental shelf.
       D. Seamount.

Answer: C. Continental shelf.
Usually off the coast of a continent the progression is the continental shelf, the continental slope, and then the continental rise. A seamount is a term used to describe any volcano that rises at least a kilometer above the seafloor.

53.   **Mount Kīlauea on the island of Hawaii, is a very active volcano that has continuous lava flow into the ocean near it. What is the name of the type of shoreline created at the point where the lava flows meet the water?** ***(Rigorous) (Skill 4.7)***

       A. Stacking.
       B. Submerged.
       C. Developing.
       D. Emergent.

Answer: D. Emergent.
Answers (A) and (C) are not technical names for types of shorelines, although a stacked shoreline occurs when an island worn down to rocks. In this case the lava is building on previously deposited lava and although the lava itself is submerging under the water to develop the shoreline the over all effect is the raising of the land out of the water. Thus the correct answer is (D).

54. **The salinity of ocean water is closest to _____ .**
(Average Rigor) (Skill 4.8)

    A. 0.035 %
    B. 0.35 %
    C. 3.5 %
    D. 35 %

Answer: C. 3.5 %
Salinity, or concentration of dissolved salt, can be measured in mass ratio (i.e. mass of salt divided by mass of sea water). For Earth's oceans, the salinity is approximately 3.5 %, or 35 parts per thousand. Note that answers (A) and (D) can be eliminated, because (A) is so dilute as to be hardly saline, while (D) is so concentrated that it would not support ocean life. Therefore, the answer is (C).

55. **Fossils are usually found in _____ rock.**
(Easy) (Skill 4.9)

    A. igneous
    B. sedimentary
    C. metamorphic
    D. cumulus

Answer: B. sedimentary
Fossils are formed by layers of dirt and sand settling around organisms, hardening, and taking an imprint of the organisms. When the organism decays, the hardened imprint is left behind. This is most likely to happen in rocks that form from layers of settling dirt and sand, i.e. sedimentary rock. Note that igneous rock is formed from molten rock from volcanoes (lava), while metamorphic rock can be formed from any rock under very high temperature and pressure changes. 'Cumulus' is a descriptor for clouds, not rocks. The best answer is therefore (B).

56. **Which of the following is a type of igneous rock?**
    (Rigorous) (Skill 4.9)

    A. Quartz.
    B. Granite.
    C. Obsidian.
    D. All of the above.

Answer: D. All of the above.
Igneous rocks are formed from the crystallization of molten lava. Quartz takes the longest to crystallize (also slowest to cool) and tends to form large, distinct crystals. Obsidian cools very quickly and forms a crystalline structure that appears to be smooth like glass. Granite is between Quartz and Obsidian, and is formed from a large number of small course crystals. Therefore, the answer is (D).

57. **Igneous rocks can be classified according to which of the following?**
    (Easy) (Skill 4.10)

    A. Texture.
    B. Composition.
    C. Formation process.
    D. All of the above.

Answer: D. All of the above.
Igneous rocks, which form from the crystallization of molten lava, are classified according to many of their characteristics, including texture, composition, and how they were formed. Therefore, the answer is (D).

58. **Which of these is a true statement about loamy soil?**
    (Average Rigor) (Skill 4.10)

    A. Loamy soil is gritty and porous.
    B. Loamy soil is smooth and a good barrier to water.
    C. Loamy soil is hostile to microorganisms.
    D. Loamy soil is velvety and clumpy.

Answer: D. Loamy soil is velvety and clumpy.
The three classes of soil by texture are: Sandy (gritty and porous), clay (smooth, greasy, and most impervious to water), and loamy (velvety, clumpy, and able to hold water and let water flow through). In addition, loamy soils are often the most fertile soils. Therefore, the answer must be (D).

59.   Recently, New Hampshire's famous Old Man in the Mountain collapsed. What type of erosion was the principal cause of this? *(Rigorous) (Skill 4.11)*

A. Physical weathering.
B. Chemical weathering.
C. Exfoliation.
D. Frost wedging.

Answer: D. Frost wedging.
The granite that the Old Man in the Mountain was composed of tends to be fairly resislent to the first three types of erosion, however the natural cracks in the cliff face gave plently of places for frost to form and thus widen the cracks. Eventually the widening cracks became to large for the weight of the face to continue to be supported, at which point it collapsed. Even man-made attempts to prevent the collaps, which included cables and spikes, were unable to prevent the natural end result of erosion.

60.   Which layer of the atmosphere would you expect most weather to occur? *(Average Rigor) (Skill 4.12)*

A. Troposphere.
B. Thermosphere.
C. Mesosphere.
D. Stratosphere.

Answer: A. Troposphere
The troposphere is the lowest portion of the Earth's atmosphere. It contains the highest amount of water and aerosol. Because it touches the Earth's surface features, friction builds. For all of these reasons, weather is most likely to occur in the Troposphere.

61. **Which of the following instruments measures wind speed?**
    (Easy) (Skill 4.13)

    A. A barometer.
    B. An anemometer.
    C. A thermometer.
    D. A weather vane.

Answer: B. An anemometer.
An anemometer is a device to measure wind speed, while a barometer measures pressure, a thermometer measures temperature, and a weather vane indicates wind direction. This is consistent only with answer (B).

If you chose "barometer," here is an old physics joke to console you:

A physics teacher asks a student the following question:
"Suppose you want to find out the height of a building, and the only tool you have is a barometer. How could you find out the height?"
(The teacher hopes that the student will remember that pressure is inversely proportional to height, and will measure the pressure at the top of the building and then use the data to calculate the height of the building.)
"Well," says the student, "I could tie a string to the barometer and lower it from the top of the building, and then measure the amount of string required."
"You could," answers the teacher, "but try to think of a method that uses your physics knowledge from our class."
"All right," replies the student, "I could drop the barometer from the roof and measure the time it takes to fall, and then use free-fall equations to calculate the height from which it fell."
"Yes," says the teacher, "but what about using the barometer per se?"
"Oh," answers the student, "I could find the building superintendent, and offer to exchange the barometer for a set of blueprints, and look up the height!"

62.   **The theory of continental drift is supported by which of the following?**
       (Average Rigor) (Skill 4.14)

    A. The way the shapes of South America and Europe fit together.
    B. The way the shapes of Europe and Asia fit together.
    C. The way the shapes of South America and Africa fit together.
    D. The way the shapes of North America and Antarctica fit together.

Answer: C. The way the shapes of South America and Africa fit together.
The theory of continental drift states that many years ago, there was one land mass on the Earth (Pangea). This land mass broke apart via Earth crust motion, and the continents drifted apart as separate pieces. This is supported by the shapes of South America and Africa, which seem to fit together like puzzle pieces if you look at a globe. Note that answer choices (A), (B), and (D) give either land masses that do not fit together, or those that are still attached to each other. Therefore, the answer must be (C).

63. **A fossils of a dinosaur genus known as Saurolophus have been found in both Western North America, and in Mongolia. What is the most likely explanation for these findings?**
(Rigorous) (Skill 4.14)

A. Convergent evolution

B. This genus of dinosaurs were powerful swimmers that swam across the Bering Strait.

C. At one time all land masses were connected in a land form known as Pangaea, and so the dinosaurs could have easily walked from what is now Mongolia to what is now Western North America.

D. Although Asia and North American were separate continents at the time, low sea levels made it possible for the dinosaurs to walk from one continent to the other.

Answer: D. Although Asia and North American were separate continents at the time, low sea levels made it possible for the dinosaurs to walk from one continent to the other.

Convergent evolution can explain how different species have developed similar traits but in this case the fossil record indicates too many similarites, and thus the Saurolophus are a single genus of dinosaurs. (An interesting example of convergent evolution, is that one of the few species other than humans to have distinct fingerprints are Koalas). Saurolophus was a land based herbivore with no evidence of strong swimming abilities. As for Pangea, this particular land mass occured roughly 180 million years before the Saurolophus was alive, so it is an unlikely candidate for how evidence of the genus ended up on two continents.

This leaves the ability to walk from Asia to North America, and this was accomplished by means of the Bering Land Bridge (where the Bering Strait is now). The Bering Land bridge exsisted because the level of the water in the oceans was lowered by Water being stored in large glaciers This lowering of ocean level was enough to expose what is now the ocean floor between Alaska and Siberia.

64.   **What is the most accurate description of the water cycle?**
       (Rigorous) (Skill 4.15)

       A. Rain comes from clouds, filling the ocean. The water then evaporates
          and becomes clouds again.
       B. Water circulates from rivers into groundwater and back, while water
          vapor circulates in the atmosphere.
       C. Water is conserved except for chemical or nuclear reactions, and any
          drop of water could circulate through clouds, rain, ground-water, and
          surface-water.
       D. Water flows toward the oceans, where it evaporates and forms clouds,
          which causes rain, which in turn flow back to the oceans after it falls.

Answer: C. Water is conserved except for chemical or nuclear reactions,
           and any drop of water could circulate through clouds, rain,
           ground-water, and surface-water.

All natural chemical cycles, including the water cycle, depend on the principle of
conservation of mass. (For water, unlike for elements such as Nitrogen,
chemical reactions may cause sources or sinks of water molecules.) Any drop of
water may circulate through the hydrologic system, ending up in a cloud, as rain,
or as surface- or ground-water. Although answers (A), (B) and (D) describe parts
of the water cycle, the most comprehensive and correct answer is (C).

65.   **When water falls to a cave floor and evaporates, it may deposit**
       calcium carbonate. This process leads to the formation of which of
       the following?
       (Easy) (Skill 4.16)

       A. Stalactites.
       B. Stalagmites.
       C. Fault lines.
       D. Sedimentary rocks.

Answer: B. Stalagmites.
To answer this question, recall the trick to remember the kinds of crystals formed
in caves. Stalactites have a 'c' in them, because they form hanging from the
ceiling. Stalagmites have a 'g' in them, because they are on the ground. Note that
fault lines and sedimentary rocks are irrelevant to this question. Therefore, the
answer must be (B).

66. **Quicksand is created by the Interaction of very fine sand and water. The process that creates quicksand is callled _____ .** *(Rigorous) (Skill 4.16)*

   A. Absorption
   B. Percolation
   C. Leaching
   D. Runoff

Answer: B. Percolation
Quicksand is created when ground water is forced up through sandy soil creating a semiliquid state. Percolation refers to this movement of water through the sand. If absorption had been the answer then beach sand, rather than being good for making sand castles, would take out an untold number of tourists daily. Leaching is the absorption of soluble compounds from the ground. Leaching is the principle method of groundwater contamination. Runoff is as simple as it sounds, the water that flows over the ground before reaching some form of surface water.

67. **What is the source for most of the United States' drinking water?** *(Rigorous) (Skill 4.17)*

   A. Desalinated ocean water.
   B. Surface water (lakes, streams, mountain runoff).
   C. Rainfall into municipal reservoirs.
   D. Groundwater.

Answer: D. Groundwater.
Groundwater currently provides drinking water for 53% of the population of the United States. (Although groundwater is often less polluted than surface water, it can be contaminated and it is very hard to clean once it is polluted. If too much groundwater is used from one area, then the ground may sink or shift, or local salt water may intrude from ocean boundaries.) The other answer choices can be used for drinking water, but they are not the most widely used. Therefore, the answer is (D).

68. **Which of the following is the best explanation of the fundamental concept of Uniformitarianism?**
    (Rigorous) (Skill 4.18)

    A. The types and varieties of life between will see a uniform progression over time.
    B. The physical, chemical and biological laws that operate in the geologic past operate in the same way today.
    C. Debris from catastrophic events (i.e. volcanoes, and meteorites) will be evenly distributed over the affected area.
    D. The frequency and intensity of major geologic events will remain consistent over long periods of time.

Answer: B. The physical, chemical and biological laws that operate in the geologic past operate in the same way today.

While answers (A), (C), and (D) all could represent theories that have been proposed in geology, none of them is an accurate explanation of uniformitarianism. The general idea can be expressed, by the quote, "the present is the key to the past." The forces that we can observe today have been at work over most of Earth's history.

69. **The phases of the moon are the result of its _____ in relation to the sun.** *(Average Rigor) (Skill 5.1)*

    A. revolution
    B. rotation
    C. position
    D. inclination

Answer: C. position

The moon is visible in varying amounts during its orbit around the Earth. One half of the moon's surface is always illuminated by the Sun (appears bright), but the amount observed can vary from full moon to none

70. Neap tides are especially weak tides that occur when the Sun and Moon are in a perpindicular arrangment to the Earth, and "Spring Tides" are espically strong tides that occur when the Sun and Moon are in line. At which combination of lunar phases do these tides occur (respectively)? *(Rigorous) (Skill 5.1)*

    A. Half-moon, and full moon.
    B. Quarter moon, and new moon.
    C. Gibbous moon, and quarter moon.
    D. Full moon and new moon.

Answer: B. Quarter Moon, and new Moon.
Spring tides are especially strong tides that occur when the Earth, Sun and Moon are in line, allowing both the Sun and the Moon to exert gravitational force on the Earth and increase tidal bulge height. These tides occur during the full moon and the new moon. Neap tides occur during quarter moons, when the sun is illuminating half of the Moon's surface, (the term quarter is used to refer to the fact that the Moon has traveled 1/2 of it's way there its cycle, not the amount of the surface illuminated by the Sun.) A Gibbous Moon describes the Moon between full and quarter.

71. A star's brightness is referred to as:
(Average Rigor) (Skill 5.2)

    A. Magnitude.
    B. Mass.
    C. Apparent magnitude.
    D. Intensity.

Answer: A. magnitude
Magnitude is a measure of a star's brightness. The brighter the object appears, the lower the number value of its magnitude. The apparent magnitude is how bright an observer perceives the object to be. Mass has to do with how much matter can be measured, not brightness. The term intensity is not defined in reference to stars. Researchers may also refer to a stars brightness, in terms of luminosity, which is an absolute value based on the amount of energy the star radiates per second.

72.   A telescope that collects light by using a concave mirror and can produce small images is called a _____.
       (Average Rigor) (Skill 5.3)

       A. radioactive telescope
       B. reflecting telescope
       C. refracting telescope
       D. optical telescope

Answer: B. reflecting telescope
Reflecting telescopes are commonly used in laboratory settings. Images are produced via the reflection of waves off of a concave mirror. The larger the image produced the more likely it is to be imperfect. Refracting telscopes use lenses to bend light to focus the image. The term optical telescope can be used to describe both reflecting and refracting telescopes.

73.   Which of the following units is not a measure of distance?
       (Easy) (Skill 5.4)

       A. AU (astronomical unit).
       B. Light year.
       C. Parsec.
       D. Lunar year.

Answer: D. Lunar year.
Although the terminology is sometimes confusing, it is important to remember that a light year (B) refers to the distance that light can travel in a year. Astronomical Units (AU) (A) also measure distance, and one AU is the distance between the Sun and the Earth. Parsecs (C) also measure distance, and are used in astronomical measurement—they are very large, and are usually used to measure interstellar distances. A lunar year, or any other kind of year for a planet or moon, is the time measure of that body's orbit. Therefore, the answer to this question is (D).

74. **Which of the following is the best definition for 'meteorite'?**
(Easy) (Skill 5.5)

A. A meteorite is a mineral composed of mica and feldspar.
B. A meteorite is material from outer space that has struck the Earth's surface.
C. A meteorite is an element that has properties of both metals and nonmetals.
D. A meteorite is a very small unit of length measurement.

Answer: B. A meteorite is material from outer space, that has struck the Earth's surface.

Meteoroids are pieces of matter in space, composed of particles of rock and metal. If a meteoroid travels through the Earth's atmosphere, friction causes burning and a shooting star—i.e. a meteor. If the meteor strikes the Earth's surface, it is known as a meteorite. Note that although the suffix –ite often means a mineral, answer (A) is incorrect. Answer (C) refers to a metalloid rather than a meteorite, and answer (D) is simply a misleading pun on *meter*. Therefore, the answer is (B).

75. **The planet with true retrograde rotation is:**
(Rigorous) (Skill 5.5)

A. Pluto.
B. Uranus.
C. Venus.
D. Saturn.

Answer: C. Venus

Venus has an axial tilt of only 3 degrees and a very slow rotation. It spins in the direction opposite of its counterparts (who spin in the same direction as the Sun). Uranus is also tilted and orbits on its side. However, this is thought to be the consequence of an impact that left the previously prograde rotating planet tilted in such a manner.

76. **What is the main difference between the 'condensation hypothesis' and the 'tidal hypothesis' for the origin of the solar system?**
    (Rigorous) (Skill 5.6)

    A. The tidal hypothesis can be tested, but the condensation hypothesis cannot.
    B. The tidal hypothesis proposes a near collision of two stars pulling on each other, but the condensation hypothesis proposes condensation of rotating clouds of dust and gas.
    C. The tidal hypothesis explains how tides began on planets such as Earth, but the condensation hypothesis explains how water vapor became liquid on Earth.
    D. The tidal hypothesis is based on Aristotelian physics, but the condensation hypothesis is based on Newtonian mechanics.

Answer: B. The tidal hypothesis proposes a near collision of two stars pulling on each other, but the condensation hypothesis proposes condensation of rotating clouds of dust and gas.
Most scientists believe the condensation hypothesis, i.e. that the solar system began when rotating clouds of dust and gas condensed into the sun and planets. A minority opinion is the tidal hypothesis, i.e. that the sun almost collided with a large star. The large star's gravitational field would have then pulled gases out of the sun; these gases are thought to have begun to orbit the sun and condense into planets. Because both of these hypotheses deal with ancient, unrepeatable events, neither can be tested, eliminating answer (A). Note that both *tidal* and *condensation* have additional meanings in physics, but those are not relevant here, eliminating answer (C). Both hypotheses are based on best guesses using modern physics, eliminating answer (D). Therefore, the answer is (B).

77. **Identify the correct sequence of organization of living things from lower to higher order:**
    (Easy) (Skill 6.1)

    A. Cell, organelle, organ, tissue, system, organism.
    B. Cell, tissue, organ, organelle, system, organism.
    C. Organelle, cell, tissue, organ, system, organism.
    D. Organelle, tissue, cell, organ, system, organism.

Answer: C. Organelle, cell, tissue, organ, system, organism.
Organelles are parts of the cell; cells make up tissue, which makes up organs. Organs work together in systems (e.g. the respiratory system), and the organism is the living thing as a whole. Therefore, the answer must be (C).

78.   **Which of the following is not a necessary characteristic of living things?** *(Average Rigor) (Skill 6.1)*

      A. Movement.
      B. Reduction of local entropy.
      C. Ability to cause change in local energy form.
      D. Reproduction.

Answer: A. Movement.
There are many definitions of *life*, but in all cases, a living organism reduces local entropy, changes chemical energy into other forms, and reproduces. Not all living things move, however, so the correct answer is (A).

79.   **Which of the following features is/are found in eukaryotic cells but not in prokaryotic cells?**

      1. **Nucleus**
      2. **Mitochondria**
      3. **Cytoskeleton**
      4. **Vacules**

      (Easy) (Skill 6.2)

      A. 4 Only.
      B. 1 and 2.
      C. 1, 2 and 4.
      D. 1, 2 and 3.

Answer: D. 1, 2 and 3.
All cells contain vacules, which may serve a diverse number of purposes depending on the cell. The other three items can be found in all eukaryotic cells.

80.   **What cell organelle contains the cell's stored food?** *(Rigorous) (Skill 6.3)*

      A. Vacuoles.
      B. Golgi Apparatus.
      C. Ribosomes.
      D. Lysosomes.

Answer: A. Vacuoles.
In a cell, the sub-parts are called organelles. Of these, the vacuoles hold stored food (and water and pigments). The Golgi apparatus sorts molecules from other parts of the cell; the ribosomes are sites of protein synthesis; the lysosomes contain digestive enzymes. This is consistent only with answer (A).

81.   The first stage of mitosis is called _____ .
        (Average Rigor) (Skill 6.4)

        A. telophase
        B. anaphase
        C. prophase
        D. mitophase

Answer: C. prophase
In mitosis, the division of somatic cells, prophase is the stage where the cell enters mitosis. The four stages of mitosis, in order, are: prophase, metaphase, anaphase, and telophase. ("Mitophase" is not one of the steps.) During prophase, the cell begins the nonstop process of division. Its chromatin condenses, its nucleolus disappears, the nuclear membrane breaks apart, mitotic spindles form, its cytoskeleton breaks down, and centrioles push the spindles apart. Note that interphase, the stage where chromatin is loose, chromosomes are replicated, and cell metabolism is occurring, is technically not a stage of mitosis; it is a precursor to cell division.

82.   **Klinefelter syndrome is a condition in which a person is born with two X chromosomes and one Y chromosome. What process during meiosis would cause this to happen?**
        (Rigorous) (Skill 6.4)

        A. Inversion.
        B. Translocation.
        C. Non-disjunction.
        D. Arrangement failure.

Answer: C. Non-disjunction
Non-disjunction describes the process by which chromosomes (or chromatids) fail to separate, and one cell (in this case gamette) recieves both copies and the other cell receives none. Inversion is a process where a gene reverses itself within the chromosome. Translocation can lead to some gentic disorders, because a portion of one chromosome is swapped with a portion of another chromosome. As a term arrangement failure might be a good description for a number of genetic processes (including non-disjunction) but does not have a specifc meaning itself.

83. **A white flower is crossed with a red flower. Which of the following is a sign of incomplete dominance?**
(Average Rigor) (Skill 6.5)

    A. Pink flowers.
    B. Red flowers.
    C. White flowers.
    D. No flowers.

Answer: A. Pink flowers.
Incomplete dominance means that neither the red nor the white gene is strong enough to suppress the other. Therefore both are expressed, leading in this case to the formation of pink flowers. Therefore, the answer is (A).

84. **A carrier of a genetic disorder is heterozygous for a disorder that is recessive in nature. Hemophilia is a sex-linked disorder. This means that:** *(Easy) (Skill 6.6)*

    A. Only females can be carriers.
    B. Only males can be carriers.
    C. Both males and females can be carriers.
    D. Neither females nor males can be carriers.

Answer: A. Only females can be carriers
Since hemophilia is a sex-linked disorder the gene only appears on the X chromosome, with no counterpart on the Y chromosome. Since males are XY they cannot be heterozygous for the trait, what ever is on the single X chromosome will be expressed. Females being XX can be heterozygous. Answer (C) would describe a genetic disorder that is recessive and expressed on one of the somatic chromosomes (not sex-linked). Answer (D) would describe a genetic disorder that is dominant and expressed on any of the chromosomes. An example of answer (C) is sickle cell anemia. An example of answer (D) is Achondroplasia (the most common type of short-limbed dwarfism), in fact for this condition people that are homozygous dominant for the gene that creates the disorde rusually have severe health problems if they live past infancy, so almost all individuals with this disorder are carriers.

85. A child has type O blood. Her father has type A blood, and her mother has type B blood. What are the genotypes of the father and mother, respectively? *(Average Rigor) (Skill 6.6)*

   A. AO and BO.
   B. AA and AB.
   C. OO and BO.
   D. AO and BB.

Answer: A. AO and BO.
Because O blood is recessive, the child must have inherited two O's—one from each of her parents. Since her father has type A blood, his genotype must be AO; likewise her mother's blood must be BO. Therefore, only answer (A) can be correct.

86. Amino acids are carried to the ribosome in protein synthesis by

   _____ .

   (Average Rigor) (Skill 6.7)

   A. transfer RNA (tRNA)
   B. messenger RNA (mRNA)
   C. ribosomal RNA (rRNA)
   D. transformation RNA (trRNA)

Answer: A. Transfer RNA (tRNA)
The job of tRNA is to carry and position amino acids to/on the ribosomes. mRNA copies DNA code and brings it to the ribosomes; rRNA is in the ribosome itself. There is no such thing as trRNA. Thus, the answer is (A).

87. Which is the correct sequence of insect development? *(Easy) (Skill 6.8)*

   A. Egg, pupa, larva, adult.
   B. Egg, larva, pupa, adult.
   C. Egg, adult, larva, pupa.
   D. Pupa, egg, larva, adult.

Answer: B. Egg, larva, pupa, adult.
An insect begins as an egg, hatches into a larva (e.g. caterpillar), forms a pupa (e.g. cocoon), and emerges as an adult (e.g. moth). Therefore, the answer is (B).

88.   **Echinodermata are best known for what characteristic?**
        (Average Rigor) (Skill 6.8)

   A. Their slimy skin.
   B. Their dry habitat.
   C. Their tube feet.
   D. Their tentacles.

Answer: C. Their tube feet.
Echinodermata include sea urchins and starfish. They live in marine habitats, have spiny skin, and do not have tentacles. Thus, the best known characteristic choice here would have to be their tube feet, which they use for locomotion and feeding.

89.   **Laboratory researchers have classified fungi as distinct from plants because the cell walls of fungi _____ .**
        (Rigorous) (Skill 6.8)

   A. contain chitin
   B. contain yeast
   C. are more solid
   D. are less solid

Answer: A. contain chitin
Kingdom Fungi consists of organisms that are eukaryotic, multicellular, absorptive consumers. They have a chitin cell wall, which is the only universally present feature in fungi that is never present in plants. Thus, the answer is (A).

90.   Diatoms are one of the primary contributors to photosynethis in the oceans. They also have a unique cell wall made up of silicate, which often makes them sink in the water. Although some diatoms might form colonies most are single celled. Diatoms are usually nonmotile, although in many species the gametes have flagella. Based on this information which answer is the best identification of Diatoms. *(Rigorous) (Skill 6.9)*

A. Protozoans.
B. Euglenas.
C. Protists.
D. Blue-Green Algae.

Answer: C. Protists.
Euglena is a species of protozoans that uses a flagella to move, but like all protozoans they do not have chloroplasts and cannot preform photosynthesis. Although like diatoms, blue-green algae does use photosynthesis, the mechanism is considerably different, not relying on chloroplasts as in dlatoms. Blue-green algae are bacteria, which means that they will not have a cell wall, as a diatom does. Being a (usually) single cellular eukaroytic organism capable of photosynthesis means that the only one of the descriptors that is broad enough to include diatoms is protist. An interesting side note: A large portion of beach sand is made up of old diatom silicate cell walls.

91.   Which plant tissues contain chloroplasts?
        (Average Rigor) (Skill 6.11)

A. Stomata.
B. Palisade mesophyll.
C. Spongy Mesophyll.
D. Endosperm.

Answer: B. Palisade mesophyll.
Palisade mesophyll is one part of the leaf, in this case the part where chloroplasts exist and photosynthesis occurs. The spongy mesophyll is the other part of the leaf, where gas exchange occurs. The stomata is the part of the leaf that is the opening for air to enter and exit the leaf. The endosperm is the food source in the seed.

92.   The process of Transpiration requires which of the following?

    1 Xylem
    2 Stomata
    3 Roots
    4 Capillary action

    (Rigorous) (Skill 6.12)

    A. 1 and 2.
    B. 2 and 3.
    C. 1, 2, 3, and 4.
    D. 1 and 3.

Answer: C. 1, 2, 3, and 4.
Transpiration requires all four items to function successfully. The roots are required as the source of the water, and the xylem is required as the tube to carry the water. The stomata allows for evaporation which creates a pressure difference between the top of the xylem and the bottom (much the same as when you suck on a straw). Capillary action is the process by which water's cohesive nature allows it to travel up the xylem. Capillary action is also what causes water to travel up paper when an edge is dipped into a dish of water.

93.   **Enzymes speed up reactions by _____ .**
       (Average Rigor) (Skill 6.13)

    A. utilizing ATP
    B. lowering pH, allowing reaction speed to increase
    C. increasing volume of substrate
    D. lowering energy of activation

Answer: D. lowering energy of activation
Because enzymes are catalysts, they work the same way—they cause the formation of activated chemical complexes, which require a lower activation energy. Therefore, the answer is (D). ATP is an energy source for cells, and pH or volume changes may or may not affect reaction rate, so these answers can be eliminated.

94. **A product of anaerobic respiration in animals is _____.**
(*Rigorous*) (*Skill 6.13*)

    A. carbon dioxide
    B. lactic acid
    C. oxygen
    D. sodium chloride

Answer: B. lactic acid
In animals, anaerobic respiration (i.e. respiration without the presence of oxygen) generates lactic acid as a byproduct. (Note that some anaerobic bacteria generate carbon dioxide from respiration of methane, and animals generate carbon dioxide in aerobic respiration.) Oxygen is not normally a by-product of respiration, though it is a product of potosynthesis, and sodium chloride is not strictly relevant in this question. Therefore, the answer must be (B). By the way, lactic acid is believed to cause muscle soreness after anaerobic weight-lifting.

95. **Multiple sclerosis is an autoimmune disease that prevents nerves that are being attacked from being properly insulated, thus preventing normal propagation of the nerve signal. Which part of the nervous system is the most likely target of the body's immune system in this diease?**
(*Rigorous*) (*Skill 6.14*)

    A. Axon.
    B. Synapse.
    C. Dendrite.
    D. Myelin.

Answer: D. Myelin.
Answers (A), (B), and (C) are all part of the neuron, and although they all play a part in propagating a nerve impulse, only the myelin shealth composed of Schwann cells insulates these parts of the neuron. It is possible that in later stages of multiple sclerosis there will be damage to axons. This will usually only happen after the myelin sheath has been stripped away.

96.   Many male birds sing long complicated songs that describe thier identity and the area of land that they claim. Which of the answers below is the best decription of this behavior?
       (Rigorous) (Skill 6.15)

       A. Innate territorial behavior.
       B. Learned competitive behavior.
       C. Innate mating behavior.
       D. Learned territorial behavior.

Answer: D. Learned territorial behavior.
Birds often learn their songs, through a combination of trial and error, and listening to the songs of other members of their species (in some cases other species, this is called mimicry). Thus answers (A) and (C) are not correct. Typically a male bird will use a short song to impress a mate, the longer song is territorial because it is trying to convey to other males both identity, and the territory that it claims.

97.   What are the most significant and prevalent elements in the biosphere?
       (Easy) (Skill 7.1)

       A. Carbon, hydrogen, oxygen, nitrogen, phosphorus.
       B. Carbon, hydrogen, sodium, iron, calcium.
       C. Carbon, oxygen, sulfur, manganese, iron.
       D. Carbon, hydrogen, oxygen, nickel, sodium, nitrogen.

Answer: A. Carbon, Hydrogen, Oxygen, Nitrogen, Phosphorus.
Organic matter (and life as we know it) is based on carbon atoms, bonded to hydrogen and oxygen. Nitrogen and phosphorus are the next most significant elements, followed by sulfur and then trace nutrients such as iron, sodium, calcium, and others. Therefore, the answer is (A). If you know that the formula for any carbohydrate contains carbon, hydrogen, and oxygen, that will help you narrow the choices to (A) and (D) in any case.

98.   **Which of the following is found in the least abundance in organic molecules?** *(Rigorous) (Skill 7.1)*

A. Phosphorus.
B. Potassium.
C. Carbon.
D. Oxygen.

Answer: B. Potassium.
Organic molecules consist mainly of carbon, hydrogen, and oxygen, with significant amounts of nitrogen, phosphorus, and often sulfur. Other elements, such as Potassium, are present in much smaller quantities. Therefore, the answer is (B). If you were not aware of this ranking, you might have been able to eliminate carbon and oxygen because of their prevalence, in any case.

99.   **Which of the following is the most accurate definition of a non-renewable resource?** *(Average Rigor) (Skill 7.2)*

A. A nonrenewable resource is never replaced once used.
B. A nonrenewable resource is replaced on a timescale that is very long relative to human life spans.
C. A nonrenewable resource is a resource that can only be manufactured by humans.
D. A nonrenewable resource is a species that has already become extinct.

Answer: B. A nonrenewable resource is replaced on a timescale that is very long relative to human life-spans.
Renewable resources are those that are renewed, or replaced, in time for humans to use more of them. Examples include fast-growing plants, animals, or oxygen gas. (Note that while sunlight is often considered a renewable resource, it is actually a nonrenewable but extremely abundant resource.) Nonrenewable resources are those that renew themselves only on very long timescales, usually geologic timescales. Examples include minerals, metals, or fossil fuels. Therefore, the correct answer is (B).

100. **Which of the following is the best example of an explanation of the theory of evolution?** *(Rigorous) (Skill 7.3)*

   A. Giraffes need to reach higher for leaves to eat, so their necks stretch. The giraffe babies are then born with longer necks. Eventually, there are more long-necked giraffes in the population.
   B. Giraffes with longer necks are able to reach more leaves, so they eat more and have more babies than other giraffes. Eventually, there are more long-necked giraffes in the population.
   C. Giraffes want to reach higher for leaves to eat, so they release enzymes into their bloodstream, which in turn causes fetal development of longer-necked giraffes. Eventually, there are more long-necked giraffes in the population.
   D. Giraffes with long necks are more attractive to other giraffes, so they get the best mating partners and have more babies. Eventually, there are more long-necked giraffes in the population.

Answer: B. Giraffes with longer necks are able to reach more leaves, so they eat more and have more babies than other giraffes. Eventually, there are more long-necked giraffes in the population.

Although evolution is often misunderstood, it occurs via natural selection. Organisms with a life/reproductive advantage will produce more offspring. Over many generations, this changes the proportions of the population. In any case, it is impossible for a stretched neck (A) or a fervent desire (C) to result in a biologically mutated baby. Although there are traits that are naturally selected because of mate attractiveness and fitness (D), this is not the primary situation here, so answer (B) is the best choice.

101. **A wrasse (fish) cleans the teeth of other fish by eating away plaque. This is an example of _____ between the fish.**
   (Average Rigor) (Skill 7.4)

   A. parasitism
   B. symbiosis (mutualism)
   C. competition
   D. predation

Answer: B. symbiosis (mutualism)

When both species benefit from their interaction in their habitat, this is called *symbiosis*, or *mutualism*. In this example, the wrasse benefits from having a source of food, and the other fish benefit by having healthier teeth. Note that parasitism is when one species benefits at the expense of the other, competition is when two species compete with one another for the same habitat or food, and predation is when one species feeds on another. Therefore, the answer is (B).

102. **Which one of the following biomes makes up the greatest percentage of the biosphere?** *(Rigorous) (Skill 7.4)*

    A. Desert.
    B. Tropical rain forest.
    C. Marine.
    D. Temperate deciduous forest.

Answer: C. Marine
All land biomes, which includes answers (A), (B), and (D) make up approximately 25% of the Earth's surface, leaving the other 75% to the marine biome. Additionally the marine biome can range in depth from the air above the water, to several miles in depth. THis combined make answer (C) the correct answer.

103. **Which of the following is not a common type of acid in 'acid rain' or acidified surface water?** *(Average Rigor) (Skill 7.5)*

    A. Nitric acid.
    B. Sulfuric acid.
    C. Carbonic acid.
    D. Hydrofluoric acid.

Answer: D. Hydrofluoric acid.
Acid rain forms predominantly from pollutant oxides in the air (usually nitrogen-based NO_x or sulfur-based SO_x), which become hydrated into their acids (nitric or sulfuric acid). Because of increased levels of carbon dioxide pollution, carbonic acid is also common in acidified surface water environments. Hydrofluoric acid can be found, but it is much less common. In general, carbon, nitrogen, and sulfur are much more prevalent in the environment than fluorine. Therefore, the answer is (D).

104. **Viruses are responsible for many human diseases including all of the following except _____?** *(Easy) (Skill 7.6)*

    A. influenza
    B. AIDS
    C. the common cold
    D. strep throat

Answer: D. strep throat
Influenza, AIDS., and the common cold (rhinovirus infection), are all caused by viruses. (This is the reason that doctors should not be pressured to prescribe antibiotics for colds or flu—i.e. they will not be effective since the infections are not bacterial.) Strep throat (properly called *streptococcal throat* and caused by streptococcus bacteria) is not a virus, but a bacterial infection. Thus, the answer is (D).

105. **Extensive use of antibacterial soap has been found to increase the virulence of certain infections in hospitals. Which of the following might be an explanation for this phenomenon?**
(Average Rigor) (Skill 7.6)

    A. Antibacterial soaps do not kill viruses.
    B. Antibacterial soaps do not incorporate the same antibiotics used as medicine.
    C. Antibacterial soaps kill a lot of bacteria, and only the hardiest ones survive to reproduce.
    D. Antibacterial soaps can be very drying to the skin.

Answer: C. Antibacterial soaps kill a lot of bacteria, and only the hardiest ones survive to reproduce.
All of the answer choices in this question are true statements, but the question specifically asks for a cause of increased disease virulence in hospitals. This phenomenon is due to natural selection. The bacteria that can survive contact with antibacterial soap are the strongest ones, and without other bacteria competing for resources, they have more opportunity to lourish. This problem has led to several antibiotic-resistant bacterial diseases in hospitals nationwide. Therefore, the answer is (C). However, note that answers (A) and (D) may be additional problems with over reliance on antibacterial products.

106. **Which of the following hormones is least involved in the process of osmoregulation?** *(Rigorous) (Skill 7.7)*

    A. Antidiuretic hormone.
    B. Melatonin.
    C. Calcitonin.
    D. Gulcagon.

Answer: B. Melatonin.
Osmoregulation relates to the body's attempt to control the concentration of water and different soluble materials in the body. Antidiruetic Hormone (ADH) regulates the kidneys' reabsorption of water and so directly relates to the amount of water in the body. The body's failure to produce ADH can lead to a life threatening condition where an individual die of dehydration within a matter of hours. Calcitonin controls the removal of calcium from the blood. Glucagon, like insulin, controls the amount of glucose in the blood. Melatonin is involved in homostasis however it is not directly invovled in osmoregulation, rather it is involved in the regulation of body rhythms.

107. **What makes up the largest abiotic portion of the nitrogen cycle?** *(Average Rigor) (Skill 7.8)*

    A. Nitrogen fixing bacteria.
    B. Nitrates.
    C. Decomposers.
    D. Atmosphere.

Answer: D. Atomsphere.
Since answers (A) and (C) are both examples of living organisms they are biotic components of the nitrogen cycle. Nitrates are one type of nitrogen compond, (making it abiotic) that can be found in soil and in living organisms, however it makes up a small portion of the avaible nitrogen. The atmosphere being 78% Nitrogen gas (an abiotic component) makes up the largest source available to the nitrogen cycle.

108. **Which of the following abiotic factors maintains Florida's most extensive terrestrial ecosystem?** *(Rigorous) (Skill 7.9)*

    A. Rain.
    B. Flooding.
    C. Fire.
    D. Wind.

Answer: C. Fire
Florida's most extensive terrestrial ecosystem is the pine flatwoods, and although rain, flooding, droughts and wind all effect the development of this ecosystem, it is regular fires (wild and controlled) that clear away competing hardwood trees that would eventually crowd out the pines. The fires also clear out the plant coverage that might otherwise prevent the pine seedlings access to sunlight. The pines themselves are adapted to the fire conditions, they often have thick bark that helps to protect them and in the case of a few species, cones that will only release their seeds after being exposed to the extreme heat of a fire.

109. **Formaldehyde should not be used in school laboratories for the following reason:** *(Average Rigor) (Skill 8.1)*

    A. It smells unpleasant.
    B. It is a known carcinogen.
    C. It is expensive to obtain.
    D. It is explosive.

Answer: B. It is a known carcinogen.
Formaldehyde is a known carcinogen, so it is too dangerous for use in schools. In general, teachers should not use carcinogens in school laboratories. Although formaldehyde also smells unpleasant, a smell alone is not a definitive marker of danger. For example, many people find the smell of vinegar to be unpleasant, but vinegar is considered a very safe classroom/laboratory chemical. Furthermore, some odorless materials are toxic. Formaldehyde is neither particularly expensive nor explosive. Thus, the answer is (B).

110. **Experiments may be done with any of the following animals except
_____ . (Rigorous) (Skill 8.1)**

A. birds
B. invertebrates
C. lower order life
D. frogs

Answer: A. birds
No dissections may be performed on living mammalian vertebrates or birds.
Lower order life and invertebrates may be used. Biological experiments may be
done with all animals except mammalian vertebrates or birds. Therefore the
answer is (A).

111. **When measuring the volume of water in a graduated cylinder, where
does one read the measurement? (Average Rigor) (Skill 8.2)**

A. At the highest point of the liquid.
B. At the bottom of the meniscus curve.
C. At the closest mark to the top of the liquid
D. At the top of the plastic safety ring.

Answer: B. At the bottom of the meniscus curve.
To measure water in glass, you must look at the top surface at eye-level, and
ascertain the location of the bottom of the meniscus (the curved surface at the
top of the water). The meniscus forms because water molecules adhere to the
sides of the glass, which is a slightly stronger force than their cohesion to each
other. This leads to a U-shaped top of the liquid column, the bottom of which
gives the most accurate volume measurement. (Other liquids have different
forces, e.g. mercury in glass, which has a convex meniscus.) This is
consistent only with answer (B).

112. In a science experiment, a student needs to repeatedly dispense very small measured amounts of liquid into a well-mixed solution. Which of the following is the best choice for his/her equipment to use? *(Rigorous) (Skill 8.2)*

    A. Pipette, stirring rod, beaker.
    B. Burette with burette stand, stir-plate, beaker.
    C. Volumetric flask, dropper, stirring rod.
    D. Beaker, graduated cylinder, stir-plate.

Answer: B. Burette with burette stand, stir-plate, beaker.
The most accurate and convenient way to repeatedly dispense small measured amounts of liquid in the laboratory is with a burette, on a burette stand. To keep a solution well-mixed, a magnetic stir-plate is the most sensible choice, and the solution will usually be mixed in a beaker. Although other combinations of materials could be used for this experiment, choice (B) is thus the simplest and best. Choices A and C rely on a stirring a rod, which requires the student to try to mix the solution by hand while adding the liquid. Answer D relies on a graduated cylinder to add the small amounts of liquid to the solution, it is more difficult to add small quantities of a liquid with a graduated cylinder.

113. Many times science teachers are faced with the dilemna of not having enough funds to perform all the wonderful science laboratory exercises that they find. Which of these items might help with this problem? *(Easy) (Skill 8.3)*

    A. Getting supplies at hardware and grocery stores.
    B. Applying for Grant Money.
    C. Use of School Gardens or natural areas.
    D. All of the above.

Answer: D. All of the above
As a teacher anything you can get to help you teach science go for it, as long as it doesn't break any laws or put anyone (you or students) in danger. Lots of common supplies can be found in your local stores. In addition to government grant moneys there are many private sources of grant money that you can pursue. Too often we try to teach about nature while sittng in the classroom, if you can get outdoors, then do so.

114. **Who should be notified in the case of a serious chemical spill?**
(Average Rigor) (Skill 8.4)

    A. The custodian.
    B. The fire department or their municipal authority.
    C. The science department chair.
    D. The school board.

Answer: B. The fire department or other municipal authority.
Although the custodian may help to clean up laboratory messes, and the science department chair should be involved in discussions of ways to avoid spills, a serious chemical spill may require action by the fire department or other trained emergency personnel. It is best to be safe by notifying them in case of a serious chemical accident. Therefore, the best answer is (B).

115. **What is the scientific method?**
(Average Rigor) (Skill 9.1)

    A. It is the process of doing an experiment and writing a laboratory report.
    B. It is the process of using open inquiry and repeatable results to establish theories.
    C. It is the process of reinforcing scientific principles by confirming results.
    D. It is the process of recording data and observations.

Answer: B. It is the process of using open inquiry and repeatable results to establish theories.
Scientific research often includes elements from answers (A), (C), and (D), but the basic underlying principle of the scientific method is that people ask questions and do repeatable experiments to answer those questions and develop informed theories of why and how things happen. Therefore, the best answer is (B).

116. **Which of the following is not an acceptable way for a student to acknowledge sources in a laboratory report?**
(Rigorous) (Skill 9.1)

A. The student tells his/her teacher what sources s/he used to write the report.
B. The student uses footnotes in the text, with sources cited, but not in correct MLA format.
C. The student uses endnotes in the text, with sources cited, in correct MLA format.
D. The student attaches a separate bibliography, noting each use of sources.

Answer: A. The student tells his/her teacher what sources s/he used to write the report.

It may seem obvious, but students are often unaware that scientists need to cite all sources used. For the young adolescent, it is not always necessary to use official MLA format (though this should be taught at some point). Students may properly cite references in many ways, but these references must be in writing, with the original assignment. Therefore, the answer is (A).

117. **Which of the following data sets is properly represented by a bar graph?**
(Average Rigor) (Skill 9.2)

A. Number of people choosing to buy cars, vs. Color of car bought.
B. Number of people choosing to buy cars, vs. Age of car customer.
C. Number of people choosing to buy cars, vs. Distance from car lot to customer home.
D. Number of people choosing to buy cars, vs. Time since last car purchase.

Answer: A. Number of people choosing to buy cars, vs. Color of car bought.

A bar graph should be used only for data sets in which the independent variable is non-continuous (discrete), e.g. gender, color, etc. Any continuous independent variable (age, distance, time, etc.) should yield a scatter plot when the dependent variable is plotted. Therefore, the answer must be (A).

118. **Which is the correct order of methodology?**

1. **collecting data**
2. **planning a controlled experiment**
3. **drawing a conclusion**
4. **hypothesizing a result**
5. **re-visiting a hypothesis to answer a question**

(Easy) (Skill 9.3)

A. 1,2,3,4,5.
B. 4,2,1,3,5.
C. 4,5,1,3,2.
D. 1,3,4,5,2.

Answer: B. 4,2,1,3,5.
The correct methodology for the scientific method is first to make a meaningful hypothesis (educated guess), then plan and execute a controlled experiment to test that hypothesis. Using the data collected in that experiment, the scientist then draws conclusions and attempts to answer the original question related to the hypothesis. This is consistent only with answer (B).

119. **When designing a scientific experiment, a student considers all the factors that may influence the results. The process goal is to _____. *(Average Rigor) (Skill 9.3)***

A. recognize and manipulate independent variables
B. recognize and record independent variables
C. recognize and manipulate dependent variables
D. recognize and record dependent variables

Answer: A. Recognize and manipulate independent variables.
When a student designs a scientific experiment, s/he must decide what to measure, and what independent variables will play a role in the experiment. S/he must determine how to manipulate these independent variables to refine his/her procedure and to prepare for meaningful observations. Although s/he will eventually record dependent variables (D), this does not take place during the experimental design phase. Although the student will likely recognize and record the independent variables (B), this is not the process goal, but a helpful step in manipulating the variables. It is unlikely that the student will manipulate dependent variables directly in his/her experiment (C), or the data would be suspect. Thus, the answer is (A).

120. **In an experiment measuring the inhibition effect of different antibiotic discs on bacteria grown in Petri dishes, what are the independent and dependent variables respectively?** *(Rigorous) (Skill 9.4)*

    A. Number of bacterial colonies and the antibiotic type.
    B. Antibiotic type and the distance between antibiotic and the closest colony.
    C. Antibiotic type and the number of bacterial colonies.
    D. Presence of bacterial colonies and the antibiotic type.

Answer: B. Antibiotic type and the distance between antibiotic and the closest colony.

To answer this question, recall that the independent variable in an experiment is the entity that is changed by the scientist, in order to observe the effects the dependent variable. In this experiment, antibiotic used is purposely changed so it is the independent variable. Answers A and D list antibiotic type as the dependent variable and thus cannot be the answer, leaving answers B and C as the only two viable choices. The best answer is B, because it measures at what concentration of the antibiotic the bacteria are able to grow at, (as you move from the source of the antibiotic the concentration decreases). Answer C is not as effective because it could be interpreted that that a plate that shows a large number of colonies a greater distance from the antibiotic is a less effective antibiotic than a plate a smaller number of colonies in close proximity to the antibiotic disc, which is reverse of the actually result.

121. **Koch's postulates on microbiology include all of the following except:** *(Rigorous) (Skill 9.5)*

    A. The same pathogen must be found in every diseased person.
    B. The pathogen must be isolated and grown in culture.
    C. The same pathogen must be isolated from the experimental animal.
    D. Antibodies that react to the pathogen must be found in every diseased person.

Answer: D. Antibodies that react to the pathogen must be found in every diseased person.

Koch postulated that the same pathogen must be found in every diseased person, this pathogen must be isolated and grown in a culture, the disease must be induced in experimental animals from the same pathogen, and that this pathogen must then be isolated from the experimental animal. Koch's postulates do not mention antibodies being found. In fact Koch first devised his postulates in 1884 and the study of antibodies did not began until the 1890s. Thus, the answer is (D).

122. **If one inch equals 2.54 cm how many mm in 1.5 feet? (APPROXIMATELY)** *(Easy) (Skill 9.6)*

   A. 18 mm.
   B. 1800 mm.
   C. 460 mm.
   D. 4,600 mm.

Answer: C. 460 mm.
To solve this problem, note that if one inch is 2.54 centimeters, then 1.5 feet (which is 18 inches), must be 18 × 2.54 centimeters, i.e. approximately 46 centimeters. Because there are ten millimeters in a centimeter, this is approximately 460 millimeters:

(1.5 ft) (12 in/ft) (2.54 cm/in) (10 mm/cm) = (1.5) (12) (2.54) (10) mm = 457.2 mm

This is consistent only with answer (C).

123. **Separating blood into blood cells and plasma involves the process of _____ .** *(Average Rigor) (Skill 9.6)*

   A. electrophoresis
   B. centrifugation
   C. spectrophotometry
   D. chromatography

Answer: C. Centrifugation.
Electrophoresis uses electrical charges of molecules to separate them according to their size. Spectrophotometry uses percent light absorbance to measure a color change, thus giving qualitative data a quantitative value. Chromatography uses the principles of capillarity to separate substances. Centrifugation involves spinning substances at a high speed. The more dense part of a solution will settle to the bottom of the test tube, where the lighter material will stay on top. The answer is (C).

124. **Which type of student activity is most likely to expose a student's misconceptions about science?** *(Average Rigor) (Skill 9.7)*

    A. Multiple-choice and fill-in-the-blank worksheets.
    B. Laboratory activities, where the lab is laid out step by step with no active thought on the part of the student.
    C. Teacher-led demonstrations.
    D. Laboratories in which the student are forced to critically consider the steps taken and the results.

Answer: D. Laboratories in which the student are forced to critically consider the steps taken and the results.

Answer (A) is a typical retain and repeate exercise, where a student just needs to remember the answer and doesn't need to understand it. Answer (B), is often called a cookie cutter lab because everything fit to a specific plan. Students are often able to geuss the right answer without understanding the process. Teacher lead demonstrations can be interesting for the students, and my challenge a students misconceptions. A student's misconceptions are often firmly routed and will require critical thought and reflection by the student for it to change, often an attempt to illuminate a student's misconception doesn't get rid of it, but gets incorporated into their inaccurate understanding of the universe. Answer (D) requires active mental participation on the behalf of the student and thus is most likely to alter their personally understanding. These types of labs are often refered to as guided discovery laaboratories.

125. **Which of the following is not an appropriate aspect of scientific attitude?** *(Rigorous) (Skill 9.8)*

    A. Scientific curiosity.
    B. Scientific open-mindedness.
    C. Scientific conformity.
    D. Scientific skepticism

Answer: C. Scientific conformity.

Open mindedness and curiosity are two of the backbones of science. It is important not to confuse conformity with reproduceability. Scientific Skepticism is a method of obtaining knowledge through systematic doubt and continual testing. A skeptical scientist is one who refuses to accept certain types of claims without subjecting them to a systematic investigation. This is an important skill to develop in students. Thus, the answer is (C).

CPSIA information can be obtained
at www.ICGtesting.com
Printed in the USA
BVHW07s2234280718
522828BV00021B/473/P